SHAPING A MODERN ETHICS

Also Available from Bloomsbury

The Ethical Imagination in Shakespeare and Heidegger, Andy Amato
Understanding Nietzsche, Understanding Modernism,
ed. Brian Pines and Douglas Burnham
Nietzsche and Friendship, Willow Verkerk
Nietzsche's Search for Philosophy: On the Middle Writings,
Keith Ansell Pearson
Deleuze and the Schizoanalysis of Feminism,
ed. Cheri Carr and Janae Sholtz

SHAPING A MODERN ETHICS

The Humanist Legacy from Nietzsche to Feminism

Benjamin Bennett

BLOOMSBURY ACADEMIC
LONDON · NEW YORK · OXFORD · NEW DELHI · SYDNEY

BLOOMSBURY ACADEMIC
Bloomsbury Publishing Plc
50 Bedford Square, London, WC1B 3DP, UK
1385 Broadway, New York, NY 10018, USA
29 Earlsfort Terrace, Dublin 2, Ireland

BLOOMSBURY, BLOOMSBURY ACADEMIC and the Diana logo are trademarks of
Bloomsbury Publishing Plc

First published in Great Britain 2020
This paperback edition published in 2021

Copyright © Benjamin Bennett, 2020

Benjamin Bennett has asserted his right under the Copyright, Designs and Patents Act,
1988, to be identified as Author of this work.

For legal purposes the Acknowledgments on p. viii constitute an extension
of this copyright page.

Cover design by Avni Patel
Cover images: Portrait of Freidrich Nietzsche by Gustav Schultze (1882).
Portrait of Virginia Woolf by George Charles Beresford (1902).

All rights reserved. No part of this publication may be reproduced or
transmitted in any form or by any means, electronic or mechanical,
including photocopying, recording, or any information storage or retrieval
system, without prior permission in writing from the publishers.

Bloomsbury Publishing Plc does not have any control over, or responsibility for,
any third-party websites referred to or in this book. All internet addresses given
in this book were correct at the time of going to press. The author and publisher
regret any inconvenience caused if addresses have changed or sites have ceased
to exist, but can accept no responsibility for any such changes.

A catalogue record for this book is available from the British Library.

A catalog record for this book is available from the Library of Congress.

ISBN: HB: 978-1-3501-2285-7
PB: 978-1-3502-6231-7
ePDF: 978-1-3501-2286-4
eBook: 978-1-3501-2287-1

Typeset by Newgen KnowledgeWorks Pvt. Ltd., Chennai, India

To find out more about our authors and books visit www.bloomsbury.com
and sign up for our newsletters.

For Volker and Heike
Incipit vita nova

CONTENTS

Acknowledgments	viii
List of Abbreviations	ix

PRELIMINARY REMARKS 1

Chapter 1
INTRODUCTION: ETHICS, "LITERATURE," "THE HUMAN," AND IRONY ... 11

Chapter 2
NIETZSCHE AND RORTY: THE ETHICS OF IRONY ... 29

Chapter 3
KANT AND LEIBNIZ ... 55

Chapter 4
LESSING: HISTORY, IRONY, AND DIASPORA ... 65

Chapter 5
LESSING AND FREUD: THEORY, WISDOM, AND THE SCOPE OF ETHICS ... 91

Chapter 6
HABERMAS, RORTY, AND MACHIAVELLI ... 117

Chapter 7
WOOLF, BACHMANN, WITTIG: TOWARD A FEMINIST ETHICS ... 141

CONCLUSION ... 173

Notes	179
Bibliography	189
Person Index	195
Subject Index	198

ACKNOWLEDGMENTS

I have been working on this project for a long time, and the number of friends and colleagues whose advice has helped me has grown far too large for me to mention them all here. I have also aged in the process, and if I did try to mention everyone, I would be sure to forget someone important. As far as it is in my power, however, I will not forget my debt to anyone. I am also grateful to the University of Virginia for research support and technical help. Chapter 5 started life as a talk on "Freud and the Wrongness of Theoretical Closure," which I gave at a conference on "Cases and Examples" at Virginia in April 2013. I am grateful to the organizers (Volker Kaiser and Manfred Schneider) and participants for the opportunity to give that talk and for the discussion that followed. I am indebted to the Lessing Society, and to its representative Professor Carl Niekerk, for permission to use, as the basis for Chapter 4, my article "Reason, Error and the Shape of History: Lessing's Nathan and Lessing's God," *Lessing Yearbook*, IX (1977), 60–80. I am grateful to the British Psychoanalytical Society (incorporating the Institute of Psychoanalysis) for permission to use translations from *The Standard Edition of the Complete Psychological Works of Sigmund Freud*, ed. and trans. James Strachey et al., 24 vols. (London: Hogarth Press, 1953–74). And excerpts from *A Room of One's Own* by Virginia Woolf, copyright © 1929 by Houghton Mifflin Harcourt Publishing Company, renewed 1957 by Leonard Woolf, are printed by permission of Houghton Mifflin Harcourt Publishing Company (all rights reserved) and of The Society of Authors as the Literary Representative of the Estate of Vrginia Woolf. All efforts have been made to trace copyright holders. In the event of errors or omissions, please notify the publisher in writing of any corrections that need to be incorporated into future editions of this book.

ABBREVIATIONS

ADE	Association of Departments of English
ADFL	Association of Departments of Foreign Languages
BoT	Nietzsche, *The Birth of Tragedy and The Genealogy of Morals*, trans. Francis Golffing
DP	section number in the "Discours preliminaire" of Leibniz, *Théodicée*
E	section number in the "Essais" proper in Leibniz, *Théodicée*
ED	Habermas, *Erläuterungen zur Diskursethik*
F	Kant, *Kant's Foundations of Ethics*
GoM	Nietzsche, *On the Genealogy of Morals, Ecce Homo*, trans. Walter Kaufmann and R. J. Hollingdale
GW	Freud, *Gesammelte Werke*
JA	Habermas, *Justification and Application: Remarks on Discourse Ethics*
KSA	Nietzsche, *Sämtliche Werke: Kritische Studienausgabe in 15 Bänden*
LM	Lessing, *Sämtliche Werke, Sämtliche Schriften*
MC	Habermas, *Moral Consciousness and Communicative Action*
MkH	Habermas, *Moralbewußtsein und kommunikatives Handeln*
PEGS	*Publications of the English Goethe Society*
PMLA	*Publications of the Modern Language Association*
R	Kant, *Religion within the Boundaries of Mere Reason and Other Writings*
SE	*The Standard Edition of the Complete Psychological Works of Sigmund Freud*
WA	*Goethes Werke*, "Weimarer Ausgabe"

PRELIMINARY REMARKS

Wittgenstein, Strawson, and We

In Cambridge, sometime in 1929 or 1930, Ludwig Wittgenstein composed and delivered a short lecture on ethics. It was not published during his lifetime and first appeared in 1965 in *The Philosophical Review*.

The lecture is concerned solely with the question of the *existence* of ethics as a more or less scientific discipline. Starting from G. E. Moore's understanding of ethics as "the general enquiry into what is good," Wittgenstein points out that words like "good, valuable, important, right" all have at least two clearly opposed senses, "the trivial or relative sense on the one hand and the ethical or absolute sense on the other." The trivial or relative sense of such words always involves a factual state of affairs; something is good or right or important or valuable under specified circumstances or for a specified purpose. But the absolute or ethical sense creates problems for understanding.

> The right road is the road which leads to an arbitrarily predetermined end and it is quite clear to us all that there is no sense in talking about the right road apart from such a predetermined goal. Now let us see what we could possibly mean by the expression, "*the* absolutely right road." I think it would be the road which *everybody* on seeing it would, *with logical necessity*, have to go, or be ashamed for not going. And similarly the *absolute good*, if it is a describable state of affairs, would be one which everybody, independent of his tastes and inclinations, would *necessarily* bring about or feel guilty for not bringing about. And I want to say that such a state of affairs is a chimera. No state of affairs has, in itself, what I would like to call the coercive power of an absolute judge.

Which raises the question for Wittgenstein: "Then what have all of us who, like myself, are still tempted to use such expressions as 'absolute good,' 'absolute value,' etc., what have we in mind and what do we try to express?"

For his own part, says Wittgenstein, he associates the use of those expressions with personal experiences, especially the experience of wondering at the existence of the world, which brings him back to the question of relative and absolute, or of sense and nonsense. It is reasonable to wonder at any number of things in a relative sense, at an unusually large dog, for instance, or at the existence of a house one thought had been torn down. "But it is nonsense to say that I wonder at the existence of the world, because I cannot imagine it not existing." Wonder, in this case, has an absolute character, and its association with actual experience creates a paradox in Wittgenstein's thinking, since experience involves fact. "It is the paradox that an experience, a fact, should seem to have supernatural value."

Even the concept of "miracle" does not appear to help matters, since the opposition of a relative and an absolute sense still applies. Except that in this case, the relative sense of the word—the idea of a miracle as a fact one cannot explain—has the effect of undermining the concept altogether, because the very idea of a possible explanation presupposes a mode of thinking from which the concept "miracle" is excluded. "The truth is that the scientific way of looking at a fact is not the way to look at it as a miracle. For imagine whatever fact you may, it is not in itself miraculous in the absolute sense of that term." With this, Wittgenstein comes to the climax of his argument:

> And I will now describe the experience of wondering at the existence of the world by saying: it is the experience of seeing the world as a miracle. Now I am tempted to say that the right expression in language for the miracle of the existence of the world, though it is not any proposition in language, is the existence of language itself.

In the first sentence, he describes his experience by what is certainly a "proposition in language"; in the second sentence, he denies that "any proposition in language" can be "the right expression" for what he wants to say. And only the ascription of this contradiction, along with the peculiarities of the concept "miracle," to "language itself," justifies understanding the existence of the latter as the "right" expression required.

But Wittgenstein is not satisfied with this logical move. "For all I have said by shifting the expression of the miraculous from an expression *by means of* language to the expression *by the existence* of language, all I have said is again that we cannot express what we want to express and that all we *say* about the absolute miraculous remains nonsense." Indeed, a hypothetical interlocutor might object that Wittgenstein cannot even really *mean* what he says about "nonsense," that the perception of absolute value in an experience "*is just a fact like other facts*," a fact for which one happens not yet to possess an adequate explanation. And at this point, Wittgenstein brings his argument swiftly to a close:

> Now when this is urged against me I at once see clearly, as it were in a flash of light, not only that no description that I can think of would do to describe what I mean by absolute value, but that I would reject every significant description that anybody could possibly suggest, *ab initio*, on the ground of its significance. That is to say: I see now that these nonsensical expressions were not nonsensical because I had not yet found the correct expressions, but that their nonsensicality was their very essence. For all I wanted to do with them was just *to go beyond the world* and that is to say beyond significant language. My whole tendency and I believe the tendency of all men who ever tried to write or talk Ethics or Religion was to run against the boundaries of language. This running against the

walls of our cage is perfectly, absolutely hopeless .... But it is a document of a tendency in the human mind which I personally cannot help respecting deeply and I would not for my life ridicule it.

Thus a kind of retrospective clarification is offered for the idea of "expression *by the existence* of language," which we can now understand as expression constituted by the collision of language with its inherent limits.

The abruptness with which Wittgenstein ends his lecture is now also explained. For now there is simply nothing more to be said. Any development of the lecture's thought, or any comment upon it—indeed, any more talk about ethics in general—would be nothing but a repetition of the same running against walls. The rest, as at the end of the *Tractatus*, is necessarily silence.

Or is it? It seems to me that even for one who accepts Wittgenstein's argument, there is more to be said on the matter of ethics. We can still ask exactly *where*—where in the structure and operation of language—the ethical collision takes place. And information on this point is provided—indirectly—by a well-known essay of P. F. Strawson.

That essay, "Freedom and Resentment," is about ethics, but it does not question the existence of ethics as Wittgenstein does. Strawson's approach is technical. He begins with "the thesis of determinism" (hence the question of freedom) and asks whether the truth or falsity of that thesis, in whatever form, has any bearing on "the concepts of moral obligation and responsibility" and on the possibility of justifying "the practices of punishing and blaming, of expressing moral condemnation and approval" (Strawson 1). His answer to this question is no. Conceivably a complete theory of ethics (and of its limits) might be found, and one which would convince practically everybody. But Strawson's point is that such a theory—which would likely presuppose a clear answer to the question of determinism and freedom of the will—is not necessary. Usable answers to practically all significant ethical questions, he suggests, can be derived without theoretical detours from a renewed attentiveness to our normal ethical instincts, to "the facts as we know them" (2 *et passim*). (This phrase, in exactly this form, occurs ten times in the essay; and the same idea is suggested in many other ways, by references to us "as we are" [12, 14], by assertions about what is "natural" or "normal" or "ordinary" [7, 14, 17], and by the visualization of our personal attitudes and social responses as forming a "continuum" or "web" or "structure" or "network" [24–26], hence a clear object of knowledge.)

The facts Strawson has in mind are mainly our thoughts and feelings as they develop in everyday interaction with other people. "It is a pity," he says, "that talk of the moral sentiments has fallen out of favour" (25–6). It seems we must learn once again to think in the manner of Hutcheson, Hume, Adam Smith, perhaps Shaftesbury, to recognize morality in our actual daily practice rather than search for it in theory. In an age influenced by Kant, it is by no means easy to meet this demand. Our habits of mind and terminology will constantly nudge us toward formulating general theoretical ideas as a framework for the experience we want to talk about. But Strawson insists on the specific. Of course he cannot be coherent without categorizing the specifics of experience he has in mind. But he keeps his categories as simple and as theoretically untainted as possible. He distinguishes basic "*reactive* attitudes" (7 et passim), feelings occasioned immediately by my perception of others' feelings toward me; then the "vicarious" analogues to those attitudes (15), in the sense that moral indignation on another's behalf might be considered analogous to personal resentment; and finally:

> Just as there are personal and vicarious reactive attitudes associated with demands on others for oneself and demands on others for others, so there are self-reactive attitudes associated with demands on oneself for others ... such phenomena as feeling bound or obliged ... feeling compunction; feeling guilty or remorseful or at least responsible; and the more complicated phenomenon of shame. (16)

And these families of attitudes, in turn, are modified in any number of ways by what I happen to know about the persons and circumstances in each case. (Resentment, for example, might be tempered by my recognition that the offender was not conscious of offending.)

But still, are the "facts" that Strawson lays out for us really facts to begin with? He himself says, not only in his essay's title, that "resentment has a particular interest" (11), we might perhaps say a *structural centralness* in his thought. For surely we cannot speak of morality or ethics until right is distinguished from wrong, which means: until someone has been wronged by someone else, which means, in Strawson's world: until an occasion for resentment has arisen. And Strawson appears to believe, accordingly, that resentment is a universal response to wrong, at least among people we would regard as normal.

> If someone treads on my hand accidentally ... the pain may be no less acute than if he treads on it in contemptuous disregard of my existence or with a malevolent wish to injure me. But I shall generally feel in the second case a kind and degree of resentment that I shall not feel in the first. (6)

At least in the second case, it is implied, resentment is practically never absent.

Nietzsche, however—for example—would object strenuously here. Of course resentment is a fact, and of course it is what one might call a moral sentiment. But it is not a simple fact of human nature. It is a morbid psychological symptom associated with an historically morbid morality. Nor is it universal. Not only are there particular individuals, according to Nietzsche, who are immune to it—like Mirabeau *fils*, who could never forgive an injury because he had always already forgotten it (KSA 5:273)—but it is foreign to the mind of that whole segment of humanity that merits the attribute "noble." And even without going as far as Nietzsche, one might still be tempted to ask whether resentment is ever really more than a kind of moral posture by which self-pity is at once disguised and nourished. And even if these objections are dismissed—they are after all matters of opinion—must we not still be worried by the *structural centralness* of resentment in Strawson's argument? Are we sure that it is not the structure that creates the supposed "fact," rather than vice versa?

Suppose, for example, we read Strawson's essay with one of its prominent admirers, Jürgen Habermas. Of Strawson's "facts as we know them," Habermas says,

> In trying to explain this web of emotional attitudes and feelings with the tools of linguistic analysis, Strawson is interested primarily in the fact that all these emotions are embedded in a practice of everyday life that is accessible to us only in a performative attitude. This gives the web of moral feelings a certain *ineluctability*: we cannot retract at will our commitment to a lifeworld whose members we are. (MC 47, MkH 57)[1]

I don't know if Strawson himself ever read this passage; but if he did, he must have been surprised to hear of his use of "linguistic analysis," which plays no role whatever in his essay. Actually there is a mistranslation here. In the original German, Habermas speaks of a "sprachanalytisch aufklärbarer Komplex von Gefühlseinstellungen," a "complex of emotional attitudes which *can be elucidated* by linguistic analysis." But Habermas and his translators are still looking in the same direction. Habermas promises by implication that in the course of his own discussion of "discourse ethics," Strawson's work will be supported and developed by "linguistic analysis." The translators simply assume that that analysis is already present in Strawson's essay. And what is it, then, that both Habermas and his translators *miss* in Strawson's thinking, what *gap* still remains to be closed by "linguistic analysis"?

Once this question is asked, it practically answers itself. It takes only a quick look at Habermas's text (45–50/55–60) to convince us that he lays much more stress on the *structural*, on the "continuum" or "web" or "network" supposedly formed by moral feelings, than Strawson does. He requires a strong notion of structure here in order to justify his conceptual leap from the descriptive to the "normative" (48/58), a leap which Strawson never takes. And yet, Strawson also uses the notions of "continuum," "web," "network" to characterize the aggregate of moral feelings, and he does so without any apparent justification at all. Here, therefore, between "the facts as we know them" and the structure Strawson ascribes to them, arises the gap that Habermas promises to close by "linguistic analysis." (Presumably he will analyze the common vocabulary of moral feelings in order to show structure on an irreducibly basic level—although I cannot see where he actually attempts such an analysis in the text I have cited.)

And if we ask, finally, why Strawson himself does *not* feel the need for linguistic analysis here, why he is not himself moved to deal explicitly with the fairly obvious gap in his inventory of concepts, then we find ourselves back in the vicinity of questions prompted by Wittgenstein. For it is clear that in Strawson's view—a view so deeply rooted as not to require articulation—that gap is filled by implications of the word "we," the "we" who must at least codetermine "the facts as we know them." "What I have to say consists largely of commonplaces" (5), says Strawson, and the commonness of these places, of the *loci communes* which "we" presumably all experience together, is a crucial factor in his argument. Even when he says "I"—in talking about having his hand stepped on, for instance—he usually means "we," he expects us to share his sentiments. (Wittgenstein, by contrast, in his ethics lecture, never says "I" without referring exclusively to himself.)

The point is that if I, as a reader, buy into Strawson's "we," if I accept his view of "the facts as we know them," then this acceptance, along with the knowledge that presumably underlies it, already presupposes an intelligible (and communicable) structure in the facts under consideration. There is no objective reason why the facts concerning our ethical or proto-ethical emotional responses in everyday life should not *lack* structure, should not constantly explode into an irrecoverable chaos, should not be largely unconnected, or connected only in all sorts of unaccountably various ways. It is only the presupposition that those "facts" are *known to "us" in common*—not merely known to individuals in who knows how many radically different forms—that supports the idea of a "continuum" or "web" or "network" of such facts. Only the assumption of "our" common knowledge guarantees that those facts form a coherent object of knowledge in the first place.

Of course the implication also works the other way round. If a knowable structure of moral sentiments could be assumed to exist, then that structure would certainly justify the claim that "we" all know ourselves to be vessels of those sentiments. Ethical thought, as Strawson conducts it, therefore involves a logical circle that is associated eminently with our use—often our covertly or indeed unconsciously imperious or hortatory or cajoling use—of the word "we." And my contention is that this word, in this sense, is the point in language at which Wittgenstein's ethical collision with the boundaries of language occurs. (Wittgenstein himself is careful to avoid the presumptuous "we" where a collision is imminent. He says not, "*Our* whole tendency is to run against the boundaries of language," but rather, "My whole tendency and I believe the tendency of all men who have ever tried to write or talk Ethics or Religion," suggesting no opinion on whether or not I share his belief.)

Strawson would certainly have disagreed with me. His principal objections, I think, would have been two in number. First, he never claims that the "we" in his essay—whether explicit or implied—is universal. In fact he goes into considerable detail (8–14) concerning people whose moral or psychological or physical condition might disqualify them as participants in the imagined community of the essay's readers. But then, neither do I claim that his "we" is universal in anything approaching an objective sense. My point is that the essay's argument is valid *for me* only if I first make the move of buying into its implied "we." And I have suggested several reasonable responses to Strawson's notion of "resentment" that would *prevent* even a person of entirely unimpaired ethical responsibility from accepting that "we" and those "facts as we know them."

(Strawson's "we," in other words, is universal only in the sense that his argument implies no intrinsic restriction upon who may buy into it. If you understand the language and can follow and responsibly accept the reasoning, then a valid general ethics is yours for the taking. Universality is not a property of Strawson's ethics. But universalizability is such a property, as it is in Habermas's ethics.)

The second objection that would have been available to Strawson is stronger. Suppose it is true that the logical circle as I have described it is present as a danger for every reader of his essay. Suppose, therefore, that Wittgenstein is correct, that *strictly speaking* the ethical collision with the boundaries of language cannot be avoided. Is it worth the effort, is it in fact ethically responsible, to *speak strictly* in this connection? Even if I disagree on the matter of resentment—if I insist, say, on Nietzsche's view of the matter, or on Montaigne's refusal to imagine the done as undone or as not-yet-done—would it not make more sense for me to compromise a bit, in the hope of contributing to a perhaps more widely acceptable view of "the facts as we know them," hence to a more capacious "we"? By dispensing with Strawson's method altogether, am I not insisting that if we cannot have a complete ethical theory—like Kant's theory of the categorical imperative, with its peremptory answer to the question of freedom of the will—then we shall have no ethics at all?

I do not admit this dilemma. I think it is possible to accept unreservedly Wittgenstein's argument and to develop nevertheless—by concentrating on the "we," on the point where ethics "runs against the boundaries of language"—a way of talking fruitfully about ethics after all. But it cannot be expected that I will propose a general theory of the ethical "we"—which would imply exactly the objective standard of ethical validity that Wittgenstein finds impossible, Strawson unnecessary. My approach will be strictly specific. I will confine myself to the discussion of three *particular instances* of a nonuniversalizable ethical "we": the elusive but inevitable "we" of irony, the perplexing historical "we" of diasporic Jews, and a feminist "we" that refers to, but does not necessarily mean, actual women.

On the Constructionist Fallacy, on Method, and on Reading

An interesting perspective on Wittgenstein's denial that a "book" on ethics is possible is suggested by Philip Anderson's essay "More Is Different." Anderson begins with the generally accepted "reductionist hypothesis" about science: the hypothesis that "everything obeys the same fundamental laws," hence that the phenomena of molecular biology are reducible to those of chemistry, those of chemistry to those of many-body physics, those of the latter ultimately to those of elementary particle physics (393). But, he continues,

> the reductionist hypothesis does not by any means imply a "constructionist" one: The ability to reduce everything to simple fundamental laws does not imply the ability to start from those laws and reconstruct the universe …. Instead, at each [higher] level of complexity entirely new properties appear. (393)

For readers who have not studied broken symmetry in physics, which is Anderson's prime instance, an illuminating application of his thought is found in Steve Keen's treatment of the relation of microeconomics to macroeconomics (Keen 25–48).

The application to ethics has to do with the relation between what we might call microethics, meaning individuals' judgments of right or wrong, and macroethics, the domain of theories or systems that exert normative force over individuals' behavior. We have discussed Habermas's recognition, in reading Strawson, that a qualitatively new form of thinking ("linguistic analysis") is needed in order to reach the macroethical level. To generalize: macroethics requires the imposition of *authority* in some form, because normativity is by definition absent in microethics. But ethics is unlike economics, or any other science, because acceptance of the authority belonging to a supra-individual level of complexity—whether religious authority, or political or philosophical, or even language-analytic—violates its basic concept. Can a system still be called "ethics" if it might require me to suppress my own personal judgment of right or wrong? Thus we arrive at another form of Wittgenstein's conclusion: macroethics, understood in a sufficiently strict sense, cannot be carried out consistently.

(Ways of avoiding this contradiction have been suggested: most notably Kant's brilliant derivation of an inherently both micro- and macroethical "categorical imperative" from the idea of reason alone. A number of the many problems with Kantian ethics will be dealt with further on in this book, frequently in connection with Habermas's attempts to get around them, especially his claim that constructivist learning theory, coupled with regulated debate, creates a path which defies the constructionist fallacy by leading directly from individual judgment to valid ethical norms.)

It remains my opinion that Wittgenstein's point cannot be dismissed without undermining the very idea of ethics, hence that a valid ethics in propositional form (or in what Wittgenstein calls "significant language") cannot be achieved. I will defend my opinion, especially in Chapter 1 and in an extended critique of Habermas in Chapter 6. But the question that interests me principally is where this conclusion leaves us, whether it is still possible—and if so, how—to say or to learn anything useful about ethics. I have already said where I think the point is, in language, at which Wittgenstein's thought can be developed. But the question of method remains. How do we proceed?

As far as I can see, there is only one method that comes into question: the close reading of existing texts in which a Wittgensteinian "collision" is avoided, texts that possess significant general ethical force, but without, in any formulable manner, being "on" or "about" ethics. If such texts do not exist, the situation is hopeless. We can have either ethics or Wittgenstein, but not both. My claim, however, is not only that the required texts exist, but also that they form an intelligible pattern, a pattern which, in a book much larger than the present one, could likely be developed into a complete history of Western ethics, the unfolding of what I want to call a "humanist legacy."

But by "reading" these texts, we obviously cannot mean the type of reading that aims at a reasonably adequate paraphrase of its original. If reading in this sense were sufficient, then the condition that prevents Wittgenstein's collision, the condition that the texts in question not be "about" ethics, would not be met. We require what has come to be known in literary studies as "close reading," reading that seeks to take hold of its text at a level inaccessible to paraphrase.[2] We require the sort of "slow" reading that Nietzsche associates with "philology" (KSA 3:17), a patient reading, constantly suspicious of its own conclusions, constantly attentive to what might be happening behind the scenes or beneath the surface in its text.

As far as readers of the present book are concerned, I think that not many would be persuaded by anything like an expository summation of my conclusions, which are at all events only provisional. It seems to me more likely that readers who consider in detail my discussions of Nietzsche, Lessing, and Freud, or of Woolf, Wittig, and Bachmann, or of Leibniz and Machiavelli, may be persuaded that something of great ethical significance is happening in those texts, but without taking the form of ethical propositions. And I hope it may then occur to those readers that similar critical approaches are possible over a much wider range of textual material. I am aware, for my own part, of having done no more than scratch the surface. But I have done enough to convince myself, at least, that a much larger book on the history of ethics is out there waiting to be written.

Chapter 1

INTRODUCTION: ETHICS, "LITERATURE," "THE HUMAN," AND IRONY

Wittgenstein, in the lecture discussed above, describes his "feeling" about ethics "by the metaphor, that, if a man could write a book on Ethics which really was a book on Ethics, this book would, with an explosion, destroy all the other books in the world." Assuming he means that such a book would contradict the very notion of a book, I accept his view. It follows that I am, at the very least, reluctant to think of my own work as a book "on ethics."

To most readers, in fact, it will look like a book on "literature." I have reasons for disliking this term and the whole concept it tries to name, reasons I will set forth below. But it is true that mine is a book mostly about texts, as it must be. If the project of carrying ethics beyond Wittgenstein could be adequately represented in a free-standing conceptual structure, the result would be precisely a book "on ethics" and presumably an explosion. The project, accordingly, is made up mainly of finding ways to avoid this contradiction, ways of writing that have a clear ethical dimension without ever being "on ethics" in any reasonable (or explosive) sense. Nor do I mean "ways of writing" in the abstract, which would lead to the same contradiction. I mean specific texts, which I have chosen for what I hope will be their usefulness in enabling me, in my turn, to produce a text that both invokes and avoids the bedeviling contradiction of ethics.

My project, thus understood, is not new. Among philosophers and literary scholars, in fact, there has been great interest in attempting to rescue ethics by way of the attenuation it undergoes when forced into conjunction with the concept "literature." One recent book, Martin Blumenthal-Barby's *Inconceivable Effects*, starts out from the same lecture of Wittgenstein that I have cited and contains an excellent summary of recent work with an orientation similar to its own. I will use this book, further on, to situate what I am trying to do.

Ethics and Its History

But hang it all, what *is* ethics?—readers will ask. Given the problem of taking a position "on ethics," I will go as far as I can in answering.

Ethics is involved in any decision I make about what to do when my conduct is not fully determined by necessity or at least practicality. And if the idea of "acting ethically" has any meaning at all, then it must be true that in acting thus, I do not simply satisfy my personal whims or desires or needs—which implies that ethics has to be understood as a *method*.

Ethics, in this basic sense, is not the same thing as morality. My own view is that what we normally recognize as morality is a particular type of ethics, not identical with the whole. Morality, I mean, is any ethics that has a metaphysical dimension, any ethical method that is derived from a rational ideal or perhaps from the content of a revealed religion. I do not claim that this distinction is traditional, or even etymological; *mores*, after all, in Latin, can designate mere customs. But "morality," in English, does suggest something rather more elevated than "ethics," which is the basis for my terminological distinction.

Many writers—Kant foremost among them—would insist that my distinction is vacuous, that there is no such thing as ethics without an ideal or metaphysical underpinning, that if rules of conduct are to be taken seriously, they must be given by some higher authority. (For Kant, that authority is the inherent structure of reason.) I disagree. I do not even agree that the concept of ethics necessarily includes the concept of rules. Ethics is always a method. But I deny that the manner in which my ethical conduct deviates from what I would otherwise find easiest, or most comfortable or advantageous, can always be explained by formulable rules.

Ordinarily (or Kantianly) this matter is looked at the other way round. Morality is understood as the study of *duty* in the broadest sense, including my duty toward myself and toward various religious and political institutions, as well as my duty in transactions with other people. Since ethics is concerned mainly with these latter transactions, it is thought to be contained within morality, which would imply that its content can be derived from moral principles. My preference, on the contrary, is to regard ethics as the more general category and morality as one particular form. Even within the scheme I propose, morality could be understood as dominant, could be considered the *essence* of ethics. But it does not need to be considered thus.

In any case, I insist on the character of ethics as method—an idea which I borrow from Nietzsche in a manner I will explain in the next chapter. This approach excludes from ethics, for example, Emmanuel Lévinas's philosophy of encounter with the "other" and Martin Buber's dialogue philosophy of the "I–Thou," both of which play out in experience considered as a developing whole and do not originate as a methodical intervention in experience. There is plenty of room for ethical discussion in Lévinas's thought, as in Buber's. But ethical discussion and ethics are not the same thing; otherwise a book "on ethics" would be possible. The strict idea of method, moreover, raises the question of the specific collective, the "we," in which this or that method is respected; for without such a collective, method is mere idiosyncrasy. Therefore the ethical "we" is crucial in my view. Ethics in the form of propositions, as far as I can see, is inescapably universalist, in the sense that its "we" is always at least universalizable. (If the propositions make sense, they are available to anyone.) The question is whether a non-propositional ethics can be found, and what sort of non-universal "we" would accompany it. The case of Habermas, whom I will discuss in detail, is instructive. His ethics is emphatically methodical, reducible to the method of rational argumentation. But, at the same time, the strength of his insistence on a universalizable collective creates an internal tension that I claim constantly unbalances his Enlightenment project.

At this point I think I have said all I can on a general plane. I do have reasons for subordinating morality to ethics, and for positing a non-universal "we" and the idea of method. But those reasons belong wholly to the domain of practical criticism. I will argue that there are many important ethical thinkers whose thought is completely misunderstood if it is taken as universalist or moral. And I will argue further that we owe precisely to these thinkers a sense of the ethical that is entirely indispensable in the world of modern politics, science, and religion, where the contradiction suggested by Wittgenstein has become endemic and increasingly corrupting.

My argument is rooted in the eighteenth century, especially with Leibniz and Lessing, who are important not only in themselves but also because of their proximity to Kant. For the ethical side of their writing has been obscured by the pretensions of what I will call *propositional ethics*, the type of ethics that is insisted upon by Kant and then subscribed to in most post-Kantian school philosophy. (It is the type of ethics that would cause Wittgenstein's universal "explosion" if it could be realized.) But I do not mean that Leibniz and Lessing are ethical innovators. They are, rather, the *preservers* of a long tradition of non-propositional humanist ethical writing, preservers now in an increasingly inhospitable age, that age whose spirit is then captured by Kant's prodigious propositional achievement, the categorical imperative. Kant is much more the innovator, and a very successful one. But an understanding of what Leibniz and Lessing work to preserve makes it easier for us to recognize their practice of pre-Kantian ethical writing, writing in the humanistic tradition, when it reemerges later in response to more modern problems. I will call that traditional practice *rhetorical ethics* (ethics embedded in a text's rhetoric, not expressed in propositions). But rhetorical ethics must not be confused with Habermas's "discourse ethics," which is a prime example of the attempt to revive precisely propositional or Kantian ethics in a form supposedly purged of its difficulties.

I will begin my argument in Chapter 2 with the modern form of rhetorical ethics, the "ethics of irony," that is worked out by Nietzsche and then, so to speak, re-originated by Richard Rorty. Only after this matter is set forth will I go back to the eighteenth century and, in Chapter 3, attempt to show how Nietzsche's achievement in ethics is anticipated by Leibniz's non-Kantian ethical procedure—a procedure, incidentally, that is *not* derivable from his morality or theory of the good. Then, in Chapters 4 and 5, I will take up Lessing's ethics of irony and discuss the manner in which it can be regarded as a Jewish ethics, interestingly similar to the ethical dimension of psychoanalysis as understood by Freud. Chapter 6 will suggest a provisional theoretical structure by situating Habermas, Rorty, and Niccolò Machiavelli with respect to some crucial issues. And finally, in Chapter 7, using texts of Virginia Woolf, Ingeborg Bachmann, and Monique Wittig, I will try to show the unique and historically inevitable operation of ironic or rhetorical ethics in feminist thought.

Ethics of Reading?

The general idea of a modern non-propositional ethics is not new. Martin Blumenthal-Barby opens his book *Inconceivable Effects* with a lucid summary of the literary and rhetorical aspect of ethical thinking as it evolved mainly in the twentieth century (ix–xxxi).[1] Under the rubric "Philosophy's Turn to Narrative" (xi) he discusses Alasdair MacIntyre, Richard Rorty, and Martha Nussbaum, and eventually dismisses all three: MacIntyre for his insistence on community membership as a basis for ethics (xii) and the other two for being insufficiently attentive to the "figural" or "aesthetic" or "material" component of literary texts (xiv, xxiii). I think he is not fair to Rorty on this point, especially not to Rorty's idea of irony, which I will treat in Chapter 2. But he is certainly right when he talks about a modern awareness—I would say, the modern revival of a very old awareness—of the "insufficiency of propositional language in the face of ethics" (x).

After discussing the search for ethical orientation in responses to the content of more or less literary narratives, Blumenthal-Barby takes up the topic of "Literary Studies' Turn to Ethics" (xviii), his main instances being Wayne Booth, Tobin Siebers, and J. Hillis Miller. Booth's "ethical pluralism" (xix), as far as I can see, is not much different from the ethics that had been ascribed to Rorty or Nussbaum. But when we get to the matter of an *ethics of reading* in Hillis Miller and Siebers, or more specifically an ethics of critical reading, we find ourselves much closer to the center of the problem of a modern ethics—if not to a solution of that problem. The trouble is that we do not have a good idea of what we mean by "reading" in the first place. Is reading ever enough of an *act* to warrant ethical consideration and judgment? Or does it, as an act, ever have enough in the way of social or political consequences?

Blumenthal-Barby, taking a cue from Derek Attridge's response to Hillis Miller, suggests invoking the thought of Lévinas and the idea of "the ethical demand of the other" (xxii)—except that the otherness in question is here not that of another human being but that of a literary text, a "textual otherness" (xxv, xxviii) that consists in the text's resistance to the appropriative advances I make in reading it, its resistance to "the encompassing grasp of our interpretive techniques" (xxvii).[2] This conceptual move is certainly ambitious enough, but it cannot possibly succeed if we do not find a way of regarding the reading process as an "event" (xxviii)[3] in the reader's experience, comparable to the direct encounter with another person. And here a difficulty arises—in my view a crippling difficulty. For while we cannot claim much positive knowledge about what we call "reading," still there are some negative points about which we can be fairly definite. And one of them is that "reading," in any reasonable sense, does *not* have the quality of an experienced "event," for the simple reason that it cannot be located in time. An event, by definition, is chronologically locatable, whereas (as Stanley Corngold points out) every instance of reading is automatically un-located in experienced time by the components of pre-reading and re-reading that belong to its very constitution.[4]

Perhaps what we should really be talking about is not an ethics of reading, but an ethics of criticism (see Siebers, *The Ethics of Criticism*) or, more specifically, an ethics of critical writing. Miller would disagree. He says he is concerned with "something that at least has a chance to be concrete, namely the real situation of a man or woman reading a book, teaching a class, writing a critical essay" (*The Ethics of Reading* 4). But it turns out that the social reality of the classroom and the materiality of writing are not "concrete" enough. He immediately clarifies:

> No doubt that "situation" spreads out to involve institutional, historical, economic, and political "contexts," but it begins with and returns to the man or woman face to face with the words on the page. (4)

The metaphorical jump from the event of facing a person to the supposed event of "facing" a text is thus crucial here. But even without my point about the unlocatability of reading as an event, it is still hard to see how reading can have an "ethics" except by way of a *public* or at least *social* development of itself, which means by way either of writing or of the give and take of actual discussion. Miller agrees, in any case, that an "ethical moment" (8) must be located in reading before an ethics of reading can be imagined.

The problematics of this whole matter can be approached from another direction. Why, namely, do Hillis Miller and a few of his contemporaries, and nowadays everyone, invariably call their treatments of this or that text "readings," and not, for example, "interpretations"? Miller suggests an answer to this question:

> The ethics of reading is not some act of the human will to interpretation which extracts moral themes from a work, or uses it to reaffirm what the reader already knows, or imposes a meaning freely in some process of reader response or perspectivist criticism, seeing the text in a certain way. The ethics of reading is the power of the words of the text over the mind and words of the reader. This is an irresistible coercion which shapes what the reader or teacher says about the text, even when what he says is most reductive or evasive. ("The Ethics of Reading" 41)

Interpretation is associated here with will or self-assertion, whereas "reading" *submits itself* as completely as possible to "the words of the text." This is not a standard terminological distinction. "Interpretation," etymologically and in practice, suggests not an act of will but a process of negotiation between text and reader. But for Miller, even the idea of negotiation would imply too much *distance* from the text, too much perspective. I must simply open myself to a "power" from the text, a power that is describable, if at all, only in linguistic terms. Not that this opening of myself is easy or relaxed. "Reading itself is extraordinarily hard work. Clearheaded reflection on what really happens in an act of reading is even more difficult and rare …. It is so hard, too hard, to keep one's attention on the text" (*The Ethics of Reading* 3–5). Reading is thus inherently ethical, as a form of strenuous self-discipline.

But it is by no means immediately evident that the "text" by which such self-discipline is oriented really exists. The text as a material object is not enough. The text as a reservoir of "power" is needed. But not power in the sense of the creative or articulative power of the person who wrote the text; rather, a power that dwells strictly in the text's language, yet is also more specific, more tightly focused, than what we might imagine as the power of language as such or of a particular natural language.

Surely the only possible *empirical* evidence for the operation of such power, hence for the existence of a "text" in this sense, would be a general tendency toward agreement in discussions among competent readers about specific texts, especially literary texts. E. D. Hirsch asserts several times that such a tendency exists, and I can think of a large number of important thinkers who would probably concur, though for widely differing reasons, including Habermas, Gadamer, Rorty, Stanley Fish, and Wolfgang Iser. But it happens that my own experience suggests exactly the opposite: the more you talk about a literary text, the more occasion you find for disagreement. And there are theoretical initiatives of proven value that conflict (or seem to) with the idea of a text's unique potency—especially the idea of intertextuality in the strict sense in which Kristeva develops it, the idea that the things texts accomplish, the operations that show power, are never accomplished anywhere but *between* texts.[5]

At best, then, the question of whether Miller's "text" is ever actually there is undecidable. And as far as I can see, this leaves open only one possibility for imagining or asserting or practicing an "ethics of reading": we would have to be resolute in our commitment to the *idea* of "the text" as Miller understands it; in all our reading and teaching and debating and writing we would have to *presuppose* that "text" uninterruptedly, and we would have to operate *as if* it were there to guide us; in a strong sense, therefore, we would have to *create* over and over again the "text" to whose words we unfailingly submit our own words; it would have to be generated constantly as the indispensable center of our collective intellectual activity. A decision of this sort, taken by every individual member of a substantial professional community, would certainly satisfy any reasonable definition of an "ethics." Thus we find that we have come back to the idea of ethics in the form of an imperious or hortatory "we," the form that I ascribed to Strawson in the Preliminary Remarks.

But in the version implied by Miller's thinking, this ethics is potentially very dangerous. In Strawson's essay the "we" is needed in order to guarantee the presence of contour or structure in a collection of "facts" whose bare existence, as "moral sentiments," no one is likely to dispute. But in Miller's scheme, the ethical "we" is given the task of *creating* a fact, creating that ubiquitous potent entity, the "text," on which everything depends. And in order to operate properly, this pretended radical communal creativity would have to be contained exclusively within the aesthetic realm. It would require an impervious barrier between the aesthetic and the political, since any leakage would create the possibility of a politics in which respect for existing fact is subordinated to the uncompromising imperative of conviction—which adds up to a totalitarian politics. And if common sense is not already enough, then surely the history of aesthetics and politics since the eighteenth century teaches us that no such impervious barrier can be maintained. The opportunity for abuse is too obvious; the idea of a human triumph over the factual—as Hannah Arendt understood—is too seductive.[6]

I am not suggesting that literary theorists of any particular stripe are either advocates or dupes of totalitarian politics. On the contrary, I think the large intellectual movement known, since the middle of the last century, as "literary theory" has been a consistent and, at times, perhaps even effective force on the side of political liberalism. But it does not follow that every idea brought forth by that movement is necessarily liberal in its consequences, or even a good idea in itself. And the point of my argument now is that "ethics of reading" is one of those ideas that it might be wise simply to discard.

"Literary Ethics" and "Literature"

Blumenthal-Barby, in the end, is also not satisfied with the ethics proposed by Hillis Miller (though for reasons different from mine) or with Attridge's invocation of Lévinas to tweak that ethics. But the "literary ethics" he offers in its place is not easy to pin down.

> At issue is an ethics that, beyond the accumulation of moral injunctions, emanates from the fissures, chasms, and interstices of poetic enactments, an ethics that evolves as elusive effect, whose epistemic resistance this project [his present book] cannot overcome but perhaps (or that would be the hope) can invoke. (15)

Given the inherent "epistemic resistance" of the phenomena he is talking about, how can Blumenthal-Barby still speak of "*an* ethics," of a single, presumably isolable "literary ethics" (xxxi)? In his chapters on specific artifacts, he does make good on his promise to show "ethical effects" (xxxi) in a wide variety of generic situations. But on what grounds does he suggest that these effects are inherently well enough organized to merit being called *an* ethics?

I do not think there are any grounds except the assumption that ethics is a form of morality and, if it exists at all, must therefore be *one* ethics, that the business of ethics is to be unique and universally valid. It is true that Blumenthal-Barby has already accepted, by implication, a limit on the reach of the ethics he has in mind. That ethics will not pretend, like Kant's, to be valid for all rational creatures, or even for all humans. It is a "literary ethics" and will operate as a guiding or governing scheme only for those people who are fully engaged in the institution and practice of "literature"—"literature," to be sure, in a sense broad enough to embrace Hannah Arendt's totalitarianism book,

Walter Benjamin's "Critique of Violence," and the film *Germany in Autumn*, all of which figure in the development of his thought. But among the people for whom it is meant, presumably people who are distinguished by special abilities in thinking and writing, he means it to be universally valid. He has dispensed with the uncomfortable notion of reading as an ethically discussible "event" and shifted the focus to a relatively exclusive "we."

But this move raises at least two difficult questions. The first has to do with the idea of ethical universality and its application to a restricted class of individuals, especially when membership in the class depends on one's sensitivity to "the fissures, chasms, and interstices of poetic enactments." Can something like this formulation enable us to identify either the community (the "we") that defines the ethics we are seeking or the ethics that defines the community? Even if we bracket the specifics, the difficulty remains. Suppose we agree that the community in which our ethics is valid shall be defined by the concept "literature" and suppose we have a good idea of what that concept means. Precisely our grasp of the concept provides grounds for *disagreement* about whether this or that individual can claim to belong to the community it defines. And I contend that no community thus constituted can serve as the range of validity for an ethics, because a meta-ethics will first be required to decide community membership. I will come back to this point in more detail in connection with Habermas's program of "discourse ethics."

For the second question I have in mind, let us return to the concept "literature" and ask whether we really do have a good idea of what it means. In talking about whence his literary ethics will "emanate," why does Blumenthal-Barby speak of the fissures "of poetic enactments" and not of "the fissures, chasms, and interstices *of texts*"? Obviously he wants to convey a more *kinetic* idea than is normally suggested by "texts," at least if we avoid the tricky and dangerous notion of a text's "power." And it follows now that "literature" in his view—no matter how broadly one understands it—is always an *aesthetically* defined concept, that the belonging of a text to "literature" depends not on any objective qualities of that text, but on how we interact with it, on the process or kinesis by which our relation to it is engendered.

This view of literature is entirely in keeping with the history of the concept. For there is no such thing as "literature," in the normal modern sense, until close to the end of the eighteenth century. (The *word* "literature," along with other languages' versions of Latin *litteratura*, had long existed, but not in the aesthetically restricted sense common today.) The earlier material that we now retrospectively think of as "literary" consists mainly of the huge variety of different art forms in the linguistic medium that were collectively known as "poetry," plus a great deal of narrative material in prose, most of it known as "romance." What we call the "genres" of poetry, I mean, were for most of their historical existence *discrete arts*—undergoing, of course, plenty of evolution and hybridizing over time, but still essentially discrete. The collective concept "poetry," in all European languages, embraced those discrete poetic arts more or less as the concept "track and field" embraces all sorts of running, jumping, and throwing.

But in the course of the eighteenth century—with the emergence of new social and educational and commercial uses for the arts, and with the concomitant opening of rationalist thought to the suddenly fashionable idea of the "aesthetic," or to what Marian Hobson calls a "bipolar" view of art—all of poetry and romance, along with the developing novel, is gradually gathered up into the single domain of "literature." And the pleasure that for millennia had been recognized as attending the reading or hearing of those old arts is now pressed into service, in effect, as an aesthetic *definition* of the new concept.[7]

Many factors are at work here. The growth of modern middle-class society is accompanied by the enormous growth—in technical sophistication, in social resonance, and in popularity—of the novel, whence the need arises for a category of texts that will include novels while also inheriting the prestige of the "poetic." But formal rules and guides, such as had defined all the earlier poetic arts, would not be applicable here. The novel had emphatically dispensed with such regulation, and in any case, customers in the increasingly extensive book-and-periodical market were not likely to have had much poetic training. "Literature" therefore came to be defined by aesthetic criteria, criteria having to do with the type of response provoked by a text in a reader's mind. Indeed, early on in the century, in the book in which he coins the term "aesthetic," Alexander Gottlieb Baumgarten had already used such subjective criteria—the extent and manner in which a text addresses our "lower" or sensitive or affective mental faculties—to define or redefine the "poetic," well before the term "literature" ever appeared in its new aestheticized meaning.[8]

This topic has not received anything like the attention it deserves. But it appears that a crucial factor in the establishment of "literature" as an ineradicable element of the European cultural scene may have been educational politics in an atmosphere of emerging nationalism. The new concept had hardly come into being before it was put to use in manufacturing the idea of *national* literatures—German, French, and English, especially. And it is hard to believe that the concept was not thus permanently tainted. For in reality there is no such thing as a national literature, an unbroken and substantially self-contained tradition of imaginative writing in a single language. In the first place, the application of the concept "literature" to ages in which no such overarching category of imaginative writing existed is highly questionable. In the second place, we know that in the history of poetic forms, at least in the narrow confines of multilingual Europe, the main developments and innovations take place *between* languages, not in the progress of a single language here or there. The delusive idea of the national literature as a kind of organism, affected by "influences" from without but always retaining its own identity, owes its longevity primarily, I conjecture, to its usefulness for nationalist indoctrination in public schools. Which means indoctrination of a special kind: not systematic training in the principles and institutions of the polity, but rather encouragement of the notion of citizenship as a kind of aesthetic (subjective, emotional) solidarity—which is a step on the way to totalitarianism. It has been remarked often enough, in any case, that the extraordinary institutional tenacity of the idea of national literature is measurable by our need to say "comparative" literature when we wish to discuss poetic and literary phenomena as they actually arise and interact in history.

And yet, it is not difficult to see why the idea of a "literary ethics" is attractive. If one is basically in agreement with Wittgenstein about the incompatibility of ethics with "significant" language and if one nevertheless feels unable to do without clear and convincing ethical principles, then it seems that one has to restrict the community in which those principles operate. Ethics as such, universal ethics for an unrestricted community, is understood to be impossible. And what better community can be imagined for the rescue of ethics than the professional community of literary critics and scholars, people whose expertise in dealing with delicate and complicated linguistic situations suits them, better than anyone else, for the task of devising a way to talk ethics without touching off the explosion promised by Wittgenstein? What is needed, says Tobin Siebers, is an "unspoken ethics of criticism" derived from "the persistent cares and desires of people who write, read, and live together" (239).

The members of this literary community, moreover, tend to feel an especially strong need for the ethical ordering of at least their professional life, a need that is reawakened every time they look at their department letterheads and reflect on the discrepancy between what it says there (about nationality or about "literature") and what they think they actually do for a living. One can follow the ethical appetite in literary study as far back as one wishes. It is evident, for example, in Northrop Frye's idea of an "intermediate criticism," between the activity of "scholars" and that of "public critics," a criticism that would organize itself theoretically and whose possibility would imply "that at no point is there any direct learning of literature itself" and that "what one learns, transitively, is the criticism of literature" (Frye 11). In place of the ethically questionable move of accepting the conceptual instability of "literature itself," Frye's theoretical criticism would insist on a definite distance from its object, and "just as there is nothing which the philosopher cannot consider philosophically, and nothing which the historian cannot consider historically, so the critic should be able to construct and dwell in a conceptual universe of his own" (12). We have an ethical responsibility to do our own thinking as critics, says Frye, rather than contrive somehow to let literature do it for us.

The trouble is that the ethical problems associated with literature are liable to arise with the mere use of the term. As soon as I speak or write the word "literature" as if in relation to an understood referent, I have automatically opened the question of exactly how that referent is understood, or indeed constituted. At the worst, therefore, I may now find myself obliged (if only in my own thinking) to answer the charge of being complicit both in a tradition of disgraceful intellectual imprecision and in the institutional attempt to cover it up. This difficulty can be managed, perhaps even exploited, if one is careful to avoid using that suspect concept to define other concepts or if one is talking historically or speculatively. But how can it fail to poison the attempt to talk serious ethics, to establish or describe or define or somehow enact anything resembling ethical principles?

Introduction

The Human as Enemy of the Humanist

I am not necessarily opposed to the project of seeking a non-universalist position by associating ethics with the literary temper, especially if this project acknowledges its debt to *humanist tradition*, the tradition of elite classical learning in European history that leads up, in our day, to the community of people we call intellectuals. But the notion of a "literary ethics" involves such profound difficulties that its proponents constantly find themselves drifting back toward what they had by rights resolutely left behind, toward the universal in the form of "the human." (The humanistic, that is, tends to degenerate into the human, into a concept whose lack of ethical standing is brought most fully into focus by the feminist exposure of its historically inescapable masculine gendering.)

Siebers, for example, finds in "nuclear criticism" a way to come in from the cold, so to speak, a way to plead for "central human issues" (236) and against "the forms of violence that threaten community" (239), a way that leads him to his book's closing words, "The finally human is literature" (240)—words which supposedly mobilize Wallace Stevens for ethics only by way of critical irresponsibility in reading him. The title of the poem Siebers has in mind is "Lebensweisheitspielerei" (Stevens 504–5), which both *means* "fooling around" (*Spielerei*) and, by being fabricated out of incongruous German elements, *is* a kind of fooling around. It is thus not clear whether Stevens means that his poem should be taken as a fooling around *with* "the wisdom of experience" (*Lebensweisheit*) or whether that wisdom is itself an instance of fooling around. But in either case, the idea of fooling around undermines any attempt to find a new ethical stability in the lines: "The proud and the strong / Have departed. // Those that are left are the unaccomplished, / The finally human, / Natives of a dwindled sphere." And Siebers's sentence "The finally human is literature," which expresses an even further-reaching claim, also happens to paraphrase the title of an earlier Stevens poem, "Men Made out of Words," the last couplet of which exposes its joking: "The whole race is a poet that writes down / The eccentric propositions of its fate" (355–6). Surely these lines are a fooling around with Shelley's unacknowledged legislators.

Blumenthal-Barby tries to avoid the temptation of the universally human—and Wittgenstein's explosion, which he is fully aware of (x)—by going one step beyond it. His second-to-last chapter, on the film *Germany in Autumn*, is called "The Return of the Human." But that "return" is left behind emphatically in the book's final chapter, which proclaims "A Politics of Enmity"—as opposed, presumably, to an inherent "human" amity among the four erstwhile enemies of the chapter preceding. In the end, however, neither Blumenthal-Barby nor even Heiner Müller, his protagonist in that final chapter, can operate ethically without recourse to a disguised, but still thoroughly sentimental and aesthetic idea of the human.

The very concept of the human is corrupting, like the concept of literature. It is hard even to mention it without getting implicated in its history and its ethical lability. Blumenthal-Barby provides a signal instance of this difficulty:

> "Humanism is the ideology of the machine," Müller hyperbolically states in his autobiography. What he alludes to is the precarious ideological ambiguity of "humanism," which is always based on principles of selection and exclusion, mechanisms of enmity, and the expulsion of enemies, thereby producing the "inhuman" that proves to be an incessant supplement of "the" human and, perhaps ... the most genuinely and inherently "human" there is. (156)[9]

The otherwise incomprehensible transition here, in two sentences, from the scornful pleonasm of machine ideology to the idea of an achievement of genuineness—presumably via the awareness of corruption—is nothing but the twisted ethical work of "the human" as a concept. (Of course "humanism," in this passage, does *not* refer to a tradition of classical learning.)

And the same ethical work is carried out in Müller's texts, especially in the figure of the Young Bricklayer in *Germania Tod in Berlin*, who comes to visit old Hilse in the hospital and finds him dying of cancer, not of his injuries from being stoned as a strikebreaker. The task of the Young Bricklayer is reconciliation, on behalf of a community of interest that supersedes even the deadliest divisions within the workers' movement, a reconciliation made both necessary and possible by Hilse's internalization, as cancer or corruption, of the violence directed against him. A reconciliation which then also embraces Red Rosa, the party which is everybody's whore, used by everybody for everything, yet remains irresistibly attractive, as herself, and pregnant with a future which, at least for the time being, the Young Bricklayer takes as his own. Reconciliation in this form is of course never finally achieved. But for this reason it is also never sufficiently contoured or exclusive to be understood as anything but an instance of the universally human. The human by default, so to speak, like the humanness of "perhaps a puppet" in the "Nachtstück" (Night Piece) section of *Germania*, a scene which forces the roaring laughter of the clown show in Brecht's *Badener Lehrstück* into the abstract individual solitude of Beckett's "Act Without Words," where it is reduced to a scream, a single scream which provides a perfect inverted image of human (Kantian) autonomy by being identical with the mouth that screams it.

It is true enough, in general, that Müller "propels and perpetuates the bloodshed he poetically seeks to probe" (Blumenthal-Barby 176). And it is true that he handled his own cancer with considerable courage. But there is still a hedging of bets, a "human" hedging, in the idea of surgery (175–8) as a final example of radical violence. Precisely surgery *is* always addressed, from the outset by "*moral concerns*" (178).

The same basic movement, renunciation and return with respect to the human, is described on a large scale by Devin Fore in his book *Realism after Modernism: The Rehumanization of Art and Literature*. If "aesthetic modernism" is correctly characterized by Ortega y Gasset as a "dehumanization of art," and if this dehumanizing cultural project is then met, between the wars, by a realist and humanizing "countermovement," the result is a situation in which Fore finds a "glaring paradox."[10] He suggests the following questions:

If mimetic representation presupposes the inviolability of the body, how then is this neoclassical aesthetic articulated in a society in which natural anatomy has become indistinguishable from mechanical organs? How can verisimilitude and likeness be reconstructed after modernism's relentless campaign to demotivate the aesthetic sign turned the artwork from a communicative medium into mute, intractable matter? What spaces of subjective interiority and psychological depth can be claimed for a realist novel that is written in a culture where all speech has already been prefabricated for and transmitted through mass media? In sum, what happens to realism once the human is no longer a perfect integer? (4)

He approaches these questions in a manner similar to Blumenthal-Barby's, not in a single theoretical meditation but by the detailed discussion of individual artifacts. And like Blumenthal-Barby's, his interpretive arguments are often deeply illuminating—especially, to my mind, in his last chapter on Ernst Jünger.

But there are questions he never raises. We shall perhaps agree that an upheaval on the scale of the First World War is bound to produce an overturning of categories or preferences in the aesthetic realm. But does this point really account for "the aesthetic Thermidor that followed upon modernism's apparent withdrawal" (11)? Does it come anywhere near accounting for the "humanizing" form taken by that "countermovement"? With regard to both "figurative content" and "the types of anthropomorphism found within the technical matrix of the artwork itself," Fore promises to demonstrate

> that these [essentially mimetic] devices did not function in the 1920s as they did in the nineteenth century, and that, consequently, the strategies of interwar art do not signal the return of an old subject but herald the advent of a new one. Realism after modernism ... is not the same phenomenon as realism before modernism. As a consequence, each chapter [of his present book] confronts the paradoxical status of realist technique after the historical disappearance of the humanist subject to which it once corresponded. (12)

Thus the bare historical material of the book presents a considerable problem. Even assuming that an anti-modernist countermovement is bound to arise, why should it struggle to costume itself in a "human" guise which can never really fit?

I will not try to answer this question, which in any case would take another whole book. But I will suggest that it might be worth the effort to look at the large sweep of twentieth-century literature and art not as an aesthetic, but as an ethical phenomenon. The structural centralness of the concept of the human, and the combination of attracting and repelling forces associated with it, would jibe well with the general historical argument on "literary ethics" that I have sketched above. And a better explanation could then also be given of why the relation between dehumanization and rehumanization discussed by Fore has more the character of an *oscillation* than merely that of an opposition, an oscillation that appears especially in his treatment of Jünger's *Glass Bees*, where it is represented both *by* that novel, historically, and *in* it, figurally and thematically.

Habermas and "Discourse Ethics"

Let us conclude with a look at the ethics of Jürgen Habermas, which will be discussed in more detail in Chapter 6. Habermas theorizes what he calls a "discourse ethics," which is meant to be anchored in linguistic practice—like the ethics of Hillis Miller, Siebers, Blumenthal-Barby—but without the uncontrollable aesthetic component of "literary" ethics. His argument in defense of his theory is very extensive and elaborate and holds together on its own terms. But its blind spots are at least seriously damaging.

He begins by insisting on the existence of "moral phenomena,"[11] by which he means essentially Strawson's "facts as we know them" concerning moral tendencies in ordinary language. But as noted in the Preliminary Remarks, he lays much more stress than Strawson does on the supposed inherent structuration of those facts. He needs to be able to show enough structure to justify the idea that those facts possess a "normative" force (48/58) before he can reasonably characterize them as "moral phenomena." And he appears to promise, we noted, that that moral or normative structure will be demonstrated by a process of "linguistic analysis" (47/57).

As far as I can see, the only part of his subsequent argument that might be interpreted as such an analysis is his attempt to "identify a special type of validity claim connected with commands and norms" and to "identify it ... within the horizon of the lifeworld *[Lebenswelt]*, where Strawson had to look for moral phenomena when he marshalled the evidence of ordinary language against the skeptic" (57–8/68). In particular, it may be true that

> Normative claims to validity [have the special characteristic that they] *mediate a mutual dependence* of language and the social world that does not exist for the relation of language to the objective world. (61/71)

And it may also be true that this special quality of normative validity claims unfolds entirely inside a "lifeworld," despite the level of abstraction required to demonstrate it. But I cannot see what is gained thereby for bridging the gap between Strawson's "facts" and Habermas's "moral phenomena."

Perhaps the concept of "lifeworld" is meant to play a central role here. A passage was discussed in the Preliminary Remarks where the lifeworld seems almost to have the character of a moral order. The "web of moral feelings," says Habermas, has "a certain *ineluctability*" because "we cannot retract at will our commitment to a lifeworld whose members we are" (47/57). But there is a lot of conceptual slippage here. Strawson's "facts"—or "moral sentiments," as he calls them—are "moral" only in the vague sense of being potentially useful for moral purposes or suggesting an openness to such purposes. Habermas's "moral phenomena," by contrast, carry out their role in his system only by being evidence of an actual, focused moral direction in human thought, feeling, and language. And while the "lifeworld"—in any of its possible definitions—can probably be said to possess contour, its contour is fundamentally different from that of any ethical or moral framework. The very idea of a moral or ethical order, after all, includes precisely the condition that I *can* retract at will my commitment to it—with no significant alteration in my lifeworld. (Surely we still agree with Kant that a moral choice is a free choice, even if we differ on the definition of freedom.) It is in fact hard to imagine an actual systematic morality that does not at some point *prohibit* our acting upon one or the other of our "moral sentiments."

In any case, even if these objections can be answered, Habermas's "discourse ethics" has avoided the pitfalls of "literary ethics" only to find its way back to the inherent difficulties of propositional ethics. His awareness of such difficulties is expressed in the "principle of universalization" by which he tries to find a way around them. That principle, called (U) for *Universalisierungsgrundsatz*, states that "every valid norm has to fulfill the following condition":

> *All* affected can accept the consequences and the side effects its *general* observance can be anticipated to have for the satisfaction of *everyone's* interests (and these consequences are preferred to those of known alternative possibilities for regulation).

> [—daß die Folgen und Nebenwirkungen, die sich jeweils aus ihrer *allgemeinen* Befolgung für die Befriedigung der Interessen eines *jeden* Einzelnen (voraussichtlich) ergeben, von *allen* Betroffenen akzeptiert (und den Auswirkungen der bekannten alternativen Regelungsmöglichkeiten vorgezogen) werden können.] (65/75–6)

A crucial idea here, in the midst of the complicated syntax, is the restriction of the principle's application to *alle Betroffenen*, to all those people who are "affected" by the proposed norm under discussion. For this restriction has the indispensable function of ensuring that only the perspective of "participants" (not detached observers) is honored in any debate, that only a "performative" relation to proposed norms can influence a decision, not the opinion of a supposedly impartial judge, who in the strict sense does not exist anyway.

But it is hard for me to see how this needful restriction can be incorporated into procedural rules, or even mere conventions or individual rulings, without being violated by precisely the procedure (however rudimentary) in question. Without such a violation, there is no leverage by which the criterion of performativity might receive meaning. And I may be too literal-minded here, but I also do not see how Habermas's ideas could find their way into social reality without the institution of actual staged and regulated debates, which would bring with it the question of *standing*, of who gets a voice. Would another valid norm be required to adjudicate this question? Or if it is left to each individual's judgment, will the inevitable cacophony of ways in which being "affected" is interpreted not make impossible the application of the principle as a whole?[12] My dismissal of Habermas on these grounds may appear simple-minded, especially by comparison with the complexity of the arguments he deploys to defend his positions on communication and argumentation as the processes by which a practical ethics comes into being.

And it is true that one could accept most of what Habermas says if it were kept closer to the descriptive—closer, say, to Strawson—if he used his learning to create something like a broad Homeric view of the ebb and flow, the conflicts and confusions, of ethical initiatives in real social situations. But he goes a step further, into the matter of norms and their "validity," the domain of propositional ethics, where the question of competent or qualified conversation-participants constantly produces the need for prior norms and the threat of infinite regress.

Irony

There are other avenues by which Habermas's ethical thought can be questioned. In Chapter 6, I will take up his use of the idea of "lifeworld" and his insistence on an internal perspective (or "performative attitude") in discussing ethically charged situations. But the question of who belongs to an ethically competent or qualified group is useful at this point because of its wider applicability.

Suppose we agree that Wittgenstein's "explosion" refers to the impossibility of a uniform universal ethics. If such an ethics existed, it would have to be formulable in propositions—otherwise how could its availability to all human beings be guaranteed?—which means it would take the form of Wittgenstein's impossible "book on Ethics." And suppose we agree therefore that a valid ethics must *limit its reach* to a specific group of people. Habermas suggests applying this restriction case by case to the discussions by which a valid propositional ethics might gradually be coaxed into existence. Blumenthal-Barby, and several of the people he talks about, suggest limiting the ethical community to people possessing a special "literary" combination of knowledge and sensibility that would enable them to create and practice an ethics without needing to formulate it.

Once we have come this far, however, I think we need to recognize a general principle: that no non-universal group by which an ethics is defined can be such as to admit any question about who belongs to it. Because—unless the criterion of membership is ethically trivial and the ethics defined by it is therefore a joke—that question of membership will not be decidable except by a prior and more comprehensive ethics, which means we shall be driven eventually to require exactly the uniform universal ethics we had understood is impossible. This principle is the basis for my criticism of Habermas above. And its application to the question of a "literary ethics" is clear enough. We recall that Blumenthal-Barby, in staking out his position, begins by drawing an obviously questionable boundary between two classes of thinkers who seek ethical help from literature: those who are and those who are not sufficiently "literary" in their approach. Who is going to decide here?

In order to serve as the foundation for an ethics, therefore, a group must be such that the question of whether a particular individual belongs to it can never be raised in an ethically significant manner. And this condition creates a serious problem, for it is hard to imagine its being satisfied by any group except the whole human race—or perhaps, for Kant's sake, the whole class of rational beings. Which would mean that Wittgenstein's explosion signifies nothing but abandonment of the whole project of ethics.

But I contend nevertheless that there is a type of human group that is highly exclusive, yet satisfies the stated condition: I mean any group defined by the practice of *radical irony*. Wittgenstein in a sense continues to show us the way when he suggests that ethical thinking leads repeatedly to a collision with "the boundaries of language." For if such a collision belongs to my actual personal experience, then whenever I approach, in discourse, the place where it happens, I will find myself saying something fundamentally different from what I mean, I will be speaking ironically. My irony, moreover, will be radical in the sense that my true meaning will be not only unspoken but entirely incapable of being spoken (beyond the boundaries of language), which means that no clear evidence can ever be made available to anyone else for deciding whether or not I am speaking ironically. And yet, nothing prevents other people from *knowing* what I mean and so belonging, together with me, to a community of shared silent knowledge. The community in question is therefore possible; but any claim of membership in it, if valid, will be an instance of radical irony, and quibbling about its validity will be pointless. Thus our condition is satisfied. The membership of this or that individual in the community cannot be questioned meaningfully.

To say that this idea of community encounters serious problems is of course an understatement. How do its members recognize one another, if at all? And even assuming that the knowledge by which it is constituted includes a uniquely deep ethical understanding, how does that understanding produce effects in the real world? Or how does it deserve the title "ethical" if such effects are not produced? As I have suggested, I do not intend to deal with these questions in the abstract. I will try to show how they arise inescapably from the close reading of specific texts; and I will deal with them, each time, in that setting. I will approach the idea of an ironic community directly in discussing Nietzsche and Rorty; and I will then try to show the applicability and ramifications of that idea with respect to the diasporic community of the Jews and with respect to a community arising from the feminist principle that "One Is Not Born a Woman."[13]

One more point needs to be mentioned. I began above with the history of ethics, and I said that what I mean by a modern rhetorical ethics is the revival and continuation of an ethical mode that had been well established in the ages preceding Kantian propositional ethics. Am I suggesting, therefore, that the whole history of pre-Kantian ethics is characterized by radical irony? The answer is no. Radical irony is necessary only in an age of mass communications where systematic propositional ethics has become the established standard—comparable to the standard of systematic written constitutions as the bases for states, or to the idea of a "social contract." It is still true, prior to the Kantian revolution, that ethics—considered as a coherent order, not necessarily a collection of precepts—does not work except where its reach is restricted. But in those earlier ages, the restricted intellectual class that supplied the ethical vehicle—people known at various times as grammarians or *poetae* (when the term included students of poetry) or philologists or scholars or humanists or philosophers (in the broadest sense) or *sçavans*—generally satisfied the condition of unproblematic membership without the need for irony. I realize that this is a large claim, and the present book will not be large enough to justify it. I will discuss in detail below only two instances of pre-Kantian ethical thought, in Leibniz and in Machiavelli, which for the time being will have to take the place of a more complete historical argument.

Chapter 2

NIETZSCHE AND RORTY: THE ETHICS OF IRONY

Nietzsche goes out of his way to make the question of his ethics a difficult one. Surely the minimum condition, without which a text may not be reckoned to operate ethically, is that readers who have understood the text may use their understanding to orient themselves with respect to tasks or duties or obligations, or types of social behavior, in the real world. My understanding of the text must have a bearing on the question of how I craft my existence in what I do. And in the course of his career, Nietzsche strives more and more successfully to produce writings that do *not* satisfy this condition.

Socrates and Irony

This tendency is already evident in *The Birth of Tragedy*, where it has to do with the question of how I am positioned, as a reader, with respect to the figure of Socrates and the development of Socratic culture in the West. Nietzsche's idea of the Socratic certainly includes the idea of *wrongness*. Socrates himself is wrong about Greek tragedy. And the optimistic assumption underlying cultural or historical Socratism, that human existence and the world in which it unfolds can eventually be brought under the control of reason, is also clearly wrong in Nietzsche's view of the matter.

But it does not follow that I may fulfill my obligation as an understanding reader simply by rejecting a Socratic view of life, knowledge, and history. For I have not really understood *The Birth of Tragedy* until I have understood its underlying metaphysics: the doctrine (which is required by Nietzsche's non-Socratic theory of tragedy) that all articulated existence, everything that is disclosed to me as a world, is in truth nothing but a veil of illusion, *maya*, stretched over the abyss of nothingness; the doctrine that there is no such thing as a bedrock "reality" upon which our culture is erected, our system of devices for organizing experience; the doctrine that the entire range of my experiences, both natural and cultural, is constituted by a single web of illusion that stands or falls as a whole. And one of the immediate implications of this doctrine is that one *cannot reject* the specific character of one's world, including one's cultural situation, without falling into mere nihilism. If we could manage somehow to destroy the fabric of illusions by which our cultural situation is constituted (in our case, Socratic illusions), we would be left with nothing whatever, in the inconceivable condition of simply having no world.

It is only by keeping these considerations firmly in mind that we can navigate what has turned out to be one of the most difficult passages in *The Birth of Tragedy*. Toward the end of chapter 15, after remarking upon "how the insatiable zest for knowledge, prefigured in Socrates, has been transformed into tragic resignation and the need for art,"[1] Nietzsche continues:

> At this point we find ourselves, not without trepidation, knocking at the gates of present and future. Will this dialectic inversion lead to ever new configurations of genius, above all to that of Socrates as the practitioner of music? Will the all-encompassing net of art (whether under the name of religion or science) be woven ever more tightly and delicately. Or will it be torn to shreds by the restless and barbaric activities of our present day? (KSA 1:102; BoT 95–6)

The vague general idea of Nietzsche as iconoclast has led some commentators to assume that Nietzsche prefers the latter alternative here, the tearing apart of what had earlier been called "a common net of knowledge ... spread over the whole globe" in Socrates' historical wake (KSA 1:100; BoT 93–4).[2] Nothing could be less the case. The attempt to destroy that "net" would only plunge us into an uncontrolled nihilism. Indeed, the effects of the Socratic net must not even be resisted. Rather, that net must be *perfected*, in the hope that eventually it will undergo a "dialectic inversion" into something like its own opposite. But for now, this is only a hope. For the time being, our culture, our whole way of thinking, is Socratic, and we are stuck with it. This point is important because it helps us not only to understand *The Birth of Tragedy* but also to chart a central long-term continuity in Nietzsche's thought, the trend that culminates in an insistence on scientific thinking and "methods" in *The Antichrist* (e.g., KSA 6:179, 247), which we will come to below.

The Socratic worldview, for Nietzsche, is certainly wrong. But it is no more wrong, no less illusory, than any other specific worldview—no less illusory, for instance, than the brilliant Apollonian or "artistic" culture (KSA 1:115–16; BoT 108–9) that eventually produced Attic tragedy. It is true that the Socratic is involved in the demise of tragedy. "Thenceforward [after Euripides] the real antagonism was to be between the Dionysiac spirit and the Socratic, and tragedy was to perish in the conflict" (KSA 1:83; BoT 77). But it is not true that tragedy might have continued to flourish if Socrates had not been there—for its death was in truth a "suicide, in consequence of an insoluble [inner] conflict" (KSA 1:75; BoT 69).[3] And that "suicide," that internally conditioned collapse of the whole evolved culture of Hellenic art, could have had enormously destructive historical consequences. "The death of Greek tragedy ... created a tremendous vacuum that was felt far and wide" (KSA 1:75; BoT 69). Nietzsche claims, in fact, that but for the rise of the Socratic as an "elemental power" (KSA 1:91; BoT 85), Western civilization would not have survived. Without the focus provided by an optimistic

Socratic worldview (comparable to the artistic focus of Hellenic culture), "that immense store of energy used ... for the [Socratic] purposes of knowledge" in our culture (KSA 1:100; BoT 94) would have had no focus at all and, running wild, would have produced mere anarchy.

The situation of Western culture with respect to the Socratic is thus profoundly ambivalent. As much as our culture may be indebted to Greek tragedy for *its awareness of its basic metaphysical character* (the Apollonian/Dionysian tension, the assertion of illusion against a knowledge of nothingness), it also owes *its very existence* to the antitragic Socratic worldview. And this ambivalence is translated, by one's understanding of *The Birth of Tragedy*, into a personal ambivalence. As an understanding reader of this book, I am presented with the obligation to be fully committed to the Socratic worldview, while yet also managing to include in my practice of "aesthetic *science*" (KSA 1:25, my emphasis)[4] a radically anti-Socratic idea of art. My situation, if I try to fulfill this double obligation, is very difficult. But it is not a strictly impossible situation, and therefore an ethical component may still be ascribed to the book. We might in fact reasonably speak here of an ethics of *irony*, in a sense of the term not all that different from Richard Rorty's.[5]

Or if we require a parallel from Nietzsche's own intellectual background, a parallel with which he was certainly familiar, we might recall the famous paradox stated on the first page of Johann Joachim Winckelmann's *Thoughts on the Imitation of Greek Works in Painting and Sculpture* (1755): "The only way for us to become truly great—or indeed to become inimitable, if that is possible—is imitation of the ancients."[6] Like Nietzsche, Winckelmann places his readers in what seems logically an impossible situation: How can you "become inimitable" by imitating a model which is itself shown, by your success in imitating it, not to be inimitable? Clearly the exact meaning of the concept of imitation is at issue here. Only certain readers will be able to make sense of what Winckelmann is saying, a certain class of artistic practitioners and connoisseurs who possess the "eyes" (Winckelmann 30) needed to show them the proper attitude toward Greek art. Nietzsche's text, correspondingly, is addressed only to ironists, only to minds that can combine a full commitment to the Socratic with an attitude of radical skepticism. And his discussion of Kant and Schopenhauer (KSA 1:117–19, 128; BoT 110–12, 120) is meant, among other things, to show that there is no reason to doubt the existence of such minds, hence no reason to despair of one's own ability to live the needful contradiction.

The Trap of Understanding

The Birth of Tragedy, then, can still be regarded as having an ethical use. But such is no longer the case with *On the Genealogy of Morals*. The later book is set up so that one's adequate understanding of it makes strictly impossible the derivation from it of a guide to thought or action of any sort. If we wish to regard the *Genealogy* as an ethical work, we must therefore apply a completely different idea of ethics. My contention is that the aim of the *Genealogy* is precisely to maneuver us into this position.

A great deal of historical, social, and cultural commentary is incorporated into the *Genealogy*, but in its broad outlines the book is a very simple one. The first of its three "treatises" (*Abhandlungen*) deals with two opposed types of morality by way of two opposed meanings of the concept "good." The original meaning of the concept, Nietzsche says, arose from *self*-affirmation on the part of a ruling class: "it was the 'good' themselves, that is to say, the noble, powerful, high-stationed and high-minded, who felt and established themselves and their actions as good, that is, of the first rank, in contradistinction to all the low, low-minded, common and plebeian" (KSA 5:259).[7] The latter, the common people, were kept at a distance, which the "good" nobles marked by assigning them the attribute "bad" (German *schlecht*). But in Nietzsche's historical–etymological scheme, it is then these people, the low-born and low-minded, whose "*slave revolt in morality*" (KSA 5:268; GoM 34) initiates an entirely new age. The primary moral concept is now "evil," which expresses the impotent rancor of slaves against their masters; and the term "good" is now appropriated to designate everyone and everything that is *not* evil—meaning not "good" in the original sense, not high-born and high-handed. If we ask "precisely *who* is 'evil'" in this new morality, the answer is "*precisely* the 'good man' of the other morality, precisely the noble, powerful man, the ruler, but ... seen in another way by the venomous eye of *ressentiment*" (KSA 5:274; GoM 40).

Despite his association of slave morality with the Jews and with Christianity, Nietzsche is not writing history. His procedure is strictly speculative and remains so in the second treatise, where he discusses a set of concepts—"Guilt," "Bad Conscience," and the like (KSA 5:291; GoM 57)—that are related to those of the first treatise, but neither derivable from them nor exactly parallel to them. The crucial concept, that of bad conscience, strongly anticipates Freud's *Civilization and Its Discontents*.

> I regard the bad conscience as the serious illness that man was bound to contract under the stress of the most fundamental change he ever experienced—that change which occurred when he found himself finally enclosed within the walls of society and of peace .... All instincts that do not discharge themselves outwardly *turn inward*—this is what I call the *internalization* of man: thus it was that man first developed what was later called his "soul." ... Those fearful bulwarks with which the political organization protected itself against the old instincts of freedom—punishments belong among these bulwarks—brought it about that all those instincts of wild, free, prowling man turned backward *against man himself*. Hostility, cruelty, joy in persecuting, in attacking, in change, in destruction—all this turned against the possessors of such instincts: *that* is the origin of the "bad conscience." (KSA 5:321–3; GoM 84–5)

From here it is only a short step to the Judeo-Christian ideas of sin and irremediable guilt, and to the central concept of the book's third treatise, "ascetic ideals."

In that third treatise, however, Nietzsche's book begins to reflect upon itself, indeed in a strong sense to turn *against* itself—in a move that mimics the self-punishment of bad conscience. This process runs parallel to an enormous expansion of the domain of "ascetic ideals" as the essay develops. An "ascetic ideal," for most readers, would be an ideal for the sake of which one renounces some form of sensual or instinctual gratification. But after discussing at length the usefulness of such ideals in the practice of philosophy and religion, mainly from a psychological perspective, Nietzsche abruptly turns his attention to "us psychologists": "probably, we, too, are still victims of and prey to this moralized contemporary taste and ill with it, however much we think we despise it—probably it infects even *us*" (KSA 5:387; GoM 139). Probably, that is, we have been fearful of understanding fully the sickness represented by ascetic ideals. For precisely science (including "our" psychology), where it is serious about itself—"where it still inspires passion, love, ardor, and *suffering* at all"—here precisely science "is not the opposeite of the ascetic ideal but rather *the latest and noblest form of it*" (KSA 5:396–7; GoM 147). Even the best intellectuals of our time do not escape this entanglement, those thinkers in whom

> the spirit ... does without ideals of any kind—the popular expression for this abstinence is "atheism"—*except for its will to truth*. But this will, this *remnant* of an ideal, is, if you will believe me, the ideal itself in its strictest, most spiritual formulation, esoteric through and through, with all external additions abolished, and thus not so much its remnant as its *kernel*. (KSA 5:409; GoM 160)

Can readers of this book—however often Nietzsche may flatter them with being "men of knowledge" (KSA 5:247; GoM 15)—possibly hope to avoid that universal infection?

In order to understand this situation in detail, we must begin with the internal dynamics of the ascetic ideal, the mechanism by which it extends its range constantly, occupies constantly the position of "non plus ultra" (KSA 5:395; GoM 145). The ascetic ideal is to bad conscience as mill is to grist. "'Sin' ... is the priestly name for the animal's 'bad conscience'" (KSA 5:389; GoM 140). Bad conscience is interpreted by ascetic priestliness as deserved guilt for failure to resist instinctual temptation. But bad conscience is also in truth a *form* of instinctual gratification (cruelty denied an outlet and turned inward), hence an occasion for yet further guilt, a self-multiplying condition of mind. The ascetic ideal, correspondingly, must by nature become ever more unattainable and rarefied, ever more "esoteric."

Or to look at it the other way round, the ascetic ideal, while ostensibly an attack upon life, is always in truth "an artifice for the *preservation* of life" (KSA 5:366; GoM 120). Hence, again, the self-overleaping quality of the ascetic ideal in history. The only source of vitality for a morbidly dispirited humanity is the energy of a renewed attack on life, which means an attack upon, and a supersedure of, the latest version of the ascetic ideal itself.

> In this way Christianity *as a dogma* was destroyed by its own morality [in the Reformation]; in the same way Christianity *as morality* must now perish, too: we stand on the threshold of *this* event. After Christian truthfulness has drawn one inference [one ascetic move] after another, it must end by drawing

its *most striking inference,* its inference *against* itself; this will happen, however, when it poses the question *"what is the meaning of all will to truth?"* (KSA 5:410; GoM 161)

And this move, finally, leaves the book's reader no room to avoid responsibility for the ascetic ideal in its most perfected form: "what meaning would *our* whole being possess were it not this, that in us the will to truth becomes conscious of itself as a *problem?*"

In both *The Birth of Tragedy* and *On the Genealogy of Morals,* Nietzsche places me, his reader, in a difficult situation. But in the case of the earlier book, my understanding of the metaphysics behind the argument, the truth of ultimate nothingness—even if that truth is not usable as a basis for systematic development—affords me the perspective upon my cultural situation that I require in order to adopt the needful ironic stance of an anti-Socratic Socratist. My understanding of the later book provides me with no such perspective. On the contrary, understanding has now become a kind of trap. The depth to which I understand the book's argument is exactly the depth to which my thought is immersed in the business of the ascetic ideal, precisely in my constant adoption of critical distance from it. And suppose that I fall in with Nietzsche's occasional *hopeful* view of this situation: "morality will gradually *perish* now: this is the great spectacle in a hundred acts reserved for the next two centuries in Europe— the most terrible, most questionable, and perhaps also the most hopeful of all spectacles" (KSA 5:410–11; GoM 161). What I shall be doing in nurturing such "hope" is nothing but what the ascetic ideal always does, making sense of suffering, giving our suffering a "meaning" or "purpose" (KSA 5:411; GoM 162). Affirming Socratism (with the needful irony) means contributing to its demise. Affirming the ascetic ideal means nothing of the kind, however deeply I may recognize that the demise of that ideal would be desirable.

The dilemma in which I find myself as an understanding reader of the *Genealogy* is ethical. It cannot be considered a mere philosophical conundrum, for to take it as such would itself be an ethical move, an act of dishonesty—"All honor to the ascetic ideal *insofar as it is honest!*" (KSA 5:407; GoM 158)—a move that would place me among those "weary and played-out people who wrap themselves in wisdom and look 'objective,'" those impotent "voluptuaries" of the intellect for whom Nietzsche reserves his deepest scorn. My situation is an ethical dilemma without an ethical solution. I cannot deny my continuing complicity in the ascetic ideal, even while recognizing that that ideal is a medicine which also "*infects the wound*" (KSA 5:373; GoM 126), a treatment which makes the sick sicker (KSA 5:391; GoM 142), even while recognizing that "one may without any exaggeration call it *the true calamity* in the history of European health" (KSA 5:392; GoM 143). How can I justify my inability to assert an "opposing will that might express an *opposing ideal*" (KSA 5:395; GoM 146)? Can I even take refuge in the excuse that my complicity in the ascetic ideal is *necessary,* when I am repeatedly offered examples from fairly recent history of individuals who have avoided it: Mirabeau, Napoleon, Goethe, Beethoven?[8]

The only ethically acceptable course open to me, provided I take the book seriously, would be to carry out a titanic or Napoleonic act of self-assertion, an affirmation of myself as "good" in the original sense. But I cannot possibly carry out that act *as an understanding reader of the book*; for the very process of understanding—involving, as it must, either the will to truth or, at best, a critique of that will (which is the same will all over again)—is already an acceptance and development of the ascetic ideal. In order to avoid corruption, I would have to forget the book so completely as to put myself in the condition of never having read it—which is hardly conceivable, since I would be doing so precisely in response to the book. Thus, as I have suggested, the whole question of ethics is thrown open, the question of whether any such thing as a practicable ethics can still be imagined in Western culture, the question of what such an ethics would look like, where it would start. I myself am now the test case for such an ethics. It will have to be a new *kind* of ethics if it is to be applied to my situation as an understanding reader of the *Genealogy*.

The dilemma I encounter here is ethical. But it is also therefore *historical*. It is a distinguishing mark of the present historical age, in which the ascetic ideal is approaching a culmination. The historical gestures in the first two treatises of the *Genealogy*, dire as their suggestions may seem, can still be dismissed as metaphorical drapery for the else uncomfortably naked moral and psychological assertions. But in the third treatise the trap of understanding is sprung, and a far more threatening historical problem is unveiled directly for each reader, in the here and now, the problem of radical nihilism in the sense of an existence with no possibility whatever of an ethical dimension.

Writing as an Ethical Problem

How does Nietzsche get from *The Birth of Tragedy*, at the very beginning of his career, to *On the Genealogy of Morals*, toward the very end? In one sense, the distance between the books seems small enough. Remove from *The Birth of Tragedy* its level of metaphysical truth (the truth of nothingness) and you have plunged its reader into exactly the same type of ethical predicament as the *Genealogy* does. Why does it take Nietzsche most of his publicly productive life (about fifteen years) to get from the one to the other?

Except for the *Unzeitgemässe Betrachtungen* (Thoughts Out of Season), all of the works Nietzsche published in the time between the two books we have looked at are collections of aphorisms. This rule applies even to *Also sprach Zarathustra*, where the narrative framework gestures in the direction of unity and continuity but never actually controls the variegation and volatility of the thought. And in the *Genealogy*, Nietzsche then reflects upon this characteristic of his career by approaching the form of the aphorism as a *question*. In the book's "Preface" he says,

> In other cases [books other than *Zarathustra*], people find difficulty with the aphoristic form: this arises from the fact that today this form is *not taken seriously*

enough. An aphorism, properly stamped and molded, has not been "deciphered" when it has simply been read; rather, one has then to begin its *exegesis*, for which is required an art of exegesis. I have offered in the third essay of the present book an example of what I regard as "exegesis" in such a case—an aphorism is prefixed to this essay, the essay itself is a commentary on it. (KSA 5:255-6; GoM 22-3)

The "aphorism" referred to here is apparently the whole first section of the third essay, which concludes, like the essay as a whole, with the observation that "the human will ... *needs a goal*—and it will rather will *nothingness* than *not* will" (KSA 5:339, 412; GoM 97, 163).[9]

What exactly does Nietzsche mean by saying that the *form* of the aphorism is not taken seriously enough, or in German "dass man diese Form heute *nicht schwer genug* nimmt"—which suggests that the form is not given enough *weight*, or that its *difficulty* is not appreciated? The point Nietzsche insists on is that when we deal with an aphorism, our task is to explicate it in detail, to expand it exegetically into something more like an essay, as the first section is expanded in the whole third part of the *Genealogy*. And as far as I can see, the only possible reason for such exegesis would be to identify and evaluate the aphorism's truth claim. The relation between aphorisms and truth, in any case, is at the center of the very last aphorism of *Beyond Good and Evil*, where we read,

> Alas, what are you now, you my written and painted thoughts [the book's aphorisms]! Not long ago you were so colorful, young, and malicious, full of thorns and secret spices, you made me sneeze and laugh—and now? You have already put off your novelty, and I fear that some of you are ready to become truths. (KSA 5:239)

If truth is what an aphorism becomes when it is worn out, when it has been around too long—or when it has been explicated?—then at least in the context of *Beyond Good and Evil* and its "supplement," the *Genealogy*,[10] an aphorism can be defined as a piece of thought whose truth claim is concealed or held in abeyance.

But the ultimate trap by which intellectuals are implicated in the work of the ascetic ideal is their "will to truth." Hence the importance, for Nietzsche, of the form of the aphorism, which seems to offer a way of avoiding that trap, and hence also its difficulty, since such avoidance can never be more than temporary. The writing of aphorisms becomes a kind of tightrope walk—to use an image from *Zarathustra*—the constant courting of a danger that cannot be avoided, like the tightrope walker's defiance of gravity. It is a last resort, the last available stratagem for a free thinker in the age of ascetic ideals. And why, then, in the *Genealogy*, does Nietzsche repudiate that stratagem? Why, in the third part of that book—as if the first two parts, as "treatises," had not been repudiation enough—does he insist on actually carrying out the exegesis that turns an aphorism into a "truth," or at least into a compounded, self-knowing entanglement in the "will to truth"? The *Genealogy* is subtitled "Eine Streitschrift" (KSA 5:245), a polemic, a dispute. But *against whom* is Nietzsche disputing here—at least after the very beginning, where he disposes of the "English" association of morality with utility? Is he perhaps disputing against Nietzsche himself? Against Nietzsche as a writer of aphorisms?

If the dispute that is brought to a head in the *Genealogy* is a matter of Nietzsche contra Nietzsche, then in substance the dispute is ethical; it has to do with *the wrongness of specific types of writing considered as actions*. On the one hand, writing of the type represented by the *Genealogy* is wrong in the sense of furthering nihilism: nihilism, not merely pessimism, not, say, the "pessimism *bonae voluntatis*" that we hear of in *Beyond Good and Evil*, which "does not merely say No and will No, but—horrible to imagine! *does* No" (KSA 5:137); not even that willing of Nothingness about which the *Genealogy* itself tells us that humanity prefers it to not willing at all. Rather, the condition in which I find myself as an understanding reader of the *Genealogy* is precisely the condition of *not* willing, of not having any acceptable object for the will (not even Nothingness). It is the condition of "disgust with life," of spiritless "exhaustion," against which even the ascetic ideal had once struggled in the service of life (KSA 5:366; GoM 120). But as an understanding reader of the *Genealogy*, how can I now bring myself to take up that work of the ascetic ideal? And what other course is open to me for opposing the deadly weariness that is not even strong enough to say No?

Shall I, on the other hand, turn to the writing of aphorisms? The trouble is that writing aphorisms is wrong in the sense of *dishonest*. Suppose I use the form of the aphorism as a way of avoiding nihilism. Some of my readers may be energized and encouraged by my wit, but those readers are simply confused. The understanding reader—this is Nietzsche's point about aphoristic form in the *Genealogy*—is that reader whose truth-seeking exegesis of my anti-nihilist aphorisms exemplifies the mode of thinking represented by precisely the *Genealogy*. Thus he or she becomes in effect an understanding reader of the *Genealogy*, and so is now in the position of having *no* way to avoid nihilism, which means that my aphorisms have operated as a deception, a trap, an anti-nihilist advocacy of nihilism. By actually writing the *Genealogy*, Nietzsche insists on this point, and leaves his readers no room for failing to understand it.

It does not follow from these considerations that there is *no* possible way to write (or read) against nihilism. Perhaps, in fact, the very shape of the problem for Nietzsche suggests a solution, the association of ethical questions with types of writing, which is to say, with questions of *literary form*. Must it not now occur to us that we require types of writing (and reading) in which truth claims are not merely concealed or held in abeyance, but simply *absent*? It is not immediately clear how far we would have to go in this direction. In reading novels, and I think also in the reading of most poetry, we are probably too interested in truths about society and culture. Perhaps we require texts from which nothing even remotely resembling a truth claim can be derived, like Mallarmé's *Un coup de dés*. But have we then not overshot the mark? Do texts of this sort bear any relation at all to questions raised by the collision of *Beyond Good and Evil* with the *Genealogy*? In any case, if we go as far as Mallarmé, is there still any hope of finding an *ethical* dimension in our reading, anything by which to orient ourselves with respect to duties or obligations or social behavior in the real world? And what has happened to the idea of reading and understanding what we read?

"We" and Our Methods: The Instance of Buddhism

Rather than treat these questions in the abstract, let us ask: How does Nietzsche get beyond the *Genealogy*? Given the ethical dead end he has arrived at, how can he justify continuing to write? He says in the *Genealogy* itself that he is working on a fuller treatment of nihilism in a book to be called *The Will to Power: Attempt at a Revaluation of All Values* (KSA 5:408–9; GoM 159–60). And although he never completed that opus, he did write a draft of what was apparently to be the first section of a book called *Umwerthung aller Werthe* (Revaluation of All Values; KSA 13:545, also 589, 594), a manuscript work entitled *The Antichrist: Curse upon Christianity*.

This text shows occasional signs of incoherence in detail—attributable, I suppose, either to a lack of editing or to Nietzsche's deteriorating mental condition—but in its broad outlines it is lucid and well organized. It sets itself the question: "which type of human being should be *bred*, should be *willed*, as the higher valued, the more worthy of life, the more certain of a future" (KSA 6:170). Humans of such a higher type, Nietzsche continues, have existed often enough, but never "as *willed*":

> Rather, he [the man of that higher type] has been best suited as an object of fear; up to now he has been practically fearsomeness incarnate—and out of that fear the opposite type was willed, bred, *achieved*: the domestic animal man, the herd animal, man the sick animal—the Christian.

The basic thought of the *Genealogy* is still operating here, but with the addition of the idea of Christianity as *the* arch-enemy of a healthy humanity—an enemy (unlike the fluid and illimitable notion of "ascetic ideals") that can perhaps be defeated.

But the concept of Christianity is not as neatly circumscribed as we might expect. For if we (anti-Christians) ask exactly "*whom* we feel as our opposite," the answer is "theologians and everything that has theologian-blood in its body," which means in turn "our whole philosophy" (KSA 6:174). All European philosophy (especially German philosophy) is dismissed as speculation in the theological manner, hence as belonging to the Christian enemy. Kant is singled out for attack a few pages further on (KSA 6:177–8). And yet, the battle lines Nietzsche has in mind are still clear.

> Let us not underestimate this: *we ourselves*, we free spirits, are already a "Revaluation of All Values," an *incarnate* declaration of war and victory on all old concepts of "true" and "untrue." The most valuable insights are found latest; but the most valuable insights are *methods*. *All* methods, *all* the premises of our

present scientific approach, have for millennia been treated with the deepest contempt.... We have had the whole pathos of humanity against us—their idea of what truth *should* be, what the service of truth *should* be: each "thou shalt" was until now directed *against* us.... Our objects, our practices, our quiet, cautious, mistrustful ways—everything was regarded as unworthy and contemptible. (KSA 6:179)

The difference between "us" and them, in other words, is not what we think or believe or profess, but what we *are*. Our very existence declares war on them.

In particular, the opposition is between a culture of doctrines and a culture of "methods"—provided we understand this last term in an extreme manner. Methods, in the sense of ways of thinking or acting that are derived from doctrines or rules or "truths," are not what Nietzsche has in mind. What is commonly called "scientific method," for example, is excluded because it presupposes specific ideas about the regularity of nature. "Our" methods, by contrast, are coextensive with our alien, "hyperborean" existence (KSA 6:169), not separable even in the sense of representing an essence. They must somehow be pure practice, attached to no theory whatever, nothing but the "ways" or "paths" by which our existence follows "after" or conforms to itself—as the etymology of "method" suggests.

And if this idea seems obscure, it remains so only until Nietzsche embarks on an extended discussion of Buddhism in sections 20–23 of the work. Both Buddhism and Christianity, he says, are "nihilistic religions ... *décadence*-religions" (KSA 6:186), but are different in that Buddhism is "a hundred times more realistic ... it incorporates a legacy of objective and cool problem-setting, it comes *after* a centuries-old philosophical movement; the concept 'god' is already done with when it arrives." Christianity offers its unhappy adherents a doctrinal system—which means a pack of fictions or lies (KSA 6:181–2)—by which to seek an escape from reality. Buddhism, by contrast, insists on reality—in particular, on two "physiological facts" (KSA 6:186) under which its followers suffer: an "excessive sensitivity," especially to pain; and an "over-intellectuality, from living all too long in concepts and logical procedures that have damaged the person-shaping instinct in favor of the 'impersonal.'" Against the "depression" produced by these conditions Buddha proceeds not doctrinally but "hygienically," even against a weakening of the "person":

> In Buddha's teaching egoism becomes a duty: the saying "one thing is needed," specifically "how do *you* free yourself from suffering," regulates and limits one's whole intellectual diet (—one might perhaps recall that Athenian who similarly declared war on the purely "scientific," Socrates, who elevated personal egoism to a morality even in the realm of problems.) (KSA 6:187)

It is as if Nietzsche, long after the fact, were trying to carry out a kind of repair on *The Birth of Tragedy*, by finding a reason to affirm Socrates that does not depend on any specific idea of metaphysical truth.

The question of whether Nietzsche gets Buddhism right is not important here. What matters is that his idea of Buddhism offers a plausible model for how the hegemony of doctrinal (or "fictional") thinking—of ascetic ideals in general or Christianity in particular—can be evaded by an entire community, not merely by occasional individuals, how an entire community can organize its religious life as the practice of purely "hygienic" methods, method without doctrine. But Buddhism is not being offered as a cure for contemporary Europe.

> Buddhism is a religion for *late* humans, for kindly, gentle, increasingly over-intellectual races which feel pain too easily (—Europe is still far from being ready for it—): it is a bringing of those people back to peace and serenity, to a controlled diet in matters of intellect, to a certain toughening of the body. (KSA 6:189)

And if we ask, then, how this model can be at all relevant to our situation in modern Europe, the answer is rather surprising. Nietzsche's discussion of Buddhism serves as an introduction to his treatment, further on, of the figure of Jesus of Nazareth.

From Buddha to Jesus

Christianity, Nietzsche argues, gets Jesus completely wrong. In Nietzsche's understanding of the crucifixion and its aftermath, Jesus's disciples could not deal with their master's death except by assigning blame:

> "*who* killed him? *who* was his natural enemy?"—this question burst forth like a lightning bolt. Answer: the Jews as *government,* their highest class. From this moment on the disciples felt themselves to be in revolt *against* established order, and Jesus was understood ex post facto as having been *in revolt against established order.* Until now this militant, nay-saying, nay-doing feature had been *absent* in his character; more still, it contradicted his character. Evidently the little group of disciples had *not* understood precisely the main point, the exemplariness of that manner of dying, that freedom, elevated *above* every feeling of *ressentiment.* (KSA 6:213)

The single feeling that was most alien to Jesus himself, the desire for "revenge" (KSA 6:214), the anticipation of a vindictive "last judgment," thus becomes the principal driving force behind Christianity.

Nietzsche's diagnosis of Jesus is simple enough: a "case of delayed and impaired puberty, in consequence of degeneration" (KSA 6:203). But the symptoms of this supposed condition are complex and interesting:

> *Instinctive hatred of reality:* result of an extreme sensitivity and ability to suffer, which wishes simply no longer to be "touched," because every touch is too deeply felt.

> *Instinctive exclusion of all aversion, all enmity, all boundaries and distances in feeling:* result of an extreme sensitivity and ability to suffer, which instantly feels every conflict, every need for conflict, as an intolerable *non-pleasure [Unlust]* (that is, as *harmful,* as *opposed* by the instinct for self-preservation), and finds bliss (pleasure) only in resisting no longer, resisting no one, in resisting neither ills nor evil—so that love is the only possibility, the *last* possibility for living. (KSA 6:200–1)

The gospel of love, the injunction "That ye resist not evil" (Matt. 5:39), is thus physiologically determined, but is not necessarily, for that reason, any less significant *as a belief*:

> Such a faith does not rage, does not rebuke, does not defend itself…. It does not give proof of itself, either through miracles or through rewards and promises, and certainly not "through scripture": it is itself in every moment its own miracle, its own reward, its own proof, its own "kingdom of God." This faith can also not be formulated, it resists formulas. (KSA 6:203)

Jesus's way of living and believing thus sounds very much like the culture of "methods" that Nietzsche opposes to the doctrinal culture of Christianity. Just as "we … free spirits" *are* a "revaluation of all values," so Jesus "*lived* the unity of god and man" (KSA 6:215). He did not offer it as a doctrine.

And the relation of this Jesus to Buddhism, or at least to Nietzsche's view of Buddhism, is also evident:

> It is clear *what* ended with the crucifixion: the new and entirely original approach to a Buddhist peace-movement, to an actual, *not* merely promised *happiness on earth.* For this remains … the basic difference between those two *décadence* religions: Buddhism does not promise but fulfills, Christianity promises everything but *fulfills nothing.* (KSA 6:215)

This is not to say that Jesus is paralleled with Buddha. Buddha, for Nietzsche, is a realist, whereas Jesus is characterized by "hatred of reality." Jesus's significance stems from his oversensitivity to pain and suffering, and also from his over-intellectuality:

> If I understand anything about this great symbolist [Jesus], then it is this: that he accepted only *inner* realities as realities, as "truths"—that he understood everything else, everything natural, temporal, spatial, historical, only as signs, as the occasion for parables. (KSA 6:206)

But exactly these two qualities, oversensitivity and over-intellectuality, characterize the specific type of decadence, according to Nietzsche, that called forth Buddha's "hygienic" intervention.

What Nietzsche is suggesting, therefore, is this: that if the disciples had actually followed the teaching implicit in Jesus's manner of living, the result would have been a development in the direction of the type of decadent culture that can produce something like Buddhism. But what is the relevance of this point to the situation of modern-day Christian Europe? Surely Nietzsche is not advocating a new discipleship, under either Jesus or Buddha, as a cure for Europe's morbid condition. And what does any of this have to do with the supposed nascent culture of scientific "methods" to which we forward-looking thinkers, with Nietzsche, belong? And how does it help Nietzsche with the problem of writing?

The Ethical Problem of Understanding

The Antichrist is a very simple work. It is a violent attack on Christianity, ending with a seven-part "Law against Christianity: Promulgated on the Day of Salvation, the first day of Year One (30 September 1888 on the false calendar)" (KSA 6:254). And this proclamation, no matter how seriously one takes it, is obviously an expression of vengeful resentment, exactly the sort of *ressentiment* that characterizes not only Christianity but also the whole history of slave morality. In the *Genealogy*, Nietzsche's procedure had been much subtler. It takes a careful reading of that book to arrive at the recognition that in the very act of understanding it we find ourselves in the service of ascetic ideals. And even this recognition is not as disturbing as it might have been if Nietzsche had been less charitable in his treatment of the ascetic priest, if he had not emphasized, among other things, the role of that figure in the service of life.

In *The Antichrist* the need for intellectual work is reduced to a minimum. Suppose we have trouble recognizing how our situation as "free spirits"—with "our quiet, cautious, mistrustful ways"—is compromised by the ever angrier negativity of the text. Nietzsche then positively insists on this problem when he argues that the early Christians' angry rejection of Jewish hierarchy, after Jesus's death, produced nothing but that same priestly culture all over again.

> The Christian, this ultima ratio of falsehood, is the Jew all over again—*thrice* over again …—The fundamental will to employ only concepts, symbols, gestures, that are developed from priestly practice, the instinctive rejection of every *other* practice, of every *other* perspective upon value or usefulness—this is not only tradition, it is *heredity*. (KSA 6:219)

Jesus's legacy, Nietzsche had argued, could have been—perhaps should have been—a movement away from Jewish tradition in the direction of Buddhism. But the anger, the vengeful resentment of the early Christians, after Jesus's death, produced a priestly culture that was the Jewish hierarchy all over again. Can even the most obtuse reader now fail to recognize that the vengeful resentment *against* Christianity suggested by Nietzsche's text is doomed to produce nothing but Christianity all over again? Perhaps the resulting culture will not call itself "Christianity." But then neither does the tradition from Kantian philosophy call itself by that name—even though, in Nietzsche's view, it too is Christianity all over again, if not thrice over again, in the form of "theology."

The same predicament that is deployed beneath the surface of the *Genealogy*, as a trap for the most careful readers, is simply thrown at us as a challenge in *The Antichrist*. And the ethical aspect of the trap is now much more pointed. In the *Genealogy*, Nietzsche concedes that the ascetic ideal can be *honest* (KSA 5:407). But in *The Antichrist* he argues that there is no honesty whatever in Christianity. Christianity is such a perfect tissue of lies that removing just one lie would destroy the whole thing. "Let *one* concept be removed, put a single reality in its place—and all Christianity plunges into Nothingness!" (KSA 6:212). ("Reality" here apparently means any relatively dispassionate view of whatever matter is in question.) Thus the trap of understanding receives a new twist. If I understand *The Antichrist* affirmingly, and if I am honest about the consequences of doing so, then I must recognize that I am playing into the hand of Christianity, which is to say, into the hands of utter and complete dishonesty. Therefore my honesty is instantly transformed into dishonesty, in exactly the Christian manner. "The Christian church left nothing untouched by its rottenness. It has made of every merit a demerit, of every truth a lie, of every uprightness a soul-seated depravity" (KSA 6:252).

Of course there are other ways for me to position myself with respect to *The Antichrist*. I can disagree with everything in it. I can take an entirely non-affirming attitude—if, for example, I happen to be a committed Christian. But then I am not really a reader; there was never any reason for me to pick up the book in the first place. Or alternatively, even if I thoroughly disagree with everything Nietzsche says, it is still possible for me to experiment, as it were, with an affirming attitude. In which case the ethical trap of understanding lies open before me. And it draws my attention, as much as it draws the attention of more committed readers, to the question of *whether understanding as such, all understanding, is perhaps an ethically problematic intellectual procedure.*

But how can we possibly treat this matter as a "question"? Is it not rather simply an ethical blank wall, a recognition that in attending to it we place ourselves in a position where no honest move is open to us? In certain situations it may make some sense to worry about the ethical consequences of understanding. *Tout comprendre c'est tout pardonner*—and all that. But are we ever in a position to treat understanding as a matter of ethical choice? Would we not have to understand such a choice before making it?

Understanding and Irony

In the course of *The Antichrist* Nietzsche provides us with a certain amount of preparation for the idea of subjecting the process of understanding to extrinsic limits. What else can be meant by Buddhism's "controlled diet in matters of intellect"? Just as a bodily diet prohibits the eating of certain things, so an intellectual diet must prohibit the thinking or understanding of certain things—for the sake, presumably, of one's "health," for the sake of avoiding, say, the morbid experience of understanding as a trap. And Nietzsche's idea of a culture of "methods" dissociated from anything like doctrine raises the question of whether it is possible to employ a method without understanding it as such—without, in other words, being able to reduce it to some sort of formula or doctrine. Would such a reduction not have to be, as it were, hygienically repudiated in the practice of Nietzsche's "free spirits"? The *Genealogy* also provides context here, in the idea of *forgetting* as not only a characteristic talent of noble minds (KSA 5:273; GoM 39) but an indispensable element of mental health in general, comparable to good digestion (KSA 5:291–2; GoM 57–8).

All of this brings us back to the question of how to imagine an "understanding reader." Or to the question of what Nietzsche means by "reading as an *art*" or "*rumination*" (KSA 5:256; GoM 23)—or by "the art of reading well," which is that "philology" (KSA 6:233) which theologians are incapable of. Does "ruminating" mean simply taking one's time in order to understand as much as possible? Or does it include a parallel critical track in one's thinking, where careful decisions are made constantly about whether to retain or reject each element of understanding? On what basis would such decisions be made? Is the act of understanding itself dishonest in some cases? Are we talking here about *irony* as an ethical requirement? Surely the self-suppression of understanding would be a form of irony.

This matter can be approached by way of the question of who "we" are, Nietzsche's fellow "free spirits," we who constitute in our very existence a "revaluation of all values" (KSA 6:179). Immediately after completing the argument that Jesus's true legacy was a "*practice*" (KSA 6:207), not any form of doctrine or theology, Nietzsche returns to this question:

> —Only we, we spirits who have *become free* ["wir *freigewordenen* Geister"], possess the prerequisite for understanding something [Jesus' actual teaching] that nineteen centuries have misunderstood—only in us has honesty taken the form of instinct and passion, that honesty which declares war even more on the "hallowed lie" than on any other lie …. People were inexpressibly far from our loving and cautious neutrality, from that intellectual discipline by which alone it becomes possible to guess such strange and delicate things. With barefaced selfishness people wanted only *their* advantage from those things. From the antithesis of the evangel [i.e. the antithesis of Jesus' actual teaching] they built the *church*. (KSA 6:208)

How can Nietzsche, in *this* book, lay claim to a "loving and cautious neutrality"? And why does he now insist on speaking of "us" as "we spirits who have *become free*," rather than simply as "free spirits"?

This last designation suggests that at some point "we" have made the transition from a condition of unfreedom to one of freedom. And if freedom means freedom from doctrine, if it means "den freien Blick vor der Realität" (KSA 6:248; the free outlook upon reality) as opposed to the delusion of preconceived ideas, then it is not easy to see how that transition can have happened. Did "we" simply wake up one day from our dogmatic slumbers? A similar question arises in the section of *The Antichrist* devoted to the proposition "Überzeugungen sind Gefängnisse" (KSA 6:236; convictions are prisons).

> A spirit who wills great things, and also wills the means to achieve them, is necessarily a skeptic. Freedom from any sort of conviction *belongs* to strength, to the *ability* to see freely ["das Frei-Blicken-*können*"] .... The great passion, the basis and the power of that spirit's being—even more enlightened, more despotic, than he himself is—takes his whole intellect into its service; it makes him unhesitant; it gives him the courage even for unholy expedients; under certain circumstances it *permits* him even convictions. Conviction as *expedient*: much can be achieved only by way of a conviction.

But if one adopts a conviction as an expedient, as the means to an end, how does one un-adopt it once the end has been achieved? A "conviction" (German *Überzeugung*) is by definition an idea to which one is thoroughly committed. But once one has taken the plunge, committed oneself thoroughly, how does one then un-take the plunge?

This problem—the problem of a radically ironic state of mind in which one is both convinced and unconvinced on the same point—is clearly related to the problem of understanding. For understanding includes at least the conviction that one has understood correctly—the clearer the understanding, the firmer the corresponding conviction. And if one takes seriously Nietzsche's suggestion that there is no opposition between "conviction" and "lying," indeed that "convictions are more dangerous enemies of truth than lies are" (KSA 6:237), then it follows that *all understanding is mendacious*, the clearer the falser.[11] Or to put it only a bit less paradoxically, *all understanding is ironic*. For all thought, even at its most rudimentary, includes understanding, which means that when one's thinking has reached the point of recognizing that all understanding is lying, one finds oneself in a state of unresolvable mental tension, or irony, torn between understanding and its own unacceptability.

We must not try to reduce this point to a hermeneutic speculation. The conclusion at which Nietzsche's argument arrives is not that understanding is *mistaken*, but that it is *mendacious*, a lie (*Lüge*). The hermeneutic critique of understanding is included in this argument as a corollary. But Nietzsche is interested in more than just that philosophical subtlety; again, this situation is not merely a matter of philosophical interest. The equivalence of understanding and lying—lying in the sense of deliberate bad faith—confronts him with an unsurpassably profound ethical challenge.

In any case, we can now say that the understanding reader, for Nietzsche, is an ironic reader, whose irony includes violently opposed intellectual conditions: understanding and the refusal to accept one's own understanding; uncompromised anti-Christianity and "loving and cautious neutrality." And the question of how to manage such irony cannot possibly be answerable in general terms. Any general answer would require an overarching understanding by which the bow of irony would simply be unstrung. How I carry out the seemingly impossible intellectual move of un-understanding is strictly my business; how you carry it out is strictly yours. Neither of us needs to understand this move in the other. (We think perhaps of Nietzsche on Socrates, who he says "elevated personal egoism to a morality even in the realm of problems.") Which does not mean that we cannot give a name to the "method" involved. "Radical skepticism" perhaps, in the sense of a refusal to understand *anything*. Or perhaps we might find the key to "*becoming* free" in what Socrates calls "the unique beginning of philosophy": θαυμάζειν (*Theaetetus* 155D) or "wonderment," the condition of being baffled by what other people (including perhaps oneself at an earlier time) have no trouble understanding.

Rorty's Irony: His Ethics and Nietzsche's

A look at Richard Rorty's version of irony, his explicit endorsement of irony as a philosophical stance, will help us understand where Nietzsche's argument has brought us. Clearly Rorty's "ironist" would agree with Nietzsche that "convictions are prisons," except she would say not "conviction" but "final vocabulary," meaning the "set of words which [all human beings] employ to justify their actions, their beliefs, and their lives" (73). Like every human, the ironist *has* a final vocabulary, but she also

> has radical and continuing doubts about the final vocabulary she currently uses, because she has been impressed by other vocabularies ... she realizes that argument phrased in her present vocabulary can neither underwrite nor dissolve these doubts ... she does not think that her vocabulary is closer to reality than others, that it is in touch with a power not herself.

In other words, the ironist's final vocabulary is never really more than what Nietzsche calls an "expedient," always capable of being discarded if circumstances require.

But there are problems in Rorty's chapter on irony. First of all, its writer has to be an ironist, because from the point of view of either an adherent of common sense (74) or a "metaphysician" (75), the ironist's is simply a mistaken or fruitless intellectual attitude. You cannot understand the ironist's position or procedure if you are not yourself an ironist. Rorty is candid on this point: "We ironists" (79) are the group represented in the long section on Hegel and literary criticism. But the title of the whole chapter is "Private irony and liberal hope," and especially the second half of the chapter is saturated in the vocabulary of that "liberal hope." "The idea that we all have an overriding obligation to diminish cruelty, to make human beings equal in respect to their liability to suffering" (88), is central in this vocabulary, as is the necessity "of avoiding the humiliation of others" (91). And again, Rorty is candid about his personal position. "We ironists who are also liberals ..." he says (84).

But how is this vocabulary of liberalism not a "final vocabulary" about which the ironist must have "radical and continuing doubts"? This question is clearly present in the background when Rorty takes up the matter of a culture's "public rhetoric":

> I cannot … claim that there could or ought to be a culture whose public rhetoric is *ironist*. I cannot imagine a culture which socialized its youth in such a way as to make them continually dubious about their own process of socialization. Irony seems inherently a private matter. On my definition, an ironist cannot get along without the contrast between the final vocabulary she inherited and the one she is trying to create for herself. Irony is, if not intrinsically resentful, at least reactive. Ironists have to have something to have doubts about, something from which to be alienated. (87–8)

It appears thus that those "radical and continuing doubts" about the vocabulary of liberalism are present after all. Rorty simply refuses to express them. On this point, in fact, he is brutally candid: "My private purposes, and the part of my final vocabulary which is not relevant to my public actions, are none of your business" (91).

We are tempted to ask: Given that the sponsorship of liberal vocabulary *is* a public action, with possible political consequences, how are the sponsor's "radical" doubts about that vocabulary not relevant? Ways around this question are built into Rorty's presentation:

> But that distinction between a central, shared, obligatory portion and a peripheral, idiosyncratic, optional portion of one's final vocabulary is just the distinction which the ironist refuses to draw …. On her conception, human solidarity is not a matter of sharing a common truth or a common goal but of sharing a common selfish hope, the hope that one's world—the little things around which one has woven into [sic] one's final vocabulary—will not be destroyed. For public purposes, it does not matter if everybody's final vocabulary is different, as long as there is enough overlap so that everybody has some words with which to express the desirability of entering into other people's fantasies as well as into one's own … words like "kindness" or "decency" or "dignity." (92–3)

The ironist certainly draws a sharp distinction between parts of her final vocabulary when it comes to deciding what it is "my business" to know about. But Rorty now denies that that distinction has any normative effect on the public aspect of the vocabulary.

This denial is untenable. Precisely the decision about what is whose "business" is inescapably normative. If Rorty, as an ironist, is to keep his writing from dissolving into an incoherent tangle of self-qualifications, he has to draw the line somewhere. He has to mark out an area about which his radical doubts are none of our business. And the question of how such an area is decided upon is not answered by the idea of a reasonable overlap among people's final vocabularies.

What is required of the ironist author is inevitably a *political* decision, by which specific doubts are identified that it is better (for society) not to talk about. It is thus a decision which can be made only on the basis of some well-understood, if normally unspoken, propositions about how society works and what is best for it. How is the ironist's radical detachment to survive under these circumstances?

Of course it does survive, in some area where it is "none of our business" to look. But in the domain of "public rhetoric," or public discussion or public policy, its survival or failure to survive has no effect whatever; the author might just as well be a thorough dogmatist. And if we assume nevertheless that she is still authentically an ironist, it follows that her move into the public domain, a domain from which she is temperamentally "alienated," has been an act of considerable personal sacrifice, which means presumably an *ethically* grounded act. For the ironist in Rorty's sense, therefore, ethics begins where irony ends, where irony summons up the strength to deny its own operation. And the ethics in question is thus always indistinguishable from a dogmatic ethics, an ethics founded on established principles and theorems. There is no such thing as an ethics *of* irony.

This is where Rorty and Nietzsche part company. Nietzsche's view would be that the ironist's self-sacrificing move into the public domain is simply an act of mendacity. In Nietzsche's universe, Rorty's ironist is dishonest by definition. Her doubts about the final vocabulary she uses, we recall, are based not on an overriding method, but on her understanding of competing vocabularies. She thus lives by understanding, and understanding is mendacious. The one thing she always fails to understand, for Nietzsche, is the link with conviction that falsifies understanding. Rorty, we might say, attempts to suggest, with self-sacrifice, a path from Nietzsche's radical irony to a responsible public ethics. But Nietzsche himself will have none of it. For him, the only conceivable ethics is, after all, an ethics *of* irony.

The Ethical Dimension of Discourse

Putting aside for the time being the question of whether an ethics of irony is *possible*, we can at least say a good deal about what such an ethics would look like. First and most obviously: Ethical behavior, in an ethics of irony, cannot be based on conviction or on propositions whose truth one is convinced of, because all conviction involves falsity, which for Nietzsche means *transparent* falsity, in which one never escapes complicity. "I call falsehood: *not* wanting to see something that one sees, or not wanting to see something *as* one sees it: whether the falsehood occurs with or without witnesses does not matter. The most common falsehood is the one with which one deludes oneself" (KSA 6:238).

Second: There is nevertheless a general ethical standard, the preference for honesty over mendacity. And third, finally: The manner in which one adheres to this standard is strictly individual; sound ethical activity on my part need have nothing specific in common with sound ethical activity on yours. This last consequence follows logically from the first two, since any *necessary* common element in ethical behavior would imply an underlying principle or conviction. But Nietzsche also insists upon it: first, in his assertion that Christianity, the arch-falsehood, can be attacked with equal effectiveness at any point in its far-flung conceptual structure, and then, more importantly, in his development of what I have called the trap of understanding, each reader's inescapable recognition that the increasingly complete understanding of a book like the *Genealogy* or *The Antichrist* only increases his or her complicity in what the book is written *against*. The book poses a challenge; one has to respond to it by taking some form of intellectual action. But the book itself can offer no guidance whatever, because as far as its meaning is concerned, such action is impossible—this being precisely the trap of understanding.

Can we still talk about "ethics" in this situation, where no general prescriptive criteria can be applied to anyone's actions? Do the *Genealogy* and *The Antichrist* not simply refute ethics as a possibility? The one avenue that remains open, as far as I can see, is that of an ethics of *strict honesty in discourse*. Which would be, necessarily, an ethics of irony, since honesty for Nietzsche is incompatible with the commitment to any positive conviction whatever. Hence the main difficulty that Nietzsche confronts in the *Genealogy* and *The Antichrist*—and the difficulty that bedevils Rorty's ironist when she tries to write. For the production of discourse is always the production of meaning, which includes—in all but the most rudimentary factual discourse—a positive theoretical content that offers itself to the understanding in a manner that presupposes conviction on some level. And an honest discourse must be stripped of this type of content; it must be content-neutral. (What else can Nietzsche be talking about when he speaks of "our loving and cautious neutrality"?) How else does one "*become* free" if not by stripping one's discourse of the straitjacket of positive or doctrinaire content?

An honest discourse must therefore contrive to nullify or neutralize whatever elements of positive theoretical content arise in its unfolding. One possible method of carrying out such neutralization—for reasons discussed above—involves using the collection of aphorisms as a form, or the hybrid of aphoristic and narrative form in *Zarathustra*. But this method is not satisfactory—also for reasons discussed above. Hence Nietzsche's move back to the form of the extended essay—for the sake of *honesty*, because the competent reader of an aphorism, the slow, careful reader, will in effect transform that aphorism into an essay anyway.

And now the technique of the trap of understanding is developed and refined in the *Genealogy*: the technique that places me in the position of being able to make use of the text only by refusing to understand it. The text in a sense possesses a positive theoretical content (expresses an implied conviction) that is available to my understanding. But as soon as I understand it fully, to the point where I recognize the need for an ethically decisive response on my part, that content evaporates. Again, discourse cannot simply be devoid of positive theoretical content, cannot avoid suggesting conviction. But in the *Genealogy* Nietzsche shows that it is possible to compose a long and complicated argument which *becomes* conviction-free in that its content nullifies or neutralizes itself.

The ethical status of discourse is thus not determined by its content. The deciding factor must be the rhetorical shape of the discourse: not what we say, but *how* we speak or write. It may occur to some readers that we now find ourselves again in Rorty's vicinity, in the vicinity of the idea that "literary criticism" might represent a significant form of philosophical writing (79–84). One could argue, in fact, that the idea of honesty, in Nietzsche's radical sense, has played an important role in the history of the study of poetic form, the study of formal techniques for undoing the "communicative" façade of language. As far as I can see, formal considerations of this sort do not actually play any role in Rorty's idea of "literature" or "literary criticism."

But more important for now is the question of *why bother* with the problem of an ethics of radical honesty in discourse. What use have we for such an ethics? And for at least the first attempt at an answer to this question, we turn again to Rorty. The trouble with Rorty's irony is that it is "inherently a private matter." There is no way to verify its operation; Rorty's ironist, for all she knows, could be the only ironist in the world, perhaps the only true ironist in history. Rorty himself, when he identifies himself as an ironist, could be mistaken, or could simply be lying. But on the other hand, for Rorty, irony *must* exist. Irony can never be directly manifest in "public rhetoric." But without the invisible private operation of irony, a strong public movement critical of "final vocabularies" as such can never develop; and the hope for "a liberal culture whose public rhetoric is nominalist and historicist" (87) vanishes.

In this situation an ethics of irony, or of radical honesty in discourse, makes all the difference. Such an ethics—in the form of a method for neutralizing the positive content of speaking or writing—must serve as a kind of secret language for ironists, as the token of a hidden community of social benefactors, a kind of new freemasonry. Of course this community cannot be expected to promulgate or advocate a set of explicit ethical principles for the good of mankind. But it can perhaps be expected to provide the medium in which those who, for the time being, espouse different or opposed principles may do so in a manner sufficiently "nominalist and historicist" to avoid interfering with a reasonable level of well-being for the race. Surely a community of this sort is a strict prerequisite for anything like "solidarity"—although Rorty would disagree. And this community has no medium in which to know itself as such—which means simply, it cannot exist—without an ironic Nietzschean ethics, an ethics of radical honesty in discourse.

The Uses of Christianity

Nietzsche's resituating of all ethical questions in the domain of rhetoric can be derived, pretty much in its entirety, from the *Genealogy of Morals*. But there is a fundamental difficulty in that book that requires at least a supplement—in the form of something like *The Antichrist*. For while the *idea* of the trap of understanding emerges unmistakably from the thought of the *Genealogy*, the *reality* of the trap, from a reader's point of view, is questionable. Like the figure of Socrates in *The Birth of Tragedy*, the central content of the *Genealogy*, the history of ascetic ideals and ascetic priesthood, is so hedged about with ambivalence that in effect it ceases to operate as an ethically charged content even without the trap of understanding. Ascetic ideals, Nietzsche argues, are the worst disaster that has ever befallen healthy humanity, but the ascetic priest must nevertheless be recognized as an indispensable historical factor in the service of life. There may not be enough positive ethical substance here—my comprehension may not sufficiently engage me—for the trap to operate against.

Or to look at it differently, even the basic argument of the *Genealogy* strongly resists the understanding. The exact logical and historical relations between the first and second treatises emerge only gradually as the exposition unfolds; and the relatively clear definitions of "ascetic ideals" and "ascetic priesthood" collide with the tendency of the argument to find their referents universally operative in modern Western culture. Against this background, the trap of understanding takes shape, in the first instance, *as an idea*, as yet another problem for the understanding, indeed as a kind of infinite regress—I understand the trap, which understanding *is* the trap, which I understand as such, and so on. Does the immediate ethical character of the trap not tend to get lost in this process?

The Antichrist, however, is not at all ambivalent and does not offer itself as an exercise for the understanding. Here, as I have said, the trap of understanding is simply thrown in my face as a challenge. It does not gradually engulf me as the inevitable outcome of my work as a reader. There is in fact nothing inevitable about it. In order to avoid the trap, I need only either insist on a more temperate critique of Christianity or simply disagree with Nietzsche on the question of the essential identity of Christian and Jewish hierarchy. Here, as in the case of the *Genealogy*, the trap of understanding lies open before me. But whether I enter it is now a matter of *free choice*; the operation of the trap is now, from beginning to end, ethical in character. And it follows now from the argument above, I think, that the only possible criteria by which I may decide what position to take on *The Antichrist* must have to do with an ethics of irony, with the goal of radical honesty in discourse.

This is one use of Christianity for late Nietzsche. Christianity provides the target for a single-minded, violent attack, a curse, which is also, precisely in its violence, the product of careful "neutral" calculation concerning the possibility of asserting an ironic perspective in public discourse. Whether the attack on Christianity is in any sense objectively justified makes no difference. The pattern of contradictions (curse vs. "loving" neutrality) and issues (Christianity as perfect "falsity") is what counts, and whether that pattern helps "us ironists" (Rorty) to sniff each other out amid the confusions of modern mass culture.

The other use to which Nietzsche puts Christianity in *The Antichrist* is less obvious but no less significant. The figure of Jesus, as Nietzsche understands him, is an *allegory* of the ethics of irony, of the manner in which the text of *The Antichrist* is positioned ethically with respect to a reader. Just as Jesus, in Nietzsche's view, *lives* his teaching, rather than attempt to codify it in doctrine, just so does the irony of Nietzsche's text situate its teaching exclusively in the rhetorical *manner* (or "method") of its unfolding. To put it differently, Jesus's ethics, like the ethics of *The Antichrist*, is not a prescriptive but an *exemplary* ethics, which offers its recipient not a doctrine to understand but a model to imitate. Just as the true follower of Jesus (unlike Christians in the Pauline tradition) need only be like Jesus, or indeed simply *be* Jesus, in the matter of practicing a "loving" non-negation, in the matter of resisting neither ill nor evil, so the Nietzschean anti-Christ need simply *be* Nietzsche in a "loving" neutrality of rhetoric, in cultivating a radically honest discourse, emptied of all doctrine or precept.

The idea of imitation must be understood here in a very narrow sense. For if I imitate Jesus by way of an understanding of what he represents—or correspondingly, if I imitate Nietzsche by conforming to what I take to be his philosophical views or convictions—I am missing the point. I am not imitating in the strict sense, but rather I am tailoring my behavior to precepts that I claim to have derived from an understanding (!) of my teacher. Like Paul and his followers, I have refused to recognize that "this faith [of the man Jesus] cannot be formulated—it *lives*, it repels formulas" (KSA 6:203); I have refused simply to *be* Jesus, in a moment that is never other than the here and now. Or correspondingly, I have refused simply to be one of that "us" whom Nietzsche addresses in *The Antichrist*, that collective of thinkers, and especially of writers, which is held together not by common beliefs, but rather by the strict absence of belief, by the reduction of discourse to an exercise in "methods" or techniques for the removal of positive doctrine. (This notion of imitating without the mediation of any specific understanding of one's model, incidentally, also solves Winckelmann's paradox: that we become "inimitable" by imitating the Greeks.)

Irony and Community

For both Rorty and Nietzsche, the presence of "ironists" is indispensable to the future healthy development of mankind—however different their visions of that future may be. And whence can those ironists possibly derive a sense of the public and historical usefulness of their "inherently private" activity, if not from a recognition of the community (as it were, the secret society) that they constitute among themselves?

In Rorty's case, it is fairly clear that the necessary recognition of community has to do with his "liberal hope," which in this respect is a kind of compound hope. Rorty hopes that his own personal liberal hope will be more or less automatically shared by the fellow ironists with whom he requires some form of connection. If this first hope is fulfilled, then the recognition of liberal hope in other people's social and political writings will provide at least an initial step toward recognizing (and so creating) a community of irony. But this hope (that irony and liberalism go together) is *only* a hope. For all Rorty knows—for all he *can* know, given the inherently private quality of irony—all of his fellow liberals could as well be zealots as ironists. And while it is true that if you are going to be a zealot, it is probably better for society if you are a liberal than if you are, say, a fascist, still liberal zealotry, like any other zealotry, brings with it a complete inability to criticize "final vocabularies" as such, an inability which bodes ill for the future of humankind.

For Nietzsche in *The Antichrist*, by contrast, it is immediately clear that membership in the book's "us," in the community meant to arise among its readers, is not tied to any specific opinions on any subject. The only possible candidate for such a shared opinion would be hatred of Christianity. But in the first place, the mood of such hatred clashes violently with the "loving and cautious neutrality" that characterizes "our" community. And in the second place, once we recognize in the figure of Jesus an allegory of that neutrality, an allegory of the ethics of irony, it follows that "we," we properly methodical, ironic readers, constitute a *form* of Christianity, a form diametrically opposed to the Pauline version, but Christianity nonetheless. Hatred of Christianity, or the curse upon Christianity, certainly operates as a "conviction" in the text. But we must recognize that it operates thus, in the final analysis, as no more than an "expedient," as the marker, for "us ironists," of a place in the text that is in truth occupied by nothing.

These points, however, are strictly negative. How shall we formulate positively what constitutes the possibility of our recognizing in one another a community of radical ironists? We could speak of strict honesty in discourse, of imitation with no idea of a model, of method without theory, of a refusal to generalize (as if this were not itself a general idea), of an insistence on "reality," on the particular, the here and now. But none of these ideas brings us closer to what we are seeking. They are, precisely, ideas, and the very notion of an ethics of irony excludes the possibility of its reduction to anything like a formulable shape in the domain of ideas. Once we have recognized the importance of such a notion—by way, for example, of a comparative discussion of Nietzsche and Rorty—only one course lies open to us. We must search out as great a variety of further instances as possible, in order to clarify extensively what cannot be clarified otherwise. What is needed is what I propose to deliver in this book as a whole, a collection of instances.

But once again, the crucial point of the present chapter is that irony operates as an ethics not by prescribing rules of conduct for its practitioners. Its ethical significance is constituted by nothing but *the existence of the community it requires*. For upon that community—and not upon the influence of any teaching or the development of any institutions—depends the possibility of a "nominalist and historicist" future for human society or, more radically, the possibility of a communal and political existence unpoisoned by the inherent dishonesty of conviction.

Chapter 3

KANT AND LEIBNIZ

Both Aristotle and Kant, in their major treatises on ethics, start out from the notion of the good.[1] In the *Nicomachean Ethics*, however, this notion serves mainly to give contour and direction to what is essentially a collection of arguments on diverse ethical topics. Aristotle is careful to warn us at the outset not to expect too much completeness or exactness from any treatment of the matter he is taking up (1094b). His own treatment does not in the end pretend to be more than a kind of prelude to politics (1094b; 1180a–1181b).

Kant, in his *Foundation for the Metaphysics of Morals*, accepts no such limitations. The notion of the good provides him with a basis for every logical step by way of the postulate: "We cannot think of anything in the world or outside of it that could be purely good—something that is good in itself, without qualification—except a *good will*."[2] He concedes the existence and utility of an "empirical element" in ethics, a "practical anthropology" (4:388; F 7–8) which embraces most of the matters that concern Aristotle. But in his own present work he is interested only in the "pure part" of "moral philosophy," in a "metaphysics of morals" (4:389; F 9) without which morals, or ethics, has no claim to authority, hence in effect no reason to exist.

> We need it [a metaphysics of morals] not only to satisfy speculative motives and to disclose the origin of the principles residing *a priori* in our ability to reason, but also because our morals deteriorate without reason as a guiding thread and highest norm for their proper evaluation. For when we approach an action we wish to prove morally good, its mere *conformity* to moral law is not enough; rather, the action must be done also *for the sake of* the moral law. Otherwise the conformity is merely contingent and arbitrary. (4:389–90; F 9)

Ethics is thus now characterized by an independent absolute value, which it had lacked, for example, in Aristotle.

Problems in Kantian Ethics

The decoupling of ethics from politics is made possible, for Kant, by a concept of "will" (German *Wille*, also French *volonté*) which had not been available to Aristotle. (Greek βουλή and βούλησις [Aristotle, 1112a; 1111b] focus on deliberation and wish, respectively; προαίρεσις [1111b] usually means a choice from preexisting alternatives; and the opposition ἑκούσιος-ἀκούσιος [1109b] distinguishes willingness and unwillingness.) The concept of a radically active will capable of positing its own object (hence capable of being judged good or otherwise) can probably not arise except on the basis of a strict Cartesian separation between subjective and objective domains.[3] But Kant's is still an extreme position on the question of *how* the will's goodness can be judged. In Diderot's view, and Rousseau's (in the encyclopedia article "Droit naturel," and in *Du Contract social*, respectively), the only criterion suggested is conformity of the individual's will to a "volonté générale" (general will), whence the political is reintroduced, in however attenuated a form. Kant, on the other hand, recognizes that ethics cannot be "purified," or divested of its political or "empirical" component, until the proper object of the will is unambiguously *formulated*, a condition he thinks is satisfied by the idea of a categorical imperative.

The historical importance of Kant's formulative move is that it brings into focus once and for all the Enlightenment quest for a universal secular ethics: an ethics requiring no supernatural absolute, no revelation, yet both applicable and available to all human beings (unlike the ethics of irony, which needs a special sort of person to master it); an ethics, therefore, which unfolds in the domain of valid formulation; an ethics which perhaps need not be as fully reducible to propositions as Kant's (or indeed reducible to a "catechism" [Kant 6:480–5]) but is still an ethics we can talk *about* without resorting to the forms of irony found in Rorty and Nietzsche, without telling readers to mind their own business or attacking our own ironic stance in a Christian allegory.

There are plenty of problems in Kant's ethical theory. How do you identify and isolate a single "action" (*Handlung*) for ethical scrutiny? How do you associate unambiguously a "maxim" with an "action," except perhaps after the fact? Does a difference in one's awareness of the conditions and consequences of a proposed action not entail a difference in its maxim? Is there not, therefore, for practically any action that is not an outright crime, a calculus of consequences and a correspondingly tailored maxim that would justify it in the terms of Kant's imperative?

Then, in addition, there is the *whole* problem of a propositional or rationalist ethics. Does a critique of the Enlightenment like Horkheimer and Adorno not call into question the very idea of such an ethics? And even assuming that a consistent and operable rational ethics could be formulated, what would be the point of working it out, what difference would it make? People of sound ethical character would not need it; people lacking such character would pay it no heed. Diderot, in developing his ethics of reasoned conformity to the general will, is aware of this difficulty and meets it with the hortatory appeal to a reasoning "we" that includes the whole human race. But by the time of his association with Catherine in Russia, he has come to recognize that sound reasoning may favor the wicked as well as the virtuous (Diderot 3:47, 513). And Kant, in the end, has recourse to the idea of a religion whose whole content and operation (along with a bloodless idea of "radical evil") is derived logically from a rational ethics, which means that while perhaps providing a frame of reference for ethical thought, it can never have any original ethical authority of its own.[4]

These problems, however, do not impair the *historical* significance of Kant's project. If the complicated ironies in Nietzsche and Rorty are recognized as a response to that project, then the need for such ironies is testimony to its inherent strength and its power of persuasion, as are also the unrelenting efforts of many important present-day thinkers, Habermas at their head, to sustain the Kantian model in ethics and repair its difficulties.

Questions for Leibniz

But for now, I would like to turn to Leibniz, who is clearly one of the main thinkers Kant is confident of having left behind or swept aside in his ethical and religious thinking. In 1791—some time after both the *Foundation for the Metaphysics of Morals* and the *Critique of Practical Reason*, perhaps now in preparation for the book on religion—Kant publishes a short but vigorous critique of the very attempt (*Versuch*) to produce a "philosophical" theodicy, a rational justification of God's choices in creating the world. Leibniz is not mentioned in this piece, but readers are obviously meant to recognize in his *Theodicy* an instance of the project that Kant declares futile. (The very word "theodicy" [originally French "Théodicée," Kant's German "Theodicee"] is Leibniz's coinage.) Therefore, in the conclusion to the piece's main argument (Kant 8:264–7), Leibniz is compared by implication to Job's comforters and is thus, in effect, accused of hypocrisy, at best of unwitting hypocrisy.

Kant's general position here has the virtue of perfect clarity. The ethical aspect of religion, he insists, is the domain of reason alone.

> The one and true religion contains nothing but laws, i.e. practical principles, of whose unconditional necessity we can become conscious and which we therefore recognize as revealed through pure reason (not empirically). Only for the sake of a church, of which there can be different and equally good forms, can there be statutes, i.e. ordinances held to be divine, though to our purely moral judgment they are arbitrary and contingent. Now to deem this statutory faith ... essential to the service of God in general ... is a *delusion of religion* ... a counterfeit service. (6:167–8)[5]

But at the same time, reason, as applied to religion, is also strictly *limited* to the domain of ethics, which is why Kant takes up the matter of theodicy.

> For to be a creature and, as a natural being, merely the result of the will of the creator; yet to be capable of responsibility as a freely acting being ... but again, to consider one's own deed at the same time also as the effect of a higher being—this is a combination of concepts which we must indeed think together in the

idea of a world and of a highest good, but which can be intuited only by one who penetrates to the cognition of the supersensible (intelligible) world and sees the manner in which this grounds the sensible world. The proof of the world-author's moral wisdom in the sensible world can be founded only on this insight ... and that is an insight to which no mortal can attain. (8:263–4; R 24)

In other words, in every aspect of religion except the ethical, not reason but only faith and revelation can guide us.

It follows now that Kant, by implication, is imputing to Leibniz's *Theodicy* at least one (possibly both) of two errors: an illegitimate use of reason, or an illegitimate expansion of the domain of ethics. The main questions he raises are thus two in number: Exactly what is the status of reason, or what sort of reason is being employed, in Leibniz's *Theodicy*? And in exactly what sense, if in any at all, may the *Theodicy* be considered a work on ethics? An examination of these questions, I think, will serve to lay bare the enormous categorical gulf between Kantian and Leibnizian ethics.

More Questions

How, and to what end, is reason employed in Leibniz's *Theodicy*? Kant's critique assumes that theodicy is a kind of juridical defense of God against three separate charges: (1) that in spite of his supposed holiness as creator and lawgiver, he has permitted moral evil in the world; (2) that in spite of his supposed benevolence, he has permitted physical evil, our ills and pains; (3) that in spite of his supposed justice, he has permitted a disproportion between crimes and punishments in the world (8:257; R 18–19). And the critique then goes on to describe in detail how theodicy normally rebuts these charges, including in the description summaries of the arguments made by Leibniz and of others that Leibniz had rejected.

What puzzles us here, however, is that this section of Kant's essay occupies exactly five pages of print (8:258–62; R 19–23), whereas Leibniz's *Theodicy* is a substantial book of over three hundred pages. What does Leibniz accomplish with all that extra verbiage? It is true that his development of the arguments by which God is meant to be justified is much more nuanced than Kant's. But it is also obvious that a difference in terminological subtlety and refinement comes nowhere close to accounting for the difference in sheer bulk between the two presentations. Either Leibniz is a ridiculously inept advocate or his book, in the end, is *not* a quasi-juridical defense of God's right to have created the world as we experience it.

Our inclination toward the latter possibility is strengthened by the recognition that the very idea of the juridical is out of place in any theodicy. The juridical presupposes a contest between advocates of opposed positions: and *against whom* is the *Theodicy* (or any theodicy) understood to be arguing? A theodicy does not argue *that* there is a God who is omnipotent, omniscient, benevolent, and just, and who possesses all these qualities in absolute perfection. (Not skeptics or atheists, therefore, can serve as envisaged opponents.) Rather, it attempts to show *how* our belief in such a God can be sustained in the presence of experiences that seem to cast doubt on it. The idea of a perfect God is a premise of the supposed trial or contest, not a conclusion to be questioned or defended, which means that there is no real opposition between parties in the discussion. Everyone starts out from the acceptance of a perfectly omnipotent, omniscient, benevolent, and just God; the only point in question is how we shall most comfortably and convincingly talk about our belief among ourselves. Nicholas Jolley puts the matter succinctly when he points out that while it is true that the "urgency" of the problem of evil for Leibniz was in part "a result of the pointed challenge thrown down by Spinoza" (who denies the applicability to God of moral predicates), still, the *Theodicy* is concerned far less with refuting Spinoza than with establishing a position distinct from those of Malebranche and Bayle, thinkers with whom Leibniz *agrees* concerning the existence and attributes of God (Jolley 157–8).

But our question has still not been answered: How, and to what end, is reason employed in the *Theodicy*? Again, theodicy aims at deciding not *whether* God is justified (he is after all justified by definition), but rather *how* his justification might best be explained. And why should this matter be important enough to write books on? Anything like an *adequate* explanation of God's justice, as Kant points out, would require a type of insight that is closed to the human mind. A debate on theodicy thus resembles a target-shooting competition for the blind. Not only are we unable to aim, we are also unable to judge the results afterward. What do Leibniz and his interlocutors (especially Bayle, with whom the *Theodicy* often becomes a single extended conversation)[6] hope to gain by their efforts?

At least it is clear now how the *Theodicy* becomes as long a book as it is. Since there can be no single correct way of explaining a perfect God's permitting evil and injustice, and since there is therefore no single standard against which to measure attempts at such an explanation, it follows that the only way to defend one's own view of the matter is to compare it, one by one, with as many as possible of all the other views that have ever been put forward. Precisely this is what Leibniz does in the *Theodicy*. He not only debates with illustrious contemporaries like Bayle; he also mines the whole past of Christian and pre-Christian thought for texts against which to test his ideas by carrying out critical appraisals: from Plato and Aristotle, Augustine, the Scholastics, to Valla, Luther, Descartes, and so on. And if we consider, in addition, the large amount of supplementary theological, metaphysical, ethical, historical, legal, anthropological, and scientific material that is brought in to provide context for the central argument—since that argument cannot pretend to settle its questions by direct demonstration—we must recognize that there is no necessary limit at all to the amount by which Leibniz could have expanded his work.

But again, *why* should such a work be written? For a work it certainly is, an *opus*, the only actual book Leibniz ever published. One is perhaps even tempted to suggest that the question of evil and the project of theodicy serve here mainly as excuses for producing a kind of philosophical compendium. This supposition might also help with the question of why Leibniz often seems more interested in the style than in the substance of philosophy, in finding not new truths but rather preferable ways of expressing or explaining truths long established: why, for example, he drags John of Ruysbroeck into a discussion of "monopsychitism" (greater Spinozism, so to speak) for no apparent reason except to excuse that author's errors as stylistic quirks[7]; why he does basically the same with Luther (DP 12, 59); why he defends the principle of "determinant reason" (or sufficient reason) on the basis not of its truth but of its usefulness in founding "an infinitude of very just and very profitable arguments" (E 44, 108); why he insists on the "true and philosophic sense" in which body and soul are related while at the same time accepting as reasonable the idea of direct interdependence that is found "in everyday converse" (E 65–6, 116); why he excuses an admittedly "crude" utterance of Descartes not by explaining the truth behind it but by repairing its metaphor (E 162–5, 164–6); why he goes out of his way to find germs of his own doctrine in the vague dissatisfaction expressed by an unnamed book reviewer in a passage Bayle happens to have quoted (E 358–9, 250)[8]; and why he concludes the whole main part of his work by reproducing a dialogue of Lorenzo Valla and tacking onto it a coda showing how Valla supposedly anticipates the best-of-all-possible-worlds doctrine (E 405–17, 269–75).

Or further: Surely Leibniz is fully committed to the system of preestablished harmony as a description of the relation between body and soul. But in the *Theodicy*, he frequently argues in favor of that system not on the basis of truth or conviction, but on that of rhetorical convenience: when he finds it "best qualified" to counteract the doctrine of a "one and universal Soul that engulfs the rest" (DP 10, 58); when he asserts that Bayle's logical undermining of spontaneity does not affect it (E 300, 227); when he points out its usefulness in supporting the idea of determined but contingent futurities (E 331, 239); and when he finds in it a kind of general solution for all the philosophical difficulties insisted upon by Bayle (E 353, 248). Exactly what is it that produces these tendencies in Leibniz's writing?

Answers?

I think this much is clear: that in the *Theodicy*, and in much of his other writing, Leibniz is talking less directly about real things or abstract ideas than about "vocabularies" (in a sense related to Rorty's use of the term), about ways in which thinkers attempt to come to grips rhetorically with their sensory and intellectual experience. And for the sake of argument, I would like now to advance the supposition that he is concerned with vocabularies in *exactly* Rorty's sense of "final" vocabularies, that he is therefore speaking from what Rorty would think of as an "ironist's" perspective, the only perspective from which final vocabularies appear as a true plurality.

Let us begin by recalling that Rorty's ironist is not exempt from the condition of needing a final vocabulary in order to carry on the business of thinking. The opposed condition of strict impartiality, of being committed to no specific views whatever, is impossible. Such impartiality (in Rorty's view) would itself have to take the form of a final vocabulary. Rorty's ironist, therefore, is as fully committed to her final vocabulary as Rorty himself (for instance) is to his political liberalism. What makes her an ironist is the depth of her understanding (even while still firmly believing what she believes) that the views by which she thinks and lives are also inherently mutable, the depth of her awareness that tomorrow's final vocabulary could be a different one, the depth of suspicion with which she regards even what she knows to be true, the depth of her attraction to other incompatible vocabularies, her uncomfortable recognition that she has no firm grounds for rejecting them. But we cannot expect her to communicate this depth of understanding. To do so would require a universal meta-vocabulary whose nonexistence is the very core of precisely what she understands. If she talks about her ironic self-positioning at all, it will be to tell us, in one way or another (as Rorty does), that it is none of our business.

That Leibniz is fully committed to certain principles and propositions, therefore, is not an argument against his being an ironist in Rorty's sense. There is no reason why an ironist should not assert, for example: "This truth, that all God does is reasonable and cannot be better done, strikes at the outset every man of good sense, and extorts, so to speak, his approbation" (E 339, 241). But what positive signs of an underlying irony can we hope to find in Leibniz's writing? In fact, all the elements of the *Theodicy* that I have described above can be regarded as such signs: the treatment of philosophical positions as if they were matters of style rather than substance; the advocacy of his own system on primarily rhetorical grounds, without any explicit claim of objective validity; the discovery of resonances with his own thought in systems apparently opposed to his; and even the sheer length of the work, which suggests that the minutiae of debate, the assertion and clash and development of vocabularies, are to be regarded as more interesting, perhaps even more fundamental, than its supposed results. (Kant's dismissive opinion of the book arises from a failure to make this inference.)

It is true that these points do not add up to a conclusive argument. It is true in general that the nature of irony (as it operates in Rorty's or Nietzsche's writing) precludes a demonstration of its presence. But in the particular case of Leibniz, there is one further characteristic of his larger philosophical work that points very strongly in the direction of a radically pluralistic idea of "vocabularies." In the "Preface" of the *Theodicy* he says,

> There are two famous labyrinths where our reason very often goes astray: one concerns the great question of the Free and the Necessary, above all in the production and the origin of Evil; the other consists in the discussion of continuity and of the indivisibles which appear to be the elements thereof, and where the consideration of the infinite must enter in .... But if the knowledge of continuity is important for speculative enquiry, that of necessity is no less so for practical application; and it, together with the questions therewith connected, to wit, the freedom of man and the justice of God, forms the object of this treatise [the *Theodicy*]. (*Theodicy* 38)[9]

The whole of philosophy is thus divided into two separate regions. And what is interesting about this duality for our purposes is that the two regions require *radically different vocabularies*.

We have already touched on this point in connection with Leibniz's distinction between a "true and philosophic" discourse and "everyday converse" (E 65–6, 116). That distinction is *ethical* in nature; indeed, it is what makes ethics possible in the first place. On the level of "true" metaphysical discourse, we understand that everything God does is good and is an infallible marker of the good. Which tells us the general direction of ethics—that all ethics is a kind of imitation of God—but cannot help us with "practical application," where we must think of our intentions and actions as having a direct effect on people and things, even though our philosophical consideration of the question of substance has proven that such a direct effect is impossible. As ethical beings, that is, we must think and speak in a manner we know to be incorrect. The *Theodicy* (which uses and acknowledges both types of discourse) thus represents a kind of prolegomenon to ethics, teaching us how we must think of God in order to preserve a sense of our freedom and activity, so that ethics becomes possible. But ethics can become actual (not merely possible), it can be put into practice, only by my firm commitment, for the time being, to "everyday converse," to a manner of thinking and speaking which I had known, and still know, to be philosophically untenable. Thinking about the manifold perfection of God is of no use whatever when I must deal with the question of whether to lend money to a particular individual whom I suspect of being irresponsible. In order to think ethically, I must think of my decisions as having a direct effect upon both material bodies and immaterial souls.

It would have been convenient for the present argument if Leibniz himself had written a treatise on "practical" ethical questions, which would have shown conclusively the difference between discourses. But he wrote no such treatise. He is after all a philosopher, not a legislator or moralist. In everyday life, like all of us, he has to think ethically, in a manner known to be philosophically incorrect. Precisely philosophy—in the idea of a morally perfect God who is represented in our own being—demands this of him! But when he sits down to write, he leaves that "practical" ethical thinking behind, as he must. If he had lived to hear Kant talking about a "metaphysics of morals," or about "pure practical reason," he would have laughed out loud. When talking about "practical" morality, we are not even speaking the same language as when discussing metaphysics.

In any case, Leibniz's acceptance of an intellectual situation in which he must work with two radically different vocabularies, in two inevitably conflicting rhetorical registers, makes it difficult for us not to regard him as an ironist in Rorty's sense, as a strict rhetorical pluralist operating in the awareness that every vocabulary is just that, a vocabulary, in competition with other vocabularies, hence subject to revision or rejection at any time, *every* vocabulary, including his own cherished final vocabulary of "best of all possible worlds" and "preestablished harmony." Moreover, if we accept this supposition, then it follows that Leibniz's ethics is an ethics *of* irony, like Nietzsche's or (save where politics interferes)

Rorty's, since only irony, only a strictly relativist view of vocabularies, makes a true ethics, ethics for a philosophical mind, possible in the first place. The parallel with Rorty is especially clear. You can be, ethically speaking, a very good person in Leibniz's sense without being an ironist, just as you need not be an ironist to be a satisfactory liberal for Rorty. But just as only the true ironist, for Rorty, can make real progress in the development of a nominalist and historicist culture, so also for Leibniz—it seems to me—only the true ironist (whose very being spans the divide between philosophical truth and ethical conduct) contributes significantly to building the city of God.

Irony, History, Manners

Irony, in the sense of this and the preceding chapter, can never be conclusively demonstrated for any particular text. But it certainly seems easier to discern in Nietzsche and Rorty than in Leibniz, assuming it is there in all three cases. This difference can be understood historically. Nietzsche and Rorty find themselves in a post-Kantian intellectual situation, where the idea of ethics is strongly associated with the idea of formulable rules or standards or principles, where no need is felt to reserve for practical ethics a discursive universe separate from that in which metaphysics or science unfolds. (If Kant had recognized that in Leibniz, ethics and metaphysics require separate discourses, he would have regarded that separateness as a methodological fault.) In Nietzsche, therefore, and even in Rorty, one senses a certain desperation. The ethics of irony is in danger of being engulfed and eradicated by mass ethics, by a specious ethics-for-all-comers. The ethical ironist is now obliged, against her own inclinations, to reach out aggressively and seek contact with others of her kind, with her "fit audience ... though few." And if Kant's ethics is as innovative as I have suggested, it follows that Leibniz, before Kant, finds himself under no such obligation. The indications of irony in his writing are merely symptoms, not desperate communicative gestures.

My contention is that in pre-Kantian Europe—or perhaps we can say, in Europe before the age of mass societies and nation-states—the exclusivity and irony later insisted upon by Nietzsche were *a normal and accepted form of ethics*, ethics for an intellectual elite. In other words, what looks to us modern readers like irony in Leibniz is not really irony at all; it is not concealed, and he has no reason to conceal it, from his fellow intellectuals. The prime indication of this state of affairs in his work is that his grasp of the philosopher's simultaneous commitment to incompatible vocabularies is not a conclusion he eventually arrives at, but rather a basic condition of philosophizing, which he is aware of throughout his career. The need for different vocabularies already figures centrally, for example, in the so-called Discourse on Metaphysics of 1686, especially sections 10, 12, 14, 15, and 27. And it is hard for me to see how one can understand that need in any philosophical depth except on the basis of a radically questioning attitude toward one's own final vocabulary, an attitude which in post-Kantian thought must produce irony.

It might be suggested, finally, that what I am taking as signs in Leibniz of a quasi- or proto-ironic posture are in the end merely the polite conventions of scholarly conversation, that the idea of alternate permissible vocabularies is simply a method for avoiding nasty collisions in debate by always leaving one's opponent a way out. My response would be that the very idea of "mere" conventions in intellectual commerce already belongs to the post-Kantian situation, the idea of strict separation between the content of an utterance and its form. Kant insists on such separation in the preface to the second edition of the *Critique of Pure Reason*, when he admits the possibility of drastically rewriting his work without altering its meaning (Kant 3:22–6). But there are no "mere" conventions for a philosophical ironist. Conventions always presuppose a group that observes them; and for the ironist precisely that group is the very substance of her thought, the "we" that her irony requires in order to become more than just a speculative game. What looks to us like irony in Leibniz is after all precisely convention, the expected rhetorical behavior by which he marks his belonging to the international society of philosophers or savants. It looks like irony to us—in effect, for us, it *is* irony, crying out for comparison with Rorty, if perhaps not with Nietzsche—only because that international society of rhetorical relativists no longer occupies the foreground of intellectual life, that society of writers whose whole practice started out from the understanding that there is no single master discourse, that discourse is irreducibly plural.

Chapter 4

LESSING: HISTORY, IRONY, AND DIASPORA

Lessing is at the historical center of my argument. Strictly speaking, he is a pre-Kantian thinker, like Leibniz. He died in the same year the *Critique of Pure Reason* was published. But he had a much deeper and clearer sense than Leibniz for the problems of the coming age, a sense which I think developed in the theological controversy he provoked in the late 1770s.

In 1774, from his position at the Ducal Library in Wolfenbüttel, he began publishing the "Fragments of an Unnamed Author," a series of essentially deist manuscript writings, including much radical Bible criticism, by the late Hermann Samuel Reimarus. By the end of 1777, after publication of the second installment of the "Fragments," polemical responses from the orthodox Christian side began to appear. The most important antagonist was the senior Lutheran pastor of Hamburg, Johann Melchior Goeze, with whom Lessing conducted an extensive debate in print until, in July and August 1778, legal moves emanating from the ducal court at Braunschweig revoked the exemption from censorship (*Zensurfreiheit*) under which he had been publishing and forbade him to publish anything further on the subject of religion.

It is not necessary, for present purposes, to understand all the issues in that theological debate. What matters for us is that in the period when he wrote *Nathan der Weise* (Nathan the Wise) and *Die Erziehung des Menschengeschlechts* (The Education of the Human Race), the two texts we shall pay most attention to below, Lessing was operating under sanctions that prevented him from stating openly anything resembling what he actually thought on matters even remotely connected to religion. The use of a dramatic fiction in *Nathan*, and in the *Erziehung* the fiction of being an "editor" (adapted from the Reimarus publications), served to put some distance between the author and the material in those texts. But even with that distance in place, Lessing could not afford to be provocative to a degree the authorities would have considered dangerous.

This fact has consequences for how we must now proceed. In discussing Leibniz, we could afford to content ourselves with a broad view. The Enlightenment intellectual ethics that prefigures an ethics of irony, as Leibniz practices it and on occasion comes close to expounding it, is simply the assumed basis for his activity as a thinker and writer. It never occurs to him to conceal it, and once his writings are placed in the proper context, it can be brought into critical focus without too much trouble.

Lessing, by contrast, has no choice but to carry out a move of deliberate self-concealment in the writings that interest us. Therefore the broad view is no longer satisfactory. It will not do to say that we understand the "basic" meaning of the *Erziehung* or *Nathan*—the meaning as one might put it together after a first cursory reading—and that we can leave the "details" for further study. The details of these texts do not merely modify the supposed basic meaning; they overthrow it completely. The details, the hints, the slightly out-of-kilter metaphors, the significant silences, make all the difference. Therefore a very close reading, at considerable length, is required.

But I think the results will justify the effort. And the emergence, at a crucial point in the development of modern ethical thought, of what can reasonably be called a Jewish ethics, affords us a perspective from which to consider any number of extremely important and interesting issues, including, as a start, the ethical dimension of psychoanalysis.

Lessing's Position

Lessing (speaking as "editor") prefaces *Die Erziehung des Menschengeschlechts* with what purports to be a summary of its main content:

> Warum wollen wir in allen positiven Religionen nicht lieber weiter nichts, als den Gang erblicken, nach welchem sich der menschliche Verstand jedes Orts einzig und allein entwickeln können, und noch ferner entwickeln soll; als über eine derselben entweder lächeln, oder zürnen? Diesen unsern Hohn, diesen unsern Unwillen, verdiente in der besten Welt nichts: und nur die Religionen sollten ihn verdienen? Gott hätte seine Hand bey allem im Spiele: nur bey unsern Irrthümern nicht?[1]
>
> [Why do we not prefer to see, in all positive religions, nothing other than the unique path by which human reason, in this or that place, has been able to develop and will develop further—rather than mock or attack one of them? This scorn of ours, this indignation, would be merited by nothing in the best of worlds, and only religions deserve them in our world? God takes a hand in everything, only not in our errors?]

Clearly there is a polemical tendency here, but a careful reader might be excused some puzzlement about whom it is directed at. The idea of mocking or attacking "one" religion suggests that the target is every orthodoxy (e.g., Goeze's) that disparages a religious attitude by which it is challenged. But the more general formulation of the next sentence appears directed against those who laugh at all traditional religion, i.e., the proponents of an ultimate religion derivable from human reason alone. And then, in the apparent equating of "Religionen" to "Irrthümer" (religions to errors), Lessing seems himself to advocate that ultimate religion of "die vernünftigen Verehrer Gottes" (the rational admirers of God).²

That Lessing wishes to steer a course between orthodoxy and pure reason is clear enough. This is, after all, the man who hoped to be considered no less a supporter of the Lutheran church than chief pastor Goeze, yet is also reported to have said, "The orthodox ideas of the deity are no longer for me; I cannot abide them. Ἓν καὶ Πᾶν! I know nothing else."³ But then, what is his real position? The Aristotelian or Masonic distinction between esoteric and exoteric doctrine does not help here, the idea that while some amalgam of pure reason and pantheistic feeling may be esoterically valid, it cannot be advocated in public without causing confusion. If Lessing were trying to conceal his difficult intellectual position, why did he go to the trouble of publicizing Reimarus's writings? Why create a scandal in the Goeze controversy? Nor can it be maintained simply that Lessing in the *Erziehung*, while asserting the ultimate invalidity of all orthodoxy, is still defending the right of various orthodoxies to exist; for these thoughts presuppose an impossible point of view. God, presumably, can at once know truth and deliberately teach errors, as adults do with children. But once a book like the *Erziehung* is published, once the logical necessity of a "new eternal gospel" (§ 86) can be shown, surely the time for orthodoxy is past; surely it is time simply to proclaim the new gospel, and the *Erziehung* does not do this.

Moreover, Lessing says specifically in the preface quoted above that human understanding has not yet reached the end of its development. Therefore, even if the doctrine of the *Erziehung*—including the idea of a new eternal gospel—were generally accepted, it would still be only a step on the way, a misguided orthodoxy needing to be superseded in its turn. Indeed, the idea of metempsychosis at the end (§§ 94–100), whatever its intended truth value, has the immediate effect of calling attention to an important weakness in the argument up to that point, by raising the question of how God, in his education of the *race*, can be so manifestly unfair to the majority of *individuals*, those who are born too early in history to enjoy the ultimate fruits of their education (§ 90). (This problem—which generalizes a perennial problem in Christian theology—has a political parallel in the problem of the conflicting interests of state and individual, as discussed in *Ernst und Falk*, Lessing's Freemason dialogues.) In any event, metempsychosis itself cannot be an ultimate truth. Otherwise, by expressing it, Lessing would be violating his own admonition to the "more capable individual" of his time: "be careful not to let your weaker fellow students suspect what you are beginning to catch a scent or even a glimpse of" (§ 68).

Nathan and Saladin

The matter of reason and orthodoxy obviously requires clarification, and it seems to me that a discussion of *Nathan der Weise* is useful in this regard. For there is a strong parallel between the character of Nathan and what we might call the character of God in the *Erziehung*. Nathan is certainly meant to be seen as the most thoroughly rational personage in his drama; but like the supremely rational Teacher of the *Erziehung*, he also not only condones but deliberately promotes error. Unlike Al-Hafi, he chooses to remain in the imperfect secular world. And this choice, which is given considerable dramatic prominence at the close of Act 2, echoes Lessing's own firm determination in *Eine Duplik*: "Und einmal muß ich doch mit der Welt leben; und will mit ihr leben" (LM 13:34: I have no choice but to live with the world, and it is my wish to live with it).

But the world in which Nathan chooses to remain, despite flashes of enlightenment in various characters, is thoroughly barbaric; and this applies not only to the Christians, whose general tendency toward narrow-mindedness is stressed repeatedly. Even some very perceptive interpreters of *Nathan* consider Saladin "enlightened";[4] I suppose they refer mainly to his religious tolerance, to statements like "I have never insisted that all trees grow a single bark" (4.4.309-10). But his tolerance springs from good-hearted indifference, not from any positive rational conviction. He is a simple man: "One cloak, one sword, one horse—and one God! What more do I need?" (2.2.203-4); he has his God, and others are welcome to theirs. His simplicity, oddly enough, is expressed most clearly in a speech that seems to deny it: "Alas I too am a thing of many sides, which often do not seem to fit together very well" (4.4.333-5). He does not care if his actions are inconsistent; he does what occurs to him at any given time and lets logic worry about itself. In the midst of an enlightened conversation with Sittah, for example, about the irrational prejudice that restricts Christians to marriage with Christians, he is capable of reverting suddenly to his own irrational obsession with the malevolence of the Knights Templar (2.1.102-13), an obsession which he expresses by removing the head of every Templar he gets his hands on—every Templar, that is, save one. And this one Templar, by being a brave, likeable, and relatively enlightened human being, is living testimony to the barbarity of his general practice.

His supposed generosity, moreover, is attacked vigorously and justifiedly by Al-Hafi: "You don't consider it an affectation to oppress, starve, plunder, martyr, strangle people in their hundreds of thousands and then play the philanthropist with individuals?" (1.3.480-3). His generosity is mere recklessness, and in this it is clearly contrasted with Nathan's. When he finally feels the pinch and sees himself becoming "hard" (4.3.230), the result is only that he becomes confused and offensive, as with the messenger Ibrahim (5.1.18-19). His generosity is sustained neither by practical seriousness (in order to stay generous, one must devote some effort to staying rich) nor by a true rational humanity which avoids the damage that can be caused by generosity misplaced—as Nathan does in the first conversation with Al-Hafi (1.3.437-41).

The world in which Nathan lives—the world in which, though tempted by Al-Hafi, he makes a decision to live—is barbaric to the core, and Lessing adds a number of gratuitous touches to emphasize this. When Sittah invites Saladin into her harem to discuss how they shall deal with Nathan, she could easily mention that she wishes to show him, say, a new set of chessmen. What she actually mentions, however, is a *slave*, "a singer that I purchased only yesterday" (2.3.355-6), and

slavery is certainly irreconcilable with enlightened humanity (see *Erziehung*, §
10). Historical accuracy is no excuse here; Lessing is not obliged to display this
motif at this point. Or we might return to Saladin's religious toleration and note
that he practices it with the same recklessness that characterizes his generosity;
for he has made a "capitulation" (4.2.193) with the Christians according to which
he admits that it will not be easy for him to avoid becoming a second Pilate
by allowing Nathan to burn at the stake (4.4.422–3). And his view of Nathan's
paternal rights—"What sort of right would Nathan have over her [Recha], as soon
as he is not her father?" (4.5.462–4)—is more narrow-minded than that of at least
two Christians, the Templar when he has calmed down (5.3.98–100) and the lay
brother (4.7.624–41).

Nathan's isolation in his enlightenment seems in fact to exceed his own
comprehension. Al-Hafi has pointed out that Saladin's good nature is dangerously
ingratiating (1.3.459–60). It apparently fools even Nathan, who at the very end
entrusts an important decision to him and expects him to consider it carefully.
Incest has been avoided; and now, at the play's end, Nathan gives Saladin the
breviary that proves Assad's identity, saying, "Noch wissen sie von nichts! Noch
stehts bey dir / Allein, was sie davon erfahren sollen!" (5.8.682–3: They [the Templar
and Recha] still know nothing; what they learn is entirely up to you!). Clearly he
hopes Saladin will consider whether it is truly in the interest of the young people
to know all the facts about their family. The Templar has said specifically that he
does not want to hear about his father (5.8.639–40). And as for Recha-Blanda,
who is going to find it difficult enough adjusting to a new family, a new name,
and a new religion (her brother's Christianity), is it really necessary to tell her that
she is also a Muslim princess by birth? But Saladin mistakes Nathan's meaning
completely and answers: "Ich meines Bruders Kinder nicht erkennen? / Ich meine
Neffen—meine Kinder nicht? / Sie nicht erkennen? ich? Sie dir wohl lassen?"
(5.8.684–6: I should not recognize my brother's children .... Perhaps I should leave
them to you?). Here, where a rationally humane consideration of others' interest
is required, Saladin is in so much of a hurry to impugn Nathan's motive that he
does not even acknowledge the existence of a question. It also does not occur to
him that if Recha were left a Christian, she would probably accompany her brother
to Europe and be lost to Nathan forever. What could be Nathan's advantage here?

Nathan's Rational Promotion of Error

The above exchange between Nathan and the Sultan brings us to the next point: that
Nathan not only accepts the existence of error in the world but in fact promotes
it. He has given Recha as rational an upbringing as possible, but he understands
that reason by itself is not a sufficient basis for ordering one's life. He understands
that without the sense of belonging firmly to a single family and culture and
religion, without the irrational but compelling ties of "nature and blood" (4.7.707),
existence becomes disordered. We are given an example of such disorder in the
person of the Templar, whose sense of belonging to his culture is disturbed by

a vague half-knowledge concerning his father. This uncertainty perhaps makes it easier for him to discard "prejudices" (3.8.618). But it also produces violent extremes of opinion and behavior. He can exhibit Christian bigotry at its worst—for which Saladin chides him by simply calling him "Christian" (4.4.405, 408)—and a few scenes later he can turn virulently anti-Christian when he says to Nathan of Recha: "Will she not have to play the Christian among Christians? And having played the part long enough, will she not become one? Will the pure grain you have sown not be choked by weeds?" (5.5.321–6). A contrast is offered in the figure of the lay brother, who, though stable as a person and firm in his Christianity, is no less open-minded than the Templar.

Precisely reason understands that the bonds of blood and tradition, rationally unjustifiable as they may be, are necessary in human existence. Nathan's love for Recha is tempered by rational altruism, which is why he has always intended to give her back to her blood relatives, and back to the institutionalized error of Christianity, as soon as possible. He has always asked of Daja not permanent resignation but merely "patience" (4.6.522–4); he has not told Recha what he knows of her background, which would only have disrupted her childhood security; he asks Saladin to think a bit before revealing the whole truth at the end: all this is required by reason. Even in his parable of the three rings he does not advocate maximum rational enlightenment, but envisions a situation in which orthodoxies compete for preeminence—"Es strebe von euch jeder um die Wette, / Die Kraft des Steins in seinem Ring' an Tag / Zu legen!" (3.7.527–9: let each of you compete to show the power of the stone in his own ring)—a situation in which moral improvement is sought not for its own sake but for the greater glory of one's own religion.

Nathan, like God in the *Erziehung*, is sufficiently rational to promote error where error is needed. This likening of divine and human abilities is found elsewhere in Lessing as well, in the *Hamburgische Dramaturgie*, for instance, where "genius," by creating a realistically consistent fiction, is said to imitate "the highest genius" (LM 9.325; no. 34) who is God. Or we think of § 73 of the *Erziehung*, where the doctrine of the Trinity is elucidated by analogy with human self-consciousness.[5] But where does all this leave the idea of a "new eternal gospel" of reason and the good for its own sake? Will a time come when reason no longer prescribes error? At least it seems clear that Lessing does not believe this time has come yet.

Error and the Activation of Reason

The interdependence of reason and error is not difficult to understand as a philosophical theorem. Lessing writes in his letter to Moses Mendelssohn of February 2, 1757: "I assume we agree, dear friend, that all passions are either violent desires or violent abhorrences? Also that in every violent desire or abhorrence we are conscious of a higher degree of our reality, and that this consciousness cannot but be pleasurable?" (LM 17:90). The association of pleasure with a consciousness of our "Realität" (or "thingishness" in the etymological sense) probably owes a good deal to Leibniz's idea of the pleasure arising from activity as opposed to passivity. The specification of such self-realizing activity as "Leidenschaften" (passions) is perhaps suggested by Dubos.⁶ And if we consider that that letter is written in reply to an essay of Mendelssohn's, "Von der Herrschaft über die Neigungen" (On Mastery over Our Inclinations), which distinguishes strictly between "upper" and "lower" mental faculties—between reason and logical processes on one hand, and the senses and passions on the other (*Ges. Schriften* 2:147–55)—then we may conclude that Lessing is ascribing specifically to the lower or irrational side of our nature an *active* power from which we receive at least a heightened sense of our reality—if not indeed our reality, our presence in the world, itself.

The distinction here between rational and irrational is similar to a distinction Lessing draws eleven years later, at the end of the *Dramaturgie*, between critical judgment and genius:

> Was in den neuerern [his own recent dramas] erträgliches ist, davon bin ich mir sehr bewußt, daß ich es einzig und allein der Critik zu verdanken habe. Ich fühle die lebendige Quelle nicht in mir, die durch eigene Kraft sich empor arbeitet, durch eigene Kraft in so reichen, so frischen, so reinen Strahlen aufschießt. (LM 10:209; nos. 101–4)
>
> [I am aware that everything tolerably good in my recent dramas is owed exclusively to my critical faculty. I do not feel in myself that vital fluid that wells upward under its own power, by its own power shoots forth in such rich, fresh, and pure streams.]

It is true that he goes on to say, "critical judgment is reputed to smother genius, and I prided myself on receiving from it something that comes very close to genius" (LM 10:210); there is thus a certain asymmetry in the distinction between critical judgment and genius. But the basic distinction remains, between a natural power that is active and creative, and a rational faculty that can approximate creativity only by squeezing its knowledge laboriously "through pumps and pipes" (LM 10:209).

And this distinction underlies the relation between reason and error in both *Nathan* and the *Erziehung*. Reason is reactive; it can dissect and reshape what it is presented with, but it does not act spontaneously; it does not create, it cannot endow life with substance. Error, on the other hand, is the condition of all true activity, of all those rationally unaccountable movements in the individual or in history—passion, genius, revelation—that give "Realität" or solid substance to our being. Genius, we hear repeatedly in the *Dramaturgie*, is useless without rational regulation, just as revelation in the *Erziehung* requires the cooperation of reason for its effectiveness (§§ 36–7, 76). But by the same token, neither the life of an individual nor the history of the race would be there for reason to work upon, if not for those vitally creative but rationally incalculable powers that necessarily produce error as well as substance. Only by virtue of error can reason *become* what it is, as an ordering power, as what Cassirer says is for Lessing "the basic structuring and synthetic power of consciousness itself" (59). Reason can approximate artistic creativity, for example, only in the form of "Critik," the faculty of judgment that presupposes error, or a difference between good and bad, in existing works. And this activation of reason by error is also the sense of the assertion in *Eine Duplik*: "Denn nicht durch den Besitz, sondern durch die Nachforschung der Wahrheit erweitern sich [des Menschen] Kräfte, worinn allein seine immer wachsende Vollkommenheit bestehet" (LM 13:24: For not the possession of truth, but rather the quest for it, expands human powers, wherein alone consists our ever-growing perfection). Reason does not develop as a force until it has material to work on; and therefore we receive even error as a divine gift, from God's left hand but still from God.

That reason as such is not a "synthetic power," that it analyzes but does not bring forth, is stated specifically in the *Erziehung*:

> Wenn auch der erste Mensch mit einem Begriffe von einem Einigen Gotte sofort ausgestattet wurde: so konnte doch dieser mitgetheilte, und nicht erworbene Begriff, unmöglich lange in seiner Lauterkeit bestehen. Sobald ihn die sich selbst überlassene menschliche Vernunft zu bearbeiten anfing, zerlegte sie den Einzigen Unermeßlichen in mehrere Ermeßlichere, und gab jedem dieser Theile ein Merkzeichen. (§ 6)
>
> [Even if the first human was equipped immediately with a concept of a single God, still this concept as a gift, not earned by thought, could not possibly persist long in its pure state. As soon as human reason, left to itself, began to work on it, it divided the immeasurable One into a number of more imaginable entities and gave to each of these fragments a characteristic mark.]

Only two sections earlier, it is true, we read that revelation provides us with "nichts, worauf die menschliche Vernunft, sich selbst überlassen, nicht auch kommen würde" (§ 4: nothing that human reason, left to itself, would not also arrive at). But this clause is in the subjunctive, whereas § 6 is in a rather surprising indicative—does Lessing mean that polytheism *did* develop from an original monotheism? Moreover, § 4 is later directly contradicted when Lessing speaks of religion's bringing us to "nähere und bessere Begriffe vom göttlichen Wesen, von unserer Natur, von unsern Verhältnissen zu Gott ... auf welche die menschliche Vernunft von selbst nimmermehr gekommen wäre" (§ 77: better and more plausible concepts of the divine, of our nature, of our connections to God ... which human reason by itself would never have arrived at). And the authenticity of this last idea is supported by its association with an argument very similar to that of both *Eine Duplik* II and the architectural "Parabel" of 1778, the argument that human and divine truth can be contained even in "a religion whose historical truth, one might say, is so awkwardly questionable" (§ 77).

But how shall we deal with the contradiction between § 4 and § 77?[7] The two sections are in fact connected by a clear development in the text. In § 4 Lessing says that reason alone ought to be sufficient for approaching truth; but immediately afterward he asks with regard to polytheism and idolatry, "who knows how many million years human reason would have drifted around in these errant paths ... if it had not pleased God to provide new impetus in a better direction?" (§ 7). How can these "millions" of years mean anything but time without end? Then Lessing argues that without the Old Testament problem of how to reconcile a divinely enforced morality with the inequitable distribution of goods in the world, human understanding would have arrived at proofs of the immortality of the soul only very late—"and perhaps never" (§ 28). And with respect to Christian doctrines other than the immortality of the soul, doctrines "whose truth is less plausible, whose usefulness is less immediate" (§ 63), he suggests both explicitly and implicitly (in the obvious incompleteness of his explanation of the Trinity [§ 73]) that reason is even now not really able to cope with them.

From here it is not difficult to reconcile § 4 and § 77. Reason follows revelation; reason, which is essentially passive, must be activated by the "Irrthümer" (errors) of arbitrary orthodoxies. And once it is thus activated, it must *appear* that reason could have arrived by itself at the quantum of truth that any given orthodoxy contains. Indeed, an activated reason, and only an activated reason, groping its way through errors, *would* eventually arrive at truth (this is the sense of the subjunctive in § 4). But activated reason does not exist in the first place except by virtue of error (this is the sense of the assertion concerning reason "by itself," or without error, in § 77). Therefore, although on specific topics of conversation he always encourages as rational a discourse as possible ("Sind / Wir unser Volk? ... Sind Christ und Jude eher Christ und Jude, / Als Mensch?" [2.5.521–4]), Nathan still does not encourage a *life* of pure reason for those he loves or respects, but rather prefers to see them ensconced in a particular tradition of belief, limited by the arbitrary bonds of "nature and blood." Only thus can reason be activated as a vital force; only thus can rational discourse *effectively* be encouraged.

Nathan says that humanity is prior to cultural citizenship, to our "Volk." But it does not follow that culture is superseded by pure humanity. The priority of humanity means that we belong to a particular culture *for the sake* of our humanity. Humanity is prior to culture in the sense that it is culture's final cause. Cultural particularity—as both the product and a source of that arbitrary creative energy, comparable to genius, without which the human race would not exist—is the vehicle by which pure humanity is actualized in the world. This truth is reflected in the fact that the word "Mensch" (man), in the conversation between Nathan and the Templar, receives its special meaning precisely from the cultural gulf between the people using it.

All this must be borne in mind when we read the words with which Nathan continues his address to the Templar: "Ah! Wenn ich einen mehr in Euch / Gefunden hätte, dem es genügt, ein Mensch / Zu heissen!" (2.5.524–6: Ah! If only I had found in you one more person whom it suffices to be called a human!). Why the unforceful verb "heissen" (be called), as opposed to "sein" (be)? The distinction between what one truly is and what one appears to be (or is called by others) figures centrally in a passage from the *Duplik* that I have already mentioned, where Lessing answers the charge that his publication of Reimarus's "Fragmente" is the action of a malicious enemy of Christian belief: "(*Being* is not an issue. That I *am* not such an enemy only One needs to know, and He knows it.) But that I should even consent to *seem* such?" (LM 13:34). Nathan therefore uses the verb "heissen" advisedly; he means not that one should *be* truly human in the secret recesses of the heart, but that one should express one's humanity, allow it to *appear* over and above one's limited cultural situation, in order that cultural particularity fulfill its true function—the function of the competing religions in the parable—which is to activate reason, to locate visibly within a coordinate system of example and contrast exactly the goal we must strive toward in order to be truly ourselves. Again, it is precisely the Templar's uncertainty concerning his basic cultural commitment that makes it *difficult* for him to follow a consistent rational or humane line in his thought and action. When Saladin poses the treacherous riddle, Nathan immediately answers, "Sultan, / Ich bin ein Jud'" (3.5.325–6: Sultan, I am a Jew); that the Templar would *not* have answered analogously under similar circumstances is shown by the scene immediately following the parable-scene, where he says, "I as a Templar am dead. I have been dead to that order from the moment that made me Saladin's prisoner" (3.8.619–21).

Thus we can understand the basic relation between reason and error in philosophical terms, and we can understand Nathan's rational promotion of error in personal and practical terms. But these points do not yet explain how the promotion of error can be compatible with reason as such, defined impersonally. Error is needed, as activation, *before* reason can operate. But once it is activated, must reason's sole task not be to eliminate error?

The Irony of God

Nathan's situation requires *irony* of him, a discrepancy between what he says and what he does. By his actions he must promote the particular cultural commitment of those he deals with; or at least he must avoid interfering with their commitment. Everything he does after his first meeting with the Templar is aimed at establishing people's "true" identity, the rationally arbitrary but realistically indispensable web of blood relationships on which their existence is based. But since the ultimate justification of cultural commitment is to provide a firm standpoint from which reason may strive in the direction of truth, it follows that he may not *teach* anything but reason itself. When he speaks, he must offer an example of the use of cultural limitedness as a means of activating reason and so contributing to universal humanity, as a means of enabling each individual "to be called a human," to bear visibly and meaningfully that title.[8]

There is only one point in the play where Nathan comes close to a direct articulation of the thought on which his activity is based, and he does this only under duress (3.7.459–74). When Saladin presses him to explain the essential equivalence among religions, he responds that all religions are founded on tradition (hence, by implication, not on truth), and that since tradition or "history" can be accepted only by way of "trust and belief," it follows that only the religion in which my trust is based on my closest personal ties (especially blood relations) can serve as the means by which I am provided a home in the world, an existential substance (including error) on which and through which reason can then operate. Nathan is revealing a personal mystery here, and it is Saladin to whom he reveals it. That Saladin appears to understand sympathetically (3.7.475–6) is why he later thinks it permissible to entrust to him the handling of the whole truth about Assad.

Lessing's situation, like Nathan's, obliges him to practice irony. But what about that God to whom Nathan is paralleled? Is God an ironist? Lessing appears to suggest this in the *Erziehung* when he says, "ewige Vorsehung! ... Laß mich an dir nicht verzweifeln, wenn selbst deine Schritte mir scheinen sollten, zurück zu gehen!" (§ 91: eternal providence! ... Let me not lose faith in you even if your steps should seem to me to go backward!). The significance of this passage is that it hints at a serious logical difficulty in the *Erziehung*. We are told that God's purpose is to teach us, "die Tugend um ihrer selbst willen zu lieben" (§ 80: to love virtue for its own sake), to bring man to the point "da er das Gute thun wird, weil es das Gute ist, nicht weil willkührliche Belohnungen darauf gesetzt sind, die seinen flatterhaften Blick ehedem blos heften und stärken sollten, die innern bessern Belohnungen desselben zu erkennen" (§ 85: where he will do the good because it is the good, not because arbitrary rewards are attached to it, which are only meant to fix and strengthen his fickle gaze for recognizing the better inner rewards). But if this is really God's purpose, then it seems He might have done better to introduce the world's religions *in reverse order*: first the doctrine of an absolutely just and inevitable eternal reward or punishment, in order that the basic "selfishness of the human heart" (§ 80), which Lessing associates with Christianity, might prompt us to do good, even without knowing the true reason; then, as a more advanced stage, something like Old Testament religion, with a hint but not a reliable promise of reward and punishment in *this* life, in order that the obvious inequity of the external world (see § 28) might prompt us to look (in this life) for "the better inner rewards"; and finally, as the last stage, perhaps something closer to Plato's idea of the Good, which is valuable strictly for its own sake—an idea which is not incompatible with polytheism.

Of course God could not give us this education in this form, since the last and truest lesson would be that there is no God, or at least no divine Teacher. Nor do I mean to say that Lessing's surface argument is implausible, the idea of an historical progression of religions toward increasing spirituality. But the argument does still hold together when turned back to front, which it has no business doing according to § 5. And by stressing the idea of a "new eternal gospel" of the good for its own sake, along with the idea of the self-servingness of a supposedly advanced Christian morality (as opposed to the Jews' "heroic obedience" [§ 32]), Lessing allows us to become aware of this difficulty, and of the whole significance of the hint in § 91, about God's moving "backward." It also makes better sense, in this light, that the most advanced morality in *Nathan* is exemplified by the representative of the oldest religion.

I think it is fair to say, therefore, that the parallel between Nathan and God holds and that God in the *Erziehung* is a kind of ironist. Just as Nathan seeks to promote rationality, but at the same time must also take care to preserve the irrational preconditions of rational activeness, so God leads us in two directions at once, both toward and away from a perfectly rational mode of existence. So much is suggested by the reversibility of the historical argument. But the idea of God's irony is still only a metaphor, only a reader's inference from faint textual hints. What is the meaning of the metaphor? And what is Lessing's actual idea of the nature of human history?[9]

The Shape of History

The idea of Christian "selfishness," which is an important indication for readers of the *Erziehung* that they must look beyond the work's surface, also figures in the discussion of Christian tragedy in the *Dramaturgie*: "Does the Christian's expectation of a blissful reward after this life not contradict the unselfishness with which we wish to see all great and good actions undertaken and accomplished on the stage?" (LM 9:189–90; no. 2). In *Nathan*, not only is "the character of the true Christian … completely untheatrical" (LM 9:189), but so is the character of the false Christian, the Patriarch who expressly despises "the theater" (4.2.144). Both the true and the false Christian are too literal-minded for the theater; both insist that the seal be set on morality by a palpable reward or punishment after death. They have not the "heroic" (thus theatrical) religious attitude of the Jew. Nor have they the Jew's capacity for irony; it cannot be said of them in one breath, as it is said of Nathan, that they *live* well and *play* well (2.2.275–6). If one wishes to write a theatrical work about monotheistic religions, then at least in Lessing's view, a Jew has to be the main character.

But why write a play in the first place? Is *Nathan*, as Lessing suggests to Elise Reimarus (LM 18:287), merely a device for circumventing official censorship, merely a substitute for an essay or sermon? Or does the parallel between Nathan and God have significance here as well? Is history perhaps not an education but rather a kind of drama, whose whole purpose is to generate and illuminate "great and good actions"? I have suggested a parallel between irrational or passionate commitments in the individual and arbitrary orthodoxies in history. Is history perhaps meant not to educate us and so to supersede orthodoxy, but rather somehow to purify orthodoxy, as tragic catharsis supposedly purifies the passions? Does *Die Erziehung des Menschengeschlechts* thus covertly overturn the idea expressed by its title?

The idea of a quasi-dramatic purification of orthodox monotheistic religions in history is not difficult in itself. Nathan reduces it to simple terms when he imagines in his ring-parable a *competition* among religions, which would oblige every individual to strive toward pure humanity—"Es eifre jeder seiner unbestochnen / Von Vorurtheilen freyen Liebe nach!" (3.7.525–6)—in order that his own religion be recognized as the most humanly beneficial.[10] Thus each religion is purified by being used as a source of activated reason. But in this view, God Himself—as the maker of meaningful order in history—must deliberately favor the existence of more than one religion ("die Ringe … die / Der Vater in der Absicht machen ließ

/ Damit sie nicht zu unterscheiden wären" [3.7.450–3]), which brings us back to the idea of God's irony.

We need here to understand the principle, if any, of *progression* in history. If a truly fruitful competition among religions can be arrived at, must it not eventually lead to a pure form of belief beyond all orthodoxy? Has Nathan himself, in the act of presenting his parable, not passed beyond all recognizably Jewish thinking? If one *knows* in general how religions are meant to interact, then surely one no longer *belongs* to any particular religion—as Nathan, at the end, does not belong to the reunited family. Thus the question of reason and error is raised all over again. If error activates reason and reason tends toward truth, how can the fruitful tension between reason and error be *maintained*, that tension by which reason receives its value as eternal striving?

How does the drama of history work? The idea that the historical succession of religions constitutes an education of the human race, the surface argument in the *Erziehung*, is itself a kind of trans-religious doctrine and must therefore take its place as an indication of the most advanced stage in our learning process, as a seed of the *newest* human religion. But that idea of history does not work without the doctrine of metempsychosis, which Lessing characterizes as the *oldest* doctrine (§ 95). Is it possible, therefore, that the oldest and the newest are the same, that Lessing understands the historical succession of religions as a huge *circle*? The Pythagoreans, after all, the sect which taught metempsychosis, also taught the Great Year, the eternal recurrence of all history. The hypothesis that Lessing sees history as a circle would fit with the hint about backward steps of Providence, and with the remark, "It is not true that the shortest line is always straight" (§ 91). But there is an even broader hint in the next section: "And what if it were pretty much certain that the large slow gear that brings the human race closer to perfection has to receive its motion from smaller faster gears, each doing its part?" (§ 92). The basic metaphor here—that of a clockwork, in which small gears drive the larger, slower gears that move the hands—is very exact, since meshing gears turn in *opposite* directions, the idea being that even if the small part of history we can observe appears to be moving backward (§ 91), precisely this motion causes the inexorable forward motion of destiny. But in a metaphor this exact, is it possible that the obvious *circular* idea suggested by the wheel as such should be gratuitous?

Or let us look at the metaphor more closely. Can history really move backward, away from the perfection of reason? This certainly seems possible if we judge by the relatively late appearance of the self-interested literal-mindedness of Christianity, after the heroism of Jewish belief. And precisely this possibility, that history moves not only toward but also away from rational perfection, is a necessary precondition for the maintenance of a fruitful tension between reason and error, the tension that must remain more or less constant in history as a repeating cycle. Hence, again, the exactness of the clockwork metaphor. Precisely the backward turnings in the development of religion, the small opposed gears, are what enable the great wheel of history to continue its onward motion *as a wheel*, in its unending circle. In any event, it is clear that the question from which we started, the question of God's irony, the question of how reason *as such* can promote error, is not answerable except in the case that history is circular.

Revelation

In order to understand *how* backward turnings in the progress of reason are possible, we must understand exactly what Lessing means by "revelation." We found it useful, earlier, to equate revelation with any arbitrarily asserted (rather than rationally derived) system of belief. But where do such systems come from? Lessing is clear on this point, for he states repeatedly that what he calls "revelation" is always *anticipated* by the insight of individuals (§§ 7, 15, 31, 56, 68, 87–90). His reading of the Book of Job is an important instance (§ 29), for he seems almost to take it as a parabolic anticipation of the "new eternal gospel" itself, which finds the true reward of a good or evil deed here and now, in the deed itself. But if inspired individuals (like the author of Job) always anticipate revelation, can we not define revelation simply as the systematized public version of individual inspiration? Revelation will thus always appear arbitrary, since its public quality can never accommodate the profundity of thought and experience that had characterized the inspiration from which it is derived.

We can now reconcile the idea of activated, forward-moving reason with the idea of a huge historical cycle, provided we keep in mind the general idea of an ironic God. For revelation itself, as codified inspiration, now provides the backward or antirational turning of religious thought without which the tension between reason and error cannot be maintained and the cyclicity of history cannot be realized. If the truth about God and man involves an ineradicable irony, then any approach to that truth must fail, must become error, as soon as it is articulated or codified. Here is where the distinction between esoteric and exoteric doctrine belongs; an esoteric doctrine is an ironic doctrine, which cannot be set forth in a systematic, publicly accessible form without losing its irony and therefore its very nature. The irony of truth can be incorporated into canonical books as "prefigurations," "innuendos," "suggestions," and stylistic subtlety (§§ 43–9), but these hints are not perceived except by the gifted mind that is already on its way to the next stage (§§ 43, 69).

Therefore the codification of an inspired insight concerning divine truth always promotes error, which in turn provides grist for the mill of reason. The erroneous component of revelation (or nascent orthodoxy) activates reason, which then pushes toward truth; reason works thus until a few individuals reach the point of inspiration, where they see through prevailing orthodoxy into the unfathomable irony of the divine; such individuals eventually attempt to express what they have seen, as Nathan does to Saladin under duress, whereupon, in due course, their ideas are codified, thus inevitably perverted, and a new revelation is at hand (a new error) so that the process can begin once more.[11] This cyclical process is the form of the many little gears that drive the great wheel of destiny. Nor is the idea of an arbitrary irrational force thus excluded, a force comparable to genius, behind all revelation. For without such a force, without a universal appetite for revelation, and without miracles and extraordinary public manifestations to feed that appetite (§§ 59–60), how could we account, in the first place, for the repeated propagation and reception of what always begins in the obscure ironic "speculations" (§§ 78–9) of a visionary who does not expect, "that the prospect that enraptures him must also enrapture other eyes" (*Erziehung*, "Vorbericht": LM 13:415)? Again, the irrational force is the force that provides "Realität"; without it the history of religion would be nothing but a catalogue of unknown and incomprehensible philosophical outpourings.

Perhaps we should take a particular example and ask about the *next* revelatory stage after Christianity. Christianity will inevitably be called into question and will be transformed, like Jewish religion and Greek and Roman religion (§ 56) before it, into a heroic or problematic belief. The form of the challenge to Christianity—both *Nathan* the play and Nathan's ring-parable suggest—will be the idea of an ironic God Who fosters a plurality of equally true religions. But it takes an unusually subtle mind to imagine an ironic God. Therefore, when this thought is finally accepted and systematized, it will be broken down by the public mind into simpler elements. The plurality of religions will have to be interpreted as a plurality of divinities; and the next major religious revelation, in who knows how many centuries, will therefore be a kind of polytheism. Irony is by definition incommensurable; and systematic reason (native passive reason, not activated reason) will have to divide "the immeasurable One into a number of more imaginable entities" (§ 6). This is how religious history turns back on itself into a circle. And thus the puzzling indicative mood in § 6 is explained as well.

Nor need we be disturbed, in interpreting his play, by Nathan's preter-Jewishness or by his exclusion from the happy family at the end. He says at one point to the Templar: "The great man always needs a lot of ground. Several such, planted too close together, only break each other's branches. But the middling-good, like us, are found everywhere in masses" (2.5.492–5). This is irony in the sense of false modesty. Surely Nathan *is* a great man, one of the ironic, activated intellects that drive the human race forward; but he does not seem to have "a lot of ground." He is hemmed in by gross misunderstanding of his motives and teaching, especially on the part of Saladin and the Templar; and the family reunion at the end is itself an image of this misunderstanding, for Nathan's aim is tension and competition among orthodoxies, not reconciliation. But precisely this communal, emotional misinterpretation of Nathan is an instance of the historical process of revelation, the repeated backward turning by which reason is enabled to maintain its activated nature as striving. Nathan's exclusion at the end—by which he does in a sense gain "ground," in that no one is near him by blood—is thus personally tragic but historically encouraging, for it promises an endless realization of his stated aims (competition, striving, activated reason) in the very process of mistaking them.

Hence also Lessing's declaration of faith at the end of the *Erziehung*: "Und was habe ich denn zu versäumen? Ist nicht die ganze Ewigkeit mein?" (§ 100: And what can I have missed out on? Is not all eternity mine?). Metempsychosis is a red herring. Even without metempsychosis, it now turns out that nothing essential in human history is ever missed by anyone, whether Jew or Christian or Mohammedan, or an ancient or future polytheist, for human history is always basically the same, always at the same radial distance from the truth about which it revolves. Nor is it therefore meaningless to speak of an education of the human race. For such an education is always in progress, in the form of the centripetal force of activated reason by which "the better ones" (§ 56) always strive toward God and toward fulfilled humanity, and by which striving they in turn move the great wheel.

Thinking the Great Year

Lessing is not the only major German thinker to hit upon a modern use for the Pythagorean doctrine of eternal circular return. What is developed as an obscure implication in the *Erziehung* is proclaimed loudly by Nietzsche in *Also sprach Zarathustra*.

Or is it? After a certain amount of preparation—connected especially with the question of the will and with the threat of "Gravity"[12]—the idea of eternal return is fully deployed in the section of Part Three of *Zarathustra* entitled "The Convalescent." Zarathustra, calling himself "the advocate of life, the advocate of suffering, the advocate of the circle" (233; KSA 4:271), confronts his "most abysmal thought" and is struck down by "disgust." After an incapacitation of seven days, without food or drink, he rises from his bed and conducts a long dialogue with his animals, the eagle and the serpent, about the content of that "abysmal thought," which is the idea of eternal return (233–8; KSA 4:271–7). But curiously enough, it is only the animals who celebrate that doctrine, while Zarathustra himself speaks exclusively of its negative aspect, of his "disgust at man" and at "eternal recurrence even for the smallest" of men. The animals are triumphant; they revel in the idea of eternal return. But Zarathustra answers, "O you buffoons and barrel-organs! ... you—have already made a hurdy-gurdy song of it?" And after the long speech in which the animals declare, "O Zarathustra ... behold, *you are the teacher of the eternal recurrence*, that is now *your* destiny!" Zarathustra does not answer at all, for he is lying "with closed eyes like a sleeper ... conversing with his soul."

Zarathustra's unwillingness to take credit for the doctrine of eternal recurrence, or to become its "teacher," is explained, I think, by his recognition that eternal recurrence is not really a doctrine to begin with. It is a *problem*, an existential problem that changes the very nature of doctrine, including itself considered (for the sake of argument) as a doctrine. The concept of doctrine ordinarily involves the possibility of teaching and learning, hence the possibility of knowing or understanding something not previously known or understood. But in the Great Year, where nothing is known or understood by anyone which had not always been known or understood in the same circumstances in exactly the same way by the same person, that possibility vanishes. The knower of eternal recurrence—say, Zarathustra—therefore cannot possibly take seriously his own principal doctrine, his "final vocabulary," the basic intellectual equipment by which, in his place, a less scrupulous thinker might pretend to press forward into the supposedly unknown and unprecedented. And yet, on the other hand, he also cannot *stop* taking his doctrine seriously. It is still, after all, his own final vocabulary, no less so now than in any earlier turning of the wheel, and he is stuck with it. The knowledge of eternal recurrence, in other words, enforces an attitude exactly analogous to the radical irony that we discussed above in connection with Nietzsche and Rorty.

Or to look at it differently, the idea of eternal recurrence, for those whose sense is attuned to it, is a kind of secret handshake among practitioners of the ethics of irony. We observed in Chapter 2 that such an ethics is exceedingly hard to lay hold of with concepts. We kept running into ideas like Christianity without religion or method without theory or imitation without a model, or into the blank wall where a philosophical author tells us to mind our own business. But the doctrine of eternal recurrence offers a way around these problems. Superficially it is an extremely easy idea, impossible to misunderstand. But when we work out its implications in detail, we find that the difficulty of *grasping* the idea of an ethics of irony has been transformed unexpectedly into the difficulty of *avoiding* such an ethics.

Consider the character of the world one lives in as a knower of eternal recurrence. On one hand, that world is predetermined down to its least detail. Nothing can happen in it that has not happened in exactly the same way millions of times before; everything is exactly as it must be. But, on the other hand, take an apple, hold it at arm's length, and open your fingers. Perhaps the apple falls to the ground. But the main reason it does so, if it does, has nothing to do with the force of gravity. It falls to the ground, primarily, because at this point in the Great Year it always *has* fallen to the ground. All other possible reasons are trumped by this one, by a reason which implies nothing whatever about any other point in the Year. Which means that there is no reason why, the next time you try it, the apple should not do something *other* than fall to the ground. Stranger things, after all, have happened. The world, in other words, is at once both wholly predetermined and unchangeable, and completely arbitrary and unpredictable. And how, in such a world, can one make even the most innocent statement of fact or opinion without already having invested it with an impenetrable irony? How can one ever be either right or wrong in what one says? How can one ever either take a position or decline to take a position?

The ascription of this line of thought to Nietzsche is made plausible by the argument on his irony in Chapter 2. The idea of something like an ironic God, in the *Erziehung* and *Nathan*, makes plausible a similar ascription to Lessing. And in both Nietzsche and Lessing, accordingly, it follows that the purpose of the idea of eternal recurrence is to say something not about the world, but about the mind that can think that idea, to sketch the possibility of such a mind without getting tangled up in the impossibility of paraphrasing what it thinks.

Lessing's Jews

If such a mind exists, a mind sufficiently ironic to think the thought of eternal recurrence through all its implications, then—as we observed in the case of Rorty's "ironist" and Nietzsche's "free spirit"—the most pressing problem for that mind, the life-and-death question, is how to find its fellows and establish contact with them. Without some form of community—however shadowy, however invisible in history—the ironist's existence is pointless, for its indispensable ethical aspect has no room in which to unfold. Irony in solitude and silence is a nihilistic notion. Irony presupposes discourse, a conversation in which what is meant is never said because it collides (says Wittgenstein) with the boundaries of language.

In discussing this problem in Nietzsche and Rorty earlier, we did not get beyond the idea of certain types of rhetorical complication as a meeting ground for ironic minds, for minds sensitive to the devices by which a text can be made to say something perfectly intelligible while at the same time it is emptied utterly of any positive conviction. But with the figure of Zarathustra, Nietzsche in a sense finds a way to go further. The idea of eternal recurrence, in Lessing, is a buried treasure in the *Erziehung*, a reward for those few readers who are prepared to follow reason even into absurdity. But in *Zarathustra*, the same idea is proclaimed aloud, at least by the animals, as if it were just one philosophical doctrine among others. It is unfurled as a kind of banner, at once both plainly visible and unfathomably cryptic, as a beacon, a gathering point, for the curious crowd, but also for those few minds who are willing to live in the complete unfolding of its implications.

How does Lessing manage the problem of irony and community? Is the ironist simply doomed to solitude, to a solitude like that of God in monotheism, or like Nathan's solitude at the end of his play? Everything Nathan does is aimed at the establishment or restoration of community: at a universal human community transcending all differences of religion or culture, and at the narrower communal structures that arise from blood relationships. At the end of the play, his ironic stance—his advocacy of both types of community, despite the inherent conflict between them—is symbolically vindicated in the recognition of a transcultural web of blood kinship to which all the play's main figures belong. All except Nathan himself. The very last words addressed to him are Saladin's monstrously unjust accusation, "Perhaps I should leave [some part of my new-found family] to you?" (5.8.686). And he has no answer. Precisely the vindication of his irony excludes him from the community that symbolizes his vision. Does this situation represent the ironist's inevitable fate?

Nathan is a Jew, the only Jew among the play's characters and the only character excluded from the family at the end. Is there something inherently solitary about being a Jew? In a much earlier play of Lessing's, *Die Juden* (The Jews), despite the plural title, there is also only one Jew among the characters, and that Jew is also excluded, by being a Jew, from a family relationship, here in the form of marriage. Do the ideas of being a Jew, being a radical ironist, and being condemned to strict solitude all belong together?

In the *Erziehung*, by contrast, Lessing occupies himself at considerable length with the Jews as a community, as a people or *Volk* (§§ 8–52). And the manner in which he introduces this section of his work is decidedly odd. He begins in § 7 with an historically very vague description of a period of "polytheism and idolatry" in which only occasional individual thinkers had achieved deeper insight into the divine. Then, in § 8, he continues as follows:

> Da er [Gott] einem jeden *einzeln Menschen* sich nicht mehr offenbaren konnte, noch wollte: so wählte er sich ein *einzelnes Volk* zu seiner besondern Erziehung; und eben das ungeschliffenste, das verwildertste, um mit ihm ganz von vorne anfangen zu können.

> [Since God no longer either could or wished to reveal himself to each *individual person,* he therefore chose an *individual people* for his special educating, and precisely the least sophisticated, the most primitive people, in order to be able to start from scratch with them.]

First oddity: Lessing suggests in § 7 that God had earlier revealed himself to *some* individuals, not to *each* individual. Second: Why did God have to change his method? Surely the individual inspiration of, say, a Moses or a Jesus can be propagated to the multitude. Third: What can possibly be meant by the very idea of direct revelation to a community, as opposed to revelation by the agency of inspired prophets?

If I am correct in my argument that the *Erziehung* is a text in which crucial elements of meaning—such as the idea of history as a circle—are buried deep beneath the surface, then the direction in which the logical difficulties of § 8 point is fairly clear. Lessing is presenting the Jews, the Jewish people, as the image of a hypothetical community of radical irony, a community in which the raw material of revelation, a radically critical attitude toward all forms of conviction, is somehow built into the collective experience, not reserved for occasional gifted individuals. I do not mean that he thinks the Jews, all of them, actually *are* such a community. But there is enough material in his discussion of the Jews to indicate why he should imagine the community of perfect irony, of eternal radial distance from the truth, as an ideal or extrapolated Jewry. I refer especially to the idea of the Jews' "heroic obedience":

> Let us also confess that it is an heroic obedience to observe God's laws purely because they are God's laws, and not because He has promised to reward the observant, here and also beyond; to observe the laws even though one has despaired utterly of any future reward and is also not very confident about rewards in this life. (§ 32)

How big a step is it here from the idea of heroic obedience to the idea of ironic obedience, the idea of being fully committed to the "final vocabulary" of Jewish observance while also finding in oneself no reason whatever for preferring that commitment to any other? How big a step is it, in the other direction, from obeying God's laws solely because they are God's laws to doing the good solely because it is the good? And how big is the difference between these two seemingly opposed directions for one who understands the eternal radial distance that separates us from truth, hence also from the indisputably good, from God's right hand?

At the end of *Nathan*, the isolation of the radical ironist is presented to us as a problem. In the *Erziehung*, precisely the suggestion that the Jews can be seen as a model for community among ironists only makes the problem more acute, because no *basis* is indicated for the establishment of such a community. God, says Lessing, decided one day to reveal himself to a community instead of to individual minds—whatever that is supposed to mean. In other words, there is no way to explain how such a community might be brought into being. The problem remains: How shall radical ironists possibly contrive to reach out and find each other? And yet, on the other hand, Lessing does offer the Jews as a device by which that otherwise practically inconceivable community of ironists might be imagined after all—in much the same way that he had offered the Freemasons as a device for thinking politically in his *Ernst und Falk* dialogues. Where does he actually stand with respect to the question of understanding among ironists and an ethics of irony?

Teaching

The thought of *Nathan* and that of the *Erziehung* seem to be pointed in different directions. But there is one clear point of intersection between the two works, in the *Erziehung*:

> But why, it will be asked, this educating of such a crude people, with which, to such an extent, God had to start from scratch? I answer: in order, with the passing of time, to be able that much more confidently to use individual members of that people as educators of all other peoples. God educated in the Jewish people the future educators of the human race. Those would be Jews, they could only be Jews, only men from a people thus educated. (§ 18)

This paragraph and the whole of *Nathan der Weise* are obviously commentaries upon one another.

But in exactly what sense? Nathan certainly acts as an educator of the Christians and Muslims in his play. And the aim of his educating, presumably, is to make available to those others the same ironic enlightenment that characterizes his own thinking. But in this he fails. The others do achieve, literally, a combination of allegiance to universal humanity (transcending all differences of nationality and religion) with allegiance to blood relationships. But this achievement is made easy by the play's plot, in which, for them, the two allegiances become identical. We can unpack the allegory here by saying that the members of that reunited Christian–Muslim family stumble into the delusion that universal humanity *is* a single huge family. They fail to understand that the two allegiances in question, the hopeless truth-seeking of the resolute ironist and the firm commitment to a native culture, are irreconcilably opposed. To sustain both at the same time (this being the ultimate aim of education) is never a solution, never anything like a stage full of people embracing each other, never anything but a *problem*.

Why, then, should it be Jews, and Jews alone, who are charged with the hopeless educative task that confronts Nathan? The superficial answer to this question, as to most others raised by this text, is unsatisfactory. God has educated the Jews "from scratch"; therefore their understanding of the divine plan is less confused by extraneous developmental forces than other peoples'; therefore they are better suited to be teachers. How can this line of thought be reconciled with the idea that the New Testament is "the second, better primer for the human race" (§ 64)? *Better* than the Old Testament which guides Jewish teaching? Are Jews the best teachers only until Christians take over? This is not at all what § 18 suggests. And in any case, § 18 is followed closely, in §§ 24, 25, by Lessing's critique of William Warburton's insistence on an uninterrupted miracle by which God, before Christ, had justified the promise of the Torah in each Jew's life. The trouble is that a superficial reading of § 18 requires just such a miracle in God's special teaching of the Jews.

We have no choice but to read § 18 together with *Nathan*, as we did § 8 above. The Jews are suited as teachers because of their aptitude for irony, their practice of an "heroic obedience" which is essentially an ironic obedience, and which—in an ironist's world, where any absolute good is eternally out of reach, at an unchanging radial distance—is practically indistinguishable from doing the good for its own sake. And if we ask now how the Jews come to develop this aptitude, the immediate historical answer is that it is *a fruit of the diaspora*. In the very next section of the *Erziehung*, Lessing carries forward the thought of § 18 as follows:

> Denn weiter. Als das Kind unter Schlägen und Liebkosungen aufgewachsen und nun zu Jahren des Verstandes gekommenn war, stieß es der Vater auf einmal in die Fremde; und hier erkannte es auf einmal das Gute, das es in seines Vaters Haus gehabt und nicht erkannt hatte. (§ 19)

> [We may continue thus. When the child had grown up under chastisements and encouragements and had come now to the age of reason, its father suddenly expelled it into foreign lands; and here it suddenly recognized the good that it had had in its father's house and had not recognized.]

Lessing does not seem to have a specific event in mind. He suggests, rather, that the whole history of Jewish scatterings and exiles, from the Babylonian Captivity down to the complete denationalization under Hadrian, and beyond, is what has made the Jews into teachers. His position is that of what we might call a radical diasporist; the Jews, in his view, do not *become what they are* except in the process of being driven forth.[13]

I do not mean that Lessing is attempting to make an objective point about the situation of the Jews in history. He is interested in the Jewish diaspora primarily as an allegorical image of the community of those radical ironists (like Nathan) who are in truth humanity's teachers. The difficulty of imagining such a community is mirrored in what Nathan's eventual isolation suggests is the difficulty of sustaining the identity of a Jewish people with no homeland. The Jews' persistence as a people is founded on nothing but the energy expended by Jews in maintaining it. (Nathan's Jewishness, in the play, is founded correspondingly on nothing but his assertion that he is a Jew.) And the same must be true of any community of true ironists. Their persistence as a community is not given them as part of their condition, but depends on repeated acts of assertion and discovery.

Ethics in the Diaspora

Why should a people living in the condition of diaspora be likely to produce mankind's best teachers? Lessing is clear enough on this point, provided we consider the thought of *Nathan* as well as that of the *Erziehung*. An individual living in the bosom of a well-integrated culture, which is dominant in its own ancestral homeland, will as a rule tend to be thoroughly submerged in the specific values and prejudices of that culture, whereas an individual living as a foreigner in a foreign land will be forced into the position, more often, of recognizing his or her cultural prejudices as mere prejudices. It does not follow that everyone living under foreign rule will use that situation as a springboard to something like Nathan's ironic wisdom, a wisdom for which the concept "humanity" denotes principally an insuperable separation from truth. The Christian patriarch in Saladin's Jerusalem, for example, is probably meant to be seen as more desperately bigoted than he would have been under a Christian ruler. But diaspora is still a condition generally favorable to ironic detachment.

And yet, on the other hand, according to § 19, diaspora is also a condition that promotes the recognition of everything that is *good* about deep cultural belonging and commitment. Thus both aspects of Nathan's wisdom, and of the wisdom he seeks to propagate, are favored in a diaspora. It follows now, moreover, that the teaching of a Nathan remains valuable even in cases where it fails of its ultimate aim. Pupils who do not reach the level of full ironic wisdom are not disoriented by this failure—which they have no viewpoint from which to experience as failure anyway—but are encouraged and confirmed in their own cultural commitment, if perhaps now in a somewhat less uncritical version of it.

Thus we arrive at something very close to a complete ethics, in the form of a universally applicable and universally beneficial method of humane teaching. It is, to be sure, not a formulable ethics, and the teaching involved in it can be carried out only by a possessor of wisdom in Nathan's mold. But once we recognize that the thought of *Nathan* and the *Erziehung* has brought us to an ethics—an ethics which is beyond all religion, perhaps beyond all morality—it must occur to us that we should have known from the outset where those texts would lead us. Surely the idea of doing the good for no other reason than that it is the good names exactly the type of ethics we have arrived at, an ethical situation where God is no longer needed. For from the ironist's perspective, permanently excluded from any usable direct knowledge of the good (of God's right hand as it were), it is hard to see how the ethics of ironic teaching is not the closest possible approximation, in practice, to doing the good strictly for its own sake. The goal of education, in any case, is no longer deferred into an indefinite future. Like truth in the Great Year, it is always here for the taking.

The ethics of irony that is adumbrated in Lessing's late writings has in common with the ethics of Nietzsche or Rorty that it restricts drastically the reference of the word "we." The benefits produced by a thinking like Nathan's are available to everyone, but the thinking itself is available only to those rare individuals who are capable of living its contradictions uninterruptedly. The exclusivity of that ethics is dramatized in the last scene of *Nathan*. When Nathan tells Saladin that the Templar and Recha still know nothing of Assad's true identity, and says, "what they learn is entirely up to you!" (5.8.682–3), he is offering him the chance to make a sacrifice comparable to his own in losing Recha as a daughter; he offers him the chance to exercise a humane wisdom (the encouragement of uncomplicated cultural commitment) that would match his own. He is testing Saladin as Saladin had tested him, seeking in him the aptitude for full ironic wisdom. (He is thus seeking an answer to the question: how shall members of an ironic ethical community make contact with one another?) And Saladin fails the test disastrously by imputing selfish motives to him. The point, clearly, is that Nathan's full wisdom is incommunicable. Saladin, in posing his conundrum and evaluating Nathan's response, has had as much opportunity as anyone could ever have to understand Nathan's ironic stance, and understanding has failed him. If there is any such thing as a community of ironists, a "we," for Nathan to belong to, then what is staged for us here is the impossibility of seeing or knowing it.

Can we perhaps imagine that community as Jewry in the diaspora? Is Nathan's ethics a Jewish ethics? If so, in what sense? Certainly Lessing does not mean to suggest either that every Jew is a radical ironist or that every radical ironist is a Jew. But the situation of Jews in the diaspora offers a clear and convenient *way to think* about a hypothetical community of radical ironists. How such a community, such an understanding of the word "we," might actually arise or be constituted—as we have seen in discussing Nietzsche and Rorty—cannot be pinned down conceptually. In order to speak or think of it at all, we must have recourse to metaphors. And in our present age, we *need* to be able to think about the community presupposed by an ethics of irony, because ethics in this form is constantly in danger of being swamped by what I have called propositional ethics in the wake of Kant.

So far, we have looked at one case, in Leibniz, where an intellectual convention whose effects are comparable to those of an ethics of irony operates without needing to be thought about, where it operates as nothing but an assumed ethical background for the discussions and debates of an intellectual elite. But Kant refuses to acknowledge the authority of such a background. He is perhaps not even aware of its presence; and he insists, in any case, that philosophy develop a single master vocabulary, rather than acknowledge plural vocabularies: a single master vocabulary for all its concerns, including ethics, which under this new regime cannot be understood as anything but a universal ethics, the ethics for a universal "we" which Wittgenstein recognizes is impossible.

Kant, in other words, does not refute Leibniz's *Theodicy* so much as he attempts to crowd it out of existence with his oversized crossbreed of metaphysics and morals. Lessing, although he does not yet have Kant to contend with, or at least not the critical Kant, undergoes a similar experience of being crowded out, in his case by a local Lutheran orthodoxy. And many of his last works, especially *Nathan* and the *Erziehung*, are devoted at least in part to the reestablishment and defense of the position he is being crowded out of.[14] Which means they set themselves the task of finding ways to think about an ethics that cannot be framed by concepts, an elite intellectual ethics that by rights ought not to need thinking about in the first place; ways of thinking that are difficult and paradoxical, but still presumably understandable by those for whom they are intended, those to whom they reach out in the attempt to preserve whatever can be preserved of an endangered, perhaps doomed intellectual community.

Jewish Ethics?

Can the position Lessing wishes to defend be understood as a Jewish ethics? This question does not admit an objective answer. The idea of a Jewish ethics, if it is important at all, is important because of its efficacy as a metaphor, its usefulness as a sign by which the adherents of an ethics of irony might recognize one another in the modern Kantian clamor of philosophy. Which means that we cannot hope to answer the question by looking at Lessing alone. If we can conclude that the idea of Jewish ethics makes a positive difference in profiling the hypothetical community of radical ironists, then in effect that radical irony, the thought that unites that "chosen people," that restricted "we," *is* a Jewish ethics.

But we can perhaps go one step further, nevertheless, in understanding an inherent Jewish focus in Lessing's ethical thought, if we consider the section of the *Erziehung* that mentions the Book of Job.

> Here and there, to be sure, an Israelite was probably inclined to extend the range of the divine promises and threats, which referred to the whole state, to include every individual member of it, in the firm belief that whoever was devout must also be happy, and that whoever was unfortunate, or became so, was suffering punishment for transgression, a punishment that would again be replaced by blessing as soon as he left off his transgression. Such an Israelite seems to have written the Book of Job; for the plan of that book is entirely in this spirit. (§29)

Here, as in much of the *Erziehung*, something strange is going on beneath the textual surface. For if there is one doctrine that the Book of Job obviously does *not* espouse, it is that every human misfortune is punishment for a transgression. It is in fact for their approach to something like that doctrine (hence to Warburton's idea of a continuing miracle!) that the three comforters are rebuked by God in Job

42. Surely Lessing cannot mean to ascribe the comforters' position to the book as a whole.

But then what does he mean? The Book of Job is unique in the Bible in that it consists of practically nothing but interpretations of itself, attempts to make sense of itself, which all turn out to be faulty. And the story in it that needs to be interpreted is nothing but the relation between God and a single individual. The "spirit" in which the book is written, therefore, is contained in the question: Does Jewish existence, Jewish belief, a commitment to Jewish culture, make any sense at all for an individual without the certainty that every blessing is God's reward, every misfortune God's punishment?

What if the answer to this question is no? Then one has no choice but to adopt the position that Lessing seems to impute to the book's author, that all blessings and misfortunes are immediate rewards and punishments. Otherwise one's existence as a Jew makes no sense. But, on the other hand, that single available position is clearly *not* the book's meaning. Therefore the imputation of that position to the book's author is wrong, or at best an instance of irony, an irony which illuminates by contrast the gulf of senselessness over which it is unfolded.

And what if precisely that gulf of senselessness (the senselessness of being a Jew)—which cannot reasonably be described as a "position" or imputed to an author (hence Lessing's irony)—is itself the true homeland of the Jews? More specifically, what if that true homeland is the homeless condition of diaspora? What if diaspora is not merely an historical accident and a convenient metaphor, but the essential condition of the Jews? Not by any means a condition universally recognized as essential among Jews, any more than such an interpretation of the Book of Job (the Book of Failed Interpretations) would be universally accepted— but a fundamentally Jewish condition nonetheless.

There is an alternative path that would have been open to the author of Job, a path that would have avoided the gulf of senselessness: the idea of reward and punishment in an afterlife, which was eventually adopted as the Christian solution. Thus our discussion of interpreting Job rejoins the main superficial argument of the *Erziehung*, the argument that the doctrinal problems in Jewish thought are God's device for guiding humanity toward the "truth" of Christianity. But if we try to take this idea seriously, then it is hard to see how we can avoid taking seriously the implied parallel argument that doctrinal problems in Christian thought— especially the question of reward or punishment for good people who lived too early for Christ—are God's way of guiding us to the truth of metempsychosis. In fact, this parallel in the end discourages us from taking seriously either of its instances and so opens before us again—as does after all the Book of Job itself— the prospect of a radically diasporic Jewish ethics.

(The reading of Job I have suggested does not differ much from that of Maimonides, which Lessing could have known.[15] Maimonides seems to identify with Job's fourth visitor, the young but wise Elihu, even while admitting "that he does not add anything to the words of Eliphaz, Bildad, and Zofar" [302]. What is new in Elihu's speeches, in other words, is thoroughly cryptic, especially the idea of a "messenger" or "interpreter" who in perhaps one case in a thousand can "shew unto man his uprightness" [Job 33:23]. That rare case spoken of by Maimonides-Elihu is apparently the achievement of wisdom: which is man's only possible "uprightness" before God; which is expressed in the gesture of *rejecting* the "dust and ashes" of a repentance that would presuppose superhuman moral understanding [301; Job 42:5–6];[16] and which—to judge from Elihu's presumably distanced, but not measurably distanced repetition of the words of the others—consists in something very like Nathan's lonely diasporic relation to all intellectual homelands, all "vocabularies," including [wherever it might be] his own.)

This point does not by any means settle the question of the Jewishness of the ethics implied in Lessing's late writings. More context is necessary, the more the better. A uniquely significant and uniquely powerful element of context, in my view, is represented by the ethical aspect and the Jewish aspect of Freud's thinking.

Chapter 5

LESSING AND FREUD: THEORY, WISDOM, AND THE SCOPE OF ETHICS

Freud was sympathetic to the Zionist project of reestablishing a Jewish homeland, but by no means enthusiastic. On February 26, 1930, he writes to Chaim Koffler, an associate of Chaim Weizmann:

> I cannot do what you wish [publicly support Jews in crisis in Palestine] .... Whoever wants to influence the masses must give them something rousing and inflammatory and my sober judgment of Zionism does not permit this. I certainly sympathize with its goals, am proud of our University in Jerusalem and am delighted with our settlements' prosperity. But, on the other hand, I do not think that Palestine could ever become a Jewish state, nor that the Christian and Islamic worlds would ever be prepared to have their holy places under Jewish care. It would have seemed more sensible to me to establish a Jewish homeland on a less historically-burdened land. But I know that such a rational viewpoint would never have gained the enthusiasm of the masses and the financial support of the wealthy. I concede with sorrow that the baseless fanaticism of our people is in part to be blamed for the awakening of Arab distrust. I can raise no sympathy at all for the misdirected piety which transforms a piece of an Herodian wall [the Wailing Wall] into a national relic, thereby offending the feelings of the natives.
> Now judge for yourself whether I, with such a critical point of view, am the right person to come forward as the solace of a people deluded by unjustified hope.[1]

At moments like this it seems that if he had had to choose between being called a Zionist and being called a "diasporist," he might have preferred the latter. But as far as I know, in his works and letters, he never expresses any clear opinion about the advantages or disadvantages, for Jews, of the condition of diaspora.

Freud's Diasporic Vision

Nevertheless, the idea of diaspora is crucial for Freud in relation to "the psychoanalytic movement." He was capable, it is true, of presenting psychoanalysis as a stable structure of concepts. (He does so with admirable clarity in the "introductory lectures" of 1915–17, where he begins with the theoretically undemanding topic of "parapraxes" [including what are now known commonly as "Freudian slips"], and only then moves on to talk about dreams and finally about the theory of neuroses.) But in general, he prefers to think about psychoanalysis *historically*, as the unfolding of a "movement."

He had already published in 1914 a lengthy essay "On the History of the Psycho-Analytic Movement," which describes how the pioneering ideas of a single individual (himself), after ten years of lonely struggle, had at last begun to attract serious and talented followers and now formed the center of a considerable international network of conferences, institutions, and publications. But this account is not the story of psychoanalysis triumphant. The network in question is essentially a diaspora, and like Jewry in the diaspora—protected by no governmental and security apparatus—it is constantly exposed to attack from without and to apostasy, internecine conflict, and perversion from within. (Adler and Jung are already available as instances.) Diaspora is a perilous and precarious condition. And Freud takes pride in his willingness to confront "the inevitable fate of psycho-analysis … to stir up contradiction and arouse bitterness."[2] He has no desire to exchange this condition for a position of establishment and security, as it were in the historical light of day.

> In conclusion, I can only express a wish that fortune may grant an agreeable upward journey to all those who have found their stay in the underworld of psycho-analysis too uncomfortable for their taste. The rest of us, I hope, will be permitted without hindrance to carry through to their conclusion our labours in the depths. (GW 10:113; SE 14:66)

These are the essay's last words, a firm farewell to all those erstwhile colleagues who have proven unable to support the diasporic "fate" of psychoanalysis.

Diaspora is also a dangerous condition for Lessing's Nathan, as for any Jew. Not only can his safety never be guaranteed in Saladin's economically unsettled and culturally barbaric Jerusalem, but (think of Job) he had also had a wife and seven sons murdered by Christians (4.7.659–88). The attacks on psychoanalysis may not be as dramatic; but in Freud's view they have in common with Lessing's idea of attacks on Jews in the diaspora that their source is more often ignorance or error than positive malice. If Nathan is the Jew as teacher in the sense of *Erziehung* § 18, the world's true universal benefactor who is doomed by his calling to a condition of homelessness and misunderstanding, then almost exactly the same, according to Freud, can be said of psychoanalysis. In his essay of 1925 on "The Resistances to Psycho-Analysis" we read,

> Thus the strongest resistances to psycho-analysis were not of an intellectual kind but arose from emotional sources. This explained their passionate character as well as their poverty in logic. The situation obeyed a simple formula: man in

mass behaved to psycho-analysis in exactly the same way as individual neurotics under treatment for their disorders …. The position was at once alarming and consoling: alarming because it was no small thing to have the whole human race as one's patient, and consoling because after all everything was taking place as the hypotheses of psycho-analysis declared that it was bound to. (GW 14:108–9; SE 19:221)

Those who attack us are only corroborating the wisdom by which we intend eventually to bring them around to health and reason. They are our allies without knowing it.

Of course the actual parallels and intersections between being a pioneer of psychoanalysis and being a European Jew were not lost on Freud. On May 3, 1908, he writes to Karl Abraham, concerning a disagreement between the latter and Jung:

> Be tolerant and don't forget that it is easier for you to follow my thinking than it is for Jung, for you are first of all entirely independent, and then you stand closer to my intellectual constitution through racial kinship, whereas he, as a Christian and son of a pastor, finds his way to me only against great inner resistances. His joining us is thus all the more valuable. I could almost have said that only his appearance on the scene has rescued psychoanalysis from the danger of becoming a Jewish national affair. (Freud/Abraham *Bfe.* 47)

And less than a year later he makes Jung into a kind of honorary Jew after all. He writes to him on January 17, 1909: "If I am Moses, then you are Joshua and will take possession of the promised land of psychiatry, which I shall only be able to glimpse from afar" (*Freud/Jung* 196–7).

While he has reason to be less outspoken on this matter in his published works, still, even as early as the "History of the Psycho-Analytic Movement," in dealing with the idea that the focus of psychoanalysis upon sex has to do with loose morals in the city of Vienna, he admits that he has "sometimes been inclined to suppose that the reproach of being a citizen of Vienna is only a euphemistic substitute for another reproach which no one would care to put forward openly" (GW 10:80; SE 14:39–40). And by the time of "The Resistances to Psycho-Analysis," while still claiming reticence, he no longer even gestures at practicing it. The last paragraph of that essay reads:

> Finally, with all reserve, the question may be raised whether the personality of the present writer as a Jew who has never sought to disguise the fact that he is a Jew may not have had a share in provoking the antipathy of his environment to psycho-analysis …. Nor is it perhaps entirely a matter of chance that the first advocate of psycho-analysis was a Jew. To profess belief in this new theory called for a certain degree of readiness to accept a situation of solitary opposition—a situation with which no one is more familiar than a Jew. (GW 14:110; SE 19:222)

The claim suggested here is enormous: that the next great teacher of mankind, in the tradition of Copernicus and Darwin (GW 14:109; SE 19:221), *had to be* a Jew in the diaspora.

But diaspora is still a precarious condition, in ways that were perhaps less important to Lessing—whose friend, Moses Mendelssohn, was a pioneer of the Haskalah movement—than to Freud. How is the identity of the Jews as a people to be preserved in the diaspora, against the forces that tend now not so much to destroy them as to assimilate them to the foreign cultures in which they reside? Freud is thinking along lines exactly parallel to this problem in his little book *The Question of Lay Analysis: Conversations with an Impartial Person* (1926). The question of the role of nonphysicians is important for a number of reasons, not least because it provides the occasion for a very broad and lucid description of both the theory and the actual practice of psychoanalysis. But the heart of the argument, Freud's ultimate reason for writing the book, appears only toward the end, where we read:

> For we do not consider it at all desirable for psycho-analysis to be swallowed up by medicine and to find its last resting-place in a text-book of psychiatry under the heading "Methods of Treatment," alongside of procedures such as hypnotic suggestion, autosuggestion, and persuasion, which, born from our ignorance, have to thank the laziness and cowardice of mankind for their short-lived effects. (GW 14:283; SE 20:248)

The hostile tone here says a great deal. The promise of institutional security offered by the medical establishment is genuinely tempting and must therefore be resisted energetically. Psychoanalysis must not be seduced, by the seeming advantages of assimilation, into violating its own unique nature and mission.

For just as the character of the Jews as a people transcends the interests of any of their host nations, so also the mission of psychoanalysis transcends the business of any particular medical or scientific discipline. The passage quoted above continues as follows:

> It [psychoanalysis] deserves a better fate and, it may be hoped, will meet with one. As a "depth-psychology," a theory of the mental unconscious, it can become indispensable to all the sciences which are concerned with the evolution of human civilization and its major institutions such as art, religion and the social order. It has already, in my opinion, afforded these sciences considerable help in solving their problems. But these are only small contributions compared with what might be achieved if historians of civilization, psychologists of religion, philologists and so on would agree themselves to handle the new instrument of research which is at their service. (GW 14:283; SE 20:248)

The imagined intellectual diaspora of psychoanalysis thus extends to all areas of the humanities and social sciences. Which means not only that researchers in these disciplines will know about psychoanalysis, but that at least a certain number of them will actually "handle" psychoanalysis as an "instrument" (*handhaben*), that they will join the psychoanalytic movement and *be* the scattered community of trained lay analysts which Freud is hoping for.

The Man Freud and the Wisdom of Psychoanalysis

It is probably true that the encouragement of lay analysis helps ensure the integrity, cohesion, and independence of psychoanalysis as both theory and practice. But the most important factor in preserving the original focus of the psychoanalytic movement is the person of Freud himself. He makes no bones about this point in "The History of the Psycho-Analytic Movement":

> For psycho-analysis is my creation; for ten years I was the only person who concerned himself with it .... Although it is a long time now since I was the only psycho-analyst, I consider myself justified in maintaining that even to-day no one can know better than I do what psycho-analysis is, how it differs from other ways of investigating the life of the mind, and precisely what should be called psycho-analysis and what would better be described by some other name. (GW 10:44; SE 14:7)

Later in his career, he mythologizes this aspect of his relation to psychoanalysis in the figure of Moses, as he had already done in the early letter to Jung we looked at above.

The most important document in his reckoning with the Jews' lawgiver is the book *Moses and Monotheism*, or in its full correct title, *The Man Moses and Monotheistic Religion*. Attention is given to many important issues in this book, especially to the question of the genetic transmission of memory traces, which had already surfaced tentatively in *Totem and Taboo* and is always present as a disturbing element, if mostly behind the scenes, in Freud's thinking on Oedipal matters. But the center of the book, around which everything else revolves, is "the man" Moses, the actual contingent individual without whom modern monotheism, embracing Judaism, Christianity, and Islam, would not exist, or at least would not exist in its present form.

This idea, that an enormous institutional, doctrinal, and intellectual structure like that of modern monotheism could owe its existence and its character to the influence of a single man—and beyond that, to a couple of pure accidents, in ancient Egyptian religious politics and in the makeup of the population of foreign workers in Egypt—flies in the face of all the common Western ideas of history as an unfolding system or organism. But Freud never takes up the general question of history. "The man" Moses monopolizes his interest, and correspondingly the man Freud, in relation to whom there is one short passage toward the end of the book in which a single word speaks volumes. In the second prefatory note to Part Three, written in London shortly after his arrival there in 1938, Freud says that he has received many letters from British people suggesting that he adopt "the way of Christ." He continues:

> The good people who wrote in this way cannot have known much about me; but I expect that when this work about Moses becomes known, in a translation, among my new compatriots, I shall probably forfeit enough of the sympathy which a number of other people as well now feel for me. (GW 16:160; SE 23:57–8)

The phrase "among my new compatriots," in the translation, would have been perfectly accurate if Freud had written, as practically any German speaker would have expected him to: *unter meinen neuen Mitbürgern*, "among my new fellow-citizens." But Freud actually writes, "unter meinen neuen Volksgenossen," which means literally: "among those with whom I share a new bond of *Volk*-membership," where *Volk* means tribe or people or nation in a sense that always suggests an original blood-kinship, a sense that clearly does not apply to his relation with his British hosts.

Is he just being careless with words? I think not. First of all, *Volksgenosse* is not a commonly used term—except among Nazis! Then, in the same sentence, he mentions the "other people" (i.e., not the Christians) who will also be offended by his Moses book. Those other people must be British Jews, people who *are*, strictly speaking, his fellow-*Volk*-members. And the general title of Part Three, which is introduced by this prefatory note, is "Moses, His People (*Volk*) and Monotheist Religion" (GW 16:156; SE 23:54)—even though the *Volk* referred to is not really "his" (Moses') except in the sense that he has appropriated it. The concept *Volk* is thus unquestionably prominent in Freud's thinking here. His use of the term *Volksgenosse* cannot be perfunctory; and yet he uses it to refer to his relation with the whole British public, which seems obviously wrong. What is he getting at?[3]

The game that is being played here—once its existence is suspected—is easy enough to identify. Here, at a moment of maximum crisis in his relation to Jewish thought and tradition, here, at the beginning of a new personal exile and at the threshold of death, Freud returns one last time to the parallel between himself and Moses.[4] Just as Moses, driven out of Egypt by religious politics, adopts a new nationality by placing himself at the head of an unsophisticated Hebrew people, so Freud, driven out of Austria by anti-Semitic politics, adopts a new nationality, joins with a new group of *Volksgenossen*, and places himself (in his own view) at the head of a people whose lack of sophistication is evident in their naive acceptance of Western religious illusions. The British people? Or do the British here not stand for "the whole human race" which Freud had once claimed as the true "patient" of psychoanalysis (GW 14:109; SE 19:221)?

Freud's claim to be a new Moses for all humanity—a Moses who will teach, this time, not monotheism but rather an "intellectuality" (*Geistigkeit*) beyond all religion[5]—is even more outrageous than his earlier implied claim to be a new Copernicus or a new Darwin (GW 14:109–10; SE 19:221–2). Especially if one considers—as is suggested by the parallel with Moses, who "created the Jews" single-handed (GW 16:213; SE 23:106)—that the "human race" taught by Moses-Freud has yet to be brought into being. And like that earlier claim, this one is made not openly but cryptically, now even more so. But then why suggest it in the first place?

The cryptic quality of Freud's presentation serves to separate, from the majority of readers, the small group that knows how to read it. And knowing how to read, here, means knowing how to read *actively*, how to generate meaning, not merely absorb it—knowing how to read like the Jewish prophets without whom Moses's project would in effect never have existed (GW 16:218–19; SE 23:111). (The book does not *show* you its truth—is it possible to judge Freud's claim objectively?—but rather enlists you in *making* its truth true.)[6] But this idea of reading—especially in connection with the *Moses* book, where psychoanalysis is confronted more directly than ever with historical reality and with the ethical and imaginative content of religion—raises the whole question of the status of psychoanalysis as a discipline. Certainly the idea of a vessel of more or less objective knowledge, a quasi-medical science or a branch of cultural history, whose content one might absorb as a passive reader, is now excluded. The content of the *Moses* book, when it is read properly, is inextricably bound up with the character and circumstances of whoever is doing the reading, as well as with the character and circumstances of its writer. (The book is not only an exercise in parallelism between the man Moses and the man Freud, but also a real-time autobiography covering the period of Freud's final exile.) And the concept that names the type of intellectual discipline to which these peculiarities of the book suggest psychoanalysis belongs, is not science or art or personal expression, but *wisdom*.

I do not mean that this condition—the quality of being a discussible body of knowledge which is also contingent upon the character and circumstances of those who happen to be engaged with it—is sufficient to define wisdom. It is certainly a necessary condition, without which the idea of wisdom makes no sense. But any attempt to go beyond that quality of contingency—which is represented for Lessing, incidentally, by Nathan's insistence on the individual's commitment to his or her particular cultural situation—faces great difficulties. How shall I even begin to talk cogently about psychoanalysis as a discipline if I must interrupt myself constantly to take account of the particular "man" Freud—not to mention the man or woman doing the talking?

We can see this problem in operation in the work of Jacques Lacan. Lacan is acutely aware of the difficult relation of contingency between Freud and psychoanalysis. In *The Four Fundamental Concepts of Psycho-Analysis*, he says:

> I would like now to make clear, astonishing as the formula may seem to you, that its status of being, which is so elusive, so unsubstantial, is given to the unconscious by the procedure of its discoverer. The status of the unconscious, which … is so fragile on the ontic plane, is ethical. In his thirst for truth, Freud says, *Whatever it is, I must go there*. (Lacan 33)

The unconscious, in this view, is not a preexisting entity that Freud comes upon in his researches, but rather it takes shape in conjunction with specific personal perceptions and decisions on his part. Yet Lacan, despite his understanding of this point, still tries to map out a path beyond Freud, a path by which "to circumscribe [the unconscious] in a structure, a temporal structure" (32), and so, presumably, to neutralize the inaccessibility of the unconscious to time (31) for the sake of theoretical mastery—a mastery that is stabilized, from the outset, only by a thoroughly non-Freudian proposition, "*the unconscious is structured like a language*" (20).

Whatever the absolute value of Lacan's theoretical move here might be, its quality *as* theory severs its connection with Freud's actual thinking. If we are seeking not understanding but wisdom—as I think we must in this situation which Lacan correctly characterizes as "ethical" at base—we must proceed differently.

Theory and Fantasy

In a late essay, "Analysis Terminable and Interminable"—which treats the eminently practical question of how to decide when, and in what sense, a course of analytic therapy may be considered complete—Freud makes a famous cryptic statement about the role of theory in psychoanalysis. "Is it possible," he asks, "to dispose of ... a pathogenic instinctual demand (*Triebanspruch*) upon the ego?" How may we effect the incorporation of that instinct or drive into the "harmony of the ego"? The answer, he concedes, is not easy. In particular,

> We can only say, "So muss denn doch die Hexe dran" [the Witch is needed]—the Witch Metapsychology. Without metapsychological speculation and theorizing—I had almost said "phantasying"—we shall not get another step forward. Unfortunately, here as elsewhere, what our Witch reveals is neither very clear nor very detailed. (GW 16:68–9; SE 23:224–5)

Theory (the "Witch") in some form is required by the question. But a theorizing that borders on the fantastic? Freud goes on, in the next sentence, to say that he will now proceed by following "a single [theoretical] clue ... a clue of the highest value ... the antithesis between the primary and the secondary processes." (This antithesis had been crucial in his thinking since *The Interpretation of Dreams* [GW 2/3:593–614; SE 5:588–609].) But in the rest of the essay, although its material can certainly be located relative to the primary/secondary distinction, the terminology never recurs and the "antithesis," as such, never figures in the argument. In the very act of invoking his own theory, Freud thus suggests a disparaging attitude toward just that theory and leaves his invocation hanging in midair.

This move is typical for Freud, as an instance of his *resistance to theoretical closure*. No theory, certainly no psychological theory, is ever closed in the strict sense of being a complete system of ideas capable of answering any question that can be stated in its terminology. But by theoretical closure, in the sense that Freud avoids or resists it, I mean the point at which a theory becomes self-developing, the point where it becomes possible to draw conclusions *about* and *beyond* the theory *from* the theory.

The passage just quoted supports the relevance of this definition. For Freud's idea of "metapsychology" can be traced at least as far back as *The Interpretation of Dreams*, where Theodor Lipps is quoted to the effect that the problem of the unconscious is "less *a* psychological problem than *the* problem of psychology" (GW 2/3:616; SE 5:611).⁷ In other words, psychoanalytic theory is not simply a type of psychological theory, but is at every step a questioning of the very idea of psychology, which means that *it cannot build upon itself* (cannot claim what I have called "closure") without risking a complete loss of contact with psychology in any commonly understood sense of the term. Psychoanalysis must always be *more* than psychology, but it loses its identity altogether if it ever becomes simply *different* from psychology. Hence also Freud's reference to Goethe (*Faust*, l. 2365), which identifies "metapsychology" with the witch by whom Faust must be magically rejuvenated, the witch whom he mistrusts because he fears that her magic will sever his contact with nature.

But we have not fully understood the remark about theorizing and fantasizing until we have understood exactly why psychoanalytic theory must be considered a "metapsychology." As time goes on and evidence accumulates, as the number of documented instances of reasonably successful therapeutic intervention increases, why should psychoanalysis in the end *not gradually become* simply a type of psychology, whose theoretical reasoning need not be subjected to any special restraints or conditions?

This is essentially the same question, for example, as the question of why Freud never attempts a theoretical resolution of the differences among three separate "points of view" by which an idea of the psyche is formed: the dynamic, the topographical, and the economic. In the essay "Analysis Terminable and Interminable," after the passage about the "Witch," Freud suggests that the problem under discussion can best be approached by quantitative considerations that tend to be underestimated because, "for the most part, our theoretical concepts have neglected to attach the same importance to the *economic* line of approach as they have to the *dynamic* and *topographical* ones" (GW 23:70-1; SE 23:226-7). We are reminded of the multiplicity of "vocabularies" in Rorty. In psychoanalysis, it appears, one sometimes makes progress simply by changing one's basic theoretical framework.

We are in fact talking here about *independent* theoretical frameworks. In his essay on "The Unconscious," Freud begins by suggesting the possibility "that conscious and unconscious ideas are distinct registrations, topographically separated, of the same content" (GW 10:275; SE 14:176). Then, however, an examination of the mechanism of repression shows that the translation of content from one psychic system to another "is not effected through the making of a new registration but through a change in its state, an alteration in its cathexis" (GW 10:279; SE 14:180). "The functional [dynamic] hypothesis," we are now told, "has here easily defeated the topographical one." But further reflection shows that we have not yet accounted for the maintenance or continuance of repression, which requires "the assumption of an *anticathexis*" (GW 10:280; SE 14:181). And in making this assumption, we find we have been "led into adopting a third point of view ... the *economic* one."

What we have here seems a straightforward theoretical argument. The first hypothesis fails and gives place to the second, which in turn leads us to a third, which, if it is not strictly final, must at least be the best available. But then Freud says, "I propose that when we have succeeded in describing a psychical process in its dynamic, topographical and economic aspects, we should speak of it as a *metapsychological* presentation" (GW 10:281; SE 14:181). The Witch thus shows herself here; and her sorcery is apparent in our understanding that even in a case where the three psychoanalytic "points of view" succeed one another logically, each at least in part refuted by the one following, *each of the three still retains its independent validity*. Not only the very idea of theory, but also the idea of *the* psyche, is thus called into question. If three different and sometimes conflicting "points of view" are required for describing an object (the psyche), and if those points of view cannot be systematically reconciled with one another, then what grounds have we for assuming the unitary existence of the object?

Freud does not hold out much hope for the requisite systematic reconciliation. In the first *Encyclopædia Britannica* article on "Psycho-Analysis," after explaining the dynamic, the economic, and the topographical points of view (in that order), he writes,

> It must not be supposed that these very general ideas are presuppositions upon which the work of psycho-analysis depends. On the contrary, they are its latest conclusions and are "open to revision." Psycho-analysis is founded securely upon the observation of the facts of mental life; and for that very reason its theoretical superstructure is still incomplete and subject to constant alteration. (GW 14:303; SE 20:266)

The "facts" (plural) are perhaps not open to doubt. But is the psyche itself (singular) a "fact"? We might recall here Lacan's doubts about the "ontic" status of the unconscious.

These considerations explain the need for an idea of "metapsychology" and the impossibility of a break with psychology in its earlier forms. The very existence of the psyche, or of the psychic "apparatus," its availability as an object of study, depends on the operation of various, often conflicting "points of view": this, I contend, is an unstated but undeniable tenet of psychoanalysis. But its contrary (the substantiality of the psyche) would be presupposed by any attempt to defend a strict separation from the history of thinking that is named "psychology." The only possible justification for such a break with the past would be the claim that psychoanalysis affords us a fundamentally clearer or more complete view of the object "psyche." And psychoanalysis cannot honestly make such a claim.

Freud's Avoidance of Closure

In order to fill out our picture of psychoanalysis as an intellectual discipline, let us begin with three instances of Freud's discomfort with the possibility or approach of theoretical closure. In *Totem and Taboo*, first of all, Freud is very definite about his conclusion "that the beginnings of religion, morals, society and art converge in the Oedipus complex," a conclusion which "is in complete agreement with the psychoanalytic finding that the same complex constitutes the nucleus of all neuroses, so far as our present knowledge goes" (GW 9:188; SE 13:156–7). But he is equally definite about not being blinded to "the uncertainties of my premises or the difficulties involved in my conclusions" (GW 9:189; SE 13:157). Specifically,

> I have taken as the basis of my whole position the existence of a collective mind, in which mental processes occur just as they do in the mind of an individual. In particular, I have supposed that the sense of guilt for an action has persisted for many thousands of years and has remained operative in generations which can have had no knowledge of that action. (SE 13:157–8)

And he never attempts to justify this supposition, except by the vague suggestion that "everyone possesses in his unconscious mental activity an apparatus which enables him to interpret other people's reactions" (GW 9:191; SE 13:159) and hence perhaps to carry on a "heritage of emotion" from older generations—as if that "heritage" could retain anything like its original strength in being transmitted thus. That is, he does not open the theoretical issue that his own theory insists upon at this point, the question of Lamarckian or soft inheritance, the inheritance of acquired characteristics including the residue of personal experiences. Or rather, he resists the idea that his own theory is sufficiently closed to raise this question.

His procedure later, in *Beyond the Pleasure Principle*, at first seems diametrically the opposite, but in the end has exactly the same effect. Here he infers from the observed fact of repetition–compulsion the existence of a class of instincts that he eventually calls "death" instincts, instincts whose violation of the pleasure and reality principles is explained by their location, *as* instincts, on an earlier and deeper level of the psychic development. But this inference has the effect of apparently requiring a dualistic theory of instincts, because it does not seem possible to subsume the sexual instincts under the theorem "*that an instinct is an urge inherent in organic life to restore an earlier state of things*" (GW 13:38; SE 18:36). "We should consequently feel relieved [!]," says Freud, "if the whole structure of our argument turned out to be mistaken" (GW 13:46; SE 18:44).

And in order to seek this supposed "relief," he now permits himself the impermissible; he treats his theory as if it were closed and builds it upon itself into the domain of general biology. Sexual instincts, he asserts, are present in all life down to the cellular level. If the same can be shown *not* to be the case with death instincts (as he claims to expect [GW 13:47]), then the latter may no longer be regarded as instincts on the same level as sexual instincts, and the dualism of instinct theory is removed. There is a certain amount of obvious irony in the thinking here. The result of an overturning of the death-instinct theory would not be a "relief" at all, because repetition–compulsion would pose a greater problem than ever.

But then Freud's summary of biological research leads to the result that while death instincts cannot be demonstrated at the cellular level, they can also not be excluded. And now, in direct contradiction to his earlier attitude, he expresses relief at the *failure* of biological experimentation to contradict his theory:

> Thus our expectation that biology would flatly contradict the recognition of death instincts has not been fulfilled. We are at liberty [!] to continue concerning ourselves with their possibility, if we have other reasons for doing so. (GW 13:53; SE 18:49)

And continue he does, in spades. Building theory upon theory to the point where he is prepared to suggest that perhaps sexual instincts do after all express "*a need to restore an earlier state of things*" (GW 13:62; SE 18:57). No less an authority than Plato supports him here, with Aristophanes' myth of the origin of love in the *Symposium*, which he now takes as a "hint" upon which to build the hypothesis of an aboriginal fragmentation of "living substance" (a single, unindividuated form of life?) whose quest for reunification is manifest in the sexual instincts (GW 13:63; SE 18:58).

In *Beyond the Pleasure Principle*, then, Freud does not avoid the assumption of theoretical closure, as in *Totem and Taboo*, but rather insists on that assumption repeatedly, until his argument becomes (at least when considered as biological science) a *reductio ad absurdum* of itself. I do not mean that its *ideas* are rendered absurd. There is no reason to conclude that the idea of a cellular reservoir of libido (GW 13:56; SE 18:52), or of a primary masochism (GW 13:58–9; SE 18:54–5), or especially the idea of an ultimately regressive quality in the sexual instincts, is necessarily wrong. It is only the *procedure* that is shown to be absurd, the procedure of assuming theoretical closure. Freud's basic view of this matter has thus not changed at all since *Totem and Taboo*. But its expression has become more complex:

> It may be asked whether and how far I am myself convinced of the truth of the hypotheses that have been set out in these pages *[Beyond the Pleasure Principle]*. My answer would be that I am not convinced myself and that I do not seek to persuade other people to believe in them. Or, more precisely, that I do not know far I believe in them. (GW 13:63–4; SE 18:59)

If Freud himself "does not know" the extent of his own belief, then who does? We will come back to this question.

Instinct and Culture

The last example I have in mind concerns *Das Unbehagen in der Kultur* (Discomfort in Civilization), the book that the Standard Edition insists on translating as *Civilization and Its Discontents*. Like *Beyond the Pleasure Principle*, it is a complicated book and becomes ever more so toward its end, where Freud feels called upon to "ask his readers' forgiveness for not having been a more skilful guide" (GW 14:493; SE 21:134). But there is more here than just a question of skill. As in the earlier books, here also unacknowledged theoretical tensions affect the shape and coherence of the presentation. Especially the question of the general character, hence the general *value* of civilization, is much more central than Freud is willing to admit (see GW 14:505; SE 21:144). He proposes, as a summary formulation,

> that the process of civilization is a modification which the vital process experiences under the influence of a task that is set it by Eros and instigated by Ananke—by the exigencies of reality; and that this task is one of uniting separate individuals into a community bound together by libidinal ties. (GW 14:499; SE 21:139)

Civilization is thus mainly the work of Eros, erected against the constant destructive operation of the aggressive or death instincts in the individuals who compose it.

But there is a completely different side to the matter, on which Freud offers us no "guidance" at all. For it is clear that the role played by the aggressive instincts in the shaping and cohesion of civilization is every bit as important as that of Eros, especially in the formation of a "cultural super-ego" (GW 14:501–4; SE 21:141–3). Freud himself carefully avoids suggesting that the death instincts are involved here. The "struggle between the individual and society," he says, "is not a derivative of the contradiction … between the primal instincts of Eros and death," but merely "a dispute within the economics of the libido" (GW 14:501; SE 21:141). But still, he cannot resist remarking, "What a potent obstacle to civilization aggressiveness must be, if the defence against it can cause as much unhappiness as aggressiveness itself!" (GW 14:504; SE 21:143). Nor can he have forgotten that in his own theory the very idea of the super-ego is inextricably bound up with that of the aggressive instincts—not only in *The Ego and the Id* (GW 13:284–7; SE 19:54–7), but in the present book as well, in the discussion of guilt (GW 14:488–93; SE 21:129–33). And he has also mentioned earlier the *direct* contribution that aggression makes to communal bonding when it is aimed outside the community toward a foe (GW 14:473–4; SE 21:114–15).

Freud's strenuous avoidance of any association of death instincts with the general aims of civilization is another instance of resistance to theoretical closure. For if death is permitted any positive function at all in the theory of civilization, it becomes difficult not to follow metapsychology toward the conclusion that civilization is *primarily* and *originally* an expression of the aggressive instincts, a kind of temple of death, a new way back to death for the newly human creature. According to Freud, after all, the initial defining move of civilization is the assertion of control over nature (GW 14:449; SE 21:90); and on the level of the individual, the aggressive character of this move is entirely apparent:

> The instinct of destruction, moderated and tamed, and, as it were, inhibited in its aim, must, when it is directed towards objects, provide the ego with satisfaction of its vital needs and with control over nature. (GW 14:480; SE 21:121)

The very next paragraph returns to the idea of civilization as "a process in the service of Eros" (GW 14:481; SE 21:122). But the analogy that Freud himself insists on repeatedly, between individual and communal development, suggests a completely different way of reading his remark on the "instinct of destruction" and "control over nature": namely, that civilization is primarily the work of the death instincts, a work made possible by the "moderating" influence of Eros. And in order to avoid this inference—I will come to the question of why it has to be avoided—the reasoning process that leads to it, the building of theory upon its own conclusions, must be aborted.

Let us note, finally, that in all these instances, the interruption or undermining of the theoretical process is not *theoretically* motivated or determined; it is not theory's turning against itself in the form of paradox or antinomy. As we will see still more clearly below, the decision about how and where to disrupt the mechanism of psychoanalytic theorizing (where to resist the Witch) is quite arbitrary. It is a decision of "the man" Freud.

The Nature of Language and the Content of the Individual Mind

The historical situation of Freud's whole project, finally, is illuminated by two crucial theoretical moves that he carefully avoids—mainly in *The Ego and the Id*—but which are picked up and used as theoretical cornerstones in post- or anti-Freudian psychoanalysis, by Lacan in one case, Jung in the other. The arbitrary quality of Freud's procedure is underscored here by the actual existence of coherent realizations of the theoretical tendencies he cuts off.

The first case concerns language. Working from insights developed in his 1915 essay on "The Unconscious," Freud asserts in *The Ego and the Id*

> that the real difference between an *Ucs.* [Unconscious] and a *Pcs.* [Preconscious] idea (thought) consists in this: that the former is carried out on some material which remains unknown, whereas the latter (the *Pcs.*) is in addition brought into connection with word-presentations [*Wortvorstellungen*] .... The question, "How does a thing become conscious?" would thus be more advantageously stated: "How does a thing become preconscious?" And the answer would be: "Through becoming connected with the word-presentations corresponding to it." (GW 13:247; SE 19:20)

Only a very short step would be needed here to embark upon Lacan's theory of the symbolic order, with its relation to Saussurean linguistics.

But Freud refuses to take that step. For him, words are not primarily semiotic entities, but simply a class of objects; and in their character as objects, they are present in the mind as "residues of memories [which] were at one time perceptions, and like all mnemic residues ... can become conscious again." The object-quality of words is crucial, because Freud interprets "clinical experience" to show that the only path for thoughts and ideas into the preconscious is by way of "the system *Pcpt.*" (GW 13:249–50; SE 19:22), the system by which the mind appropriates external sense perceptions. But thoughts and ideas as such, as internal entities, do not have any quality that can be processed directly by the system *Pcpt.*—unless that quality is supplied by their verbal associations, which take the form of remembered perceptions, primarily acoustic ones (GW 13:248; SE 19:20–1). "When a hypercathexis [involving word-memories] of the process of thinking takes place," says Freud, "thoughts are *actually* perceived—as if they came from without—and are consequently held to be true" (GW 13:250; SE 19:23). Of course clinical experience is never unambiguous, and Freud could have relaxed his interpretation of it in order to take a proto-Lacanian route. But he refuses to do so.

One could even accuse him of inconsistency here. The point he makes concerns thoughts as strictly immaterial processes, which require verbal associations before they can assume a preconscious form—although he does not insist on the notion of immateriality at the outset of his discussion (GW 13:247). And there seems to be no immediate reason why our idea of the ordinary operation of the perceptual system, of the reception of sense impressions, should be affected by his argument. But suppose we ask: what about *attention*, the process of attending to a perceived object? Is the object or sensory stimulus, in this process, not transformed into a "thought" in the sense Freud has suggested? And does it not then follow that the ordinary physical objects of our attention cannot become such without the mediation of language? (Which would suggest Saussure's theorizing, and Lacan's.) It is true that in *Beyond the Pleasure Principle*, and then especially in "A Note upon the 'Mystic Writing-Pad,' " Freud gives quite a detailed account, without recourse to the idea of language, of the relation between sensory stimuli and their traces in memory, an account which would cover, as a limiting instance, the case of momentary attention.[8] But still, he has also assigned words a special power, as gatekeepers of the preconscious. And his insistence, then, on relegating words to the status of mere remembered objects—especially by comparison with Lacan's later reflection on the symbolic—has something distinctly arbitrary about it. It is a decision on the part of the man Freud, and we shall have to ask exactly why he makes it.

My next point concerns what we might call a foundational move in *The Ego and the Id*: the replacement (or at least the supplementing) of the dynamic notion of the unconscious with the "topographical" concept of the id. The question of *whose* "unconscious" we are talking about, in any particular case, is not troublesome, because the moves of repression that shape the dynamically considered unconscious can be understood as originating in relation to a specific ego and its needs. But the question *whose* id? is much trickier. The notion of what is "mine" presupposes the notion of "I," which is the name of the ego; and the ego, topographically considered, is nothing but a specialized portion of the id, the place where the id scrapes against reality. How can the id, in any reasonable sense, "belong" to that part of itself? Freud takes up this question explicitly when he discusses the formation of the super-ego:

> Through the forming of the ideal [the super-ego], what biology and the vicissitudes of the human species have created in the id and left behind in it is taken over by the ego and re-experienced in relation to itself as an individual. Owing to the way in which the ego ideal is formed, it has the most abundant links with the phylogenetic acquisition of each individual—his archaic heritage. What has belonged to the lowest part of the mental life of each of us is changed, through the formation of the ideal, into what is highest in the human mind by our scale of values. (GW 13:264–5; SE 19:36)

But with the mention of phylogenesis, he suddenly finds himself back in the orbit of *Totem and Taboo*, faced with the problem of intergenerational transmission which he had avoided there, and which still causes him trepidation (GW 13:266; SE 19:37–8). Now, however, he presses forward:

> The super-ego, according to our hypothesis, actually originated from the experiences that led to totemism. The question whether it was the ego or the id that experienced and acquired these things soon comes to nothing [because] no external vicissitudes can be undergone by the id, except by way of the ego, which is the representative of the external world to the id. Nevertheless, it is not possible to speak of direct inheritance in the ego .... Moreover, one must not take the difference between ego and id in too hard-and-fast a sense, nor forget that the ego is a specially differentiated part of the id. The experiences of the ego seem at first to be lost for inheritance; but, when they have been repeated often enough and with sufficient strength in many individuals in successive generations, they transform themselves, so to say, into experiences of the id, the impressions of which are preserved by heredity. Thus in the id, which is capable of being inherited, are harboured residues of the existences of countless egos; and, when the ego forms its super-ego out of the id, it may perhaps only be reviving the shapes of former egos and be bringing them to resurrection. (GW 13:266–7; SE 19:38)

I will come back in a moment to this vision of the super-ego as a place for the resurrection of earlier egos.

But first, let us consider the inherited id. The Standard Edition says, "the id, which is capable of being inherited"; Freud says simply, "das erbliche Es" (GW 13:267), which means the hereditary id, the id which *is* inherited. And if individual egos leave traces in the id only gradually, by insistent repetition, it follows that the id is passed on practically unchanged from parents to offspring, whence it follows further—if we assume there is a specific class of experiences, associated with the Oedipus complex, that are "repeated often enough and with sufficient strength"—that after a succession of generations, enormous numbers of people will have essentially the same id, at least as far as Oedipal tensions are concerned. In other words, Freud is being driven here, by the logic of his own theory, toward the concept of a *collective unconscious*, not exactly the collective unconscious as theorized by Jung, but a concept of the same basic type. And as we have by now learned to expect, he refuses to make this theoretical leap, this inference from the logical shape of his own metapsychological theorizing.

That he is aware of his proximity to Jung on this point emerges clearly from a passage in the *Moses* book where he talks about the relation, in his "latency" argument, between individual and mass psychology:

> What is in question is something in a people's life which is past, lost to view, superseded and which we venture to compare with what is repressed in the mental life of an individual. We cannot at first say in what form this past existed during the time of its eclipse. It is not easy for us to carry over the concepts of individual psychology into group psychology; and I do not think we gain anything by introducing the concept of a "collective" unconscious. The content of the unconscious, indeed, is in any case a collective, universal property of mankind. (GW 16:241; SE 23:132)

One can read very subtly here. The content of Jung's collective unconscious arises prior to any possibility of acquisition through individual experience; whereas for Freud the unconscious is originally understood in a dynamic sense, as the operation of forces in actual mental life, so that its content is collective, strictly speaking, only in the sense of being *common*, the result of repeated common configurations. But Freud's theorizing also requires a topographical version of the concept of a reservoir of archaic thought, which is the id. And it is not at all clear how exactly one would differentiate the id from the collective unconscious in this sense. If Freud were a different kind of thinker, he would make the obvious move of attempting a grand synthesis, of swallowing up Jung's thought in his own presumably more powerful and comprehensive theoretical scheme. But he does not; he simply stops theorizing and leaves the theoretical loose end hanging. "For the moment, then," he continues, "we will make shift with the use of analogies." More, it in fact turns out, than just "for the moment."

The Theoretical Fallacy

With the aid of these last examples, we are now in a position to say why Freud avoids theoretical closure and how he is justified in interrupting, indeed violating, the logic of his own arguments. To put it in the form of a theorem: Psychoanalytic theory leads inexorably and repeatedly to a fundamental critique of the *activity* of theorizing, a critique of what I do when I think theoretically. Therefore the psychoanalytic theorist always finds him- or herself in a condition at least bordering on dishonesty or hypocrisy. (We recall Freud's claim not to know if he believes his own assertions.) Theorizing is necessary. One cannot move a single step forward without invoking the witch Metapsychology. But the assumption of theoretical closure—the insistence that one's theorizing is sufficiently sound to serve as a basis upon which to theorize further—would transform the unavoidable *danger* of dishonesty into a simple *fact*. Therefore the avoidance of closure, even at the expense of logical cohesion, is always a more honest move than its opposite.

Nor is it difficult to complete this argument by showing that a fundamental critique of the activity of theorizing is actually present in psychoanalytic theory. The two instances I have mentioned from *The Ego and the Id*, avoidance of a proto-Lacanian excursion into the philosophy of language and avoidance of Jung's collective unconscious, point the way.

Theorizing, first of all, is a verbal activity, a mastering of phenomena, by means of abstract concepts, in the medium of language. And as etymology suggests, it is also a quasi-visual activity, the ordering of phenomena into a pattern before the mind's eye. With respect to the verbal aspect of theorizing, we recall Freud's insistence that the only path by which immaterial ideas, like the abstract concepts of theory, may enter the verbal domain of the preconscious is by way of the system *Pcpt.* (which manages sense perceptions); thoughts are thus "*actually* perceived," he says, "and are consequently held to be true." That is to say, the mere act of verbal formulation already contains a presupposition of the *truth* of the idea being formulated, whence it follows that the activity of theorizing automatically excludes a clear critical perspective upon that activity. Theorizing, so to speak, is always one step ahead of itself, never in control of its relation to the phenomena that provoke it. We recall, at this point, our discussion in Chapter 2 of Nietzsche's critique of the inherent dishonesty of conviction and hence of understanding in general.[9] Freud's insistence that words are things is essentially a translation of that critique into psychoanalytic terms.

And as for the quasi-visual aspect: Visual experience, even the imagined visual experience of theory, cannot be characterized by clarity except where the person who sees is confident of standing in an unambiguously articulated subject–object relation to the visualized object. But precisely such a relation is denied in the argument of *The Ego and the Id*. If the id were simply an amorphous reservoir of unknowable forces interfering with the ego's self-control, theorizing could still be regarded as a defense (however hopeless) of the idea of a unified perspective, as an heroic assertion of individuality in the face of chaos. And precisely thereby, the idea of a subject–object relation would be vindicated. But this is not how things stand. The id is already present *in* the ego's structure, as the super-ego, which in turn is composed, at least in part, of countless resurrected egos from the past. Which means that my theoretical vision is in truth never strictly mine, but is constantly contaminated by the critical, often threatening operation of other envisioning agents. Therefore, like Freud, I cannot honestly say that I know how far I believe what I myself am saying.

There are still problems here. We cannot operate without theorizing, without invoking the Witch, and we must therefore cut off our theorizing before we have ventured too far into the domain of theoretical closure. But how far is too far? Surely we cannot even begin theorizing without reflecting on our activity, which must already produce a minimal degree of closure in my sense of the word. How do we decide where to stop? Freud is not consistent here. In *Totem and Taboo*, he stops before going into the question of the inheritance of acquired material; in *The*

Ego and the Id, and then in the *Moses* book, he goes into that question in detail and stops only before arriving at the concept of a collective unconscious. How far is too far? The decision is ultimately arbitrary, since any criterion for making it would presuppose the existence of a completed theory. Even in the matter of avoiding theoretical closure, we do not know whether, or to what extent, we know what we are doing.

The New Shape of Ethics

There is, however, a positive side to this delivering of psychoanalytic theory into the power of the arbitrary. Situations will arise where several theoretical paths are open to me, with no theoretical criterion for choosing among them. I am then at liberty to make a decision on ethical grounds, if such grounds are present. This is the case with Freud's decision to insist that civilization is the work of Eros, not a temple of death. It may be, for all I know, that civilization *is* a temple of death. But the activity of theorizing that I am in the midst of, whether I like it or not, is part of civilization's work. The decision facing me, between different theoretical paths, is thus affected immediately by my developing knowledge of exactly what I am doing and where I am headed. If my activity, upon reflection, makes sense to me, and if my goal seems worth working for, then it is hard to see how I can choose otherwise than to judge civilization a product of constructive Eros rather than the destructive death drive.

Precisely psychoanalysis seems destined to culminate in an ethics of this sort. All propositional ethics, whether rigidly universal, like Kant's, or attenuated by the acceptance of situational variability, like Habermas's, includes the presupposition that I know what I am doing, that my motives and goals are transparent to my own understanding (or at least can be made transparent in open debate) and are therefore subject to my surveying and adjusting them more or less at will. But psychoanalysis begins by pointing out that this presupposition enormously oversimplifies our actual mental life, that in fact I can never achieve anything anywhere close to complete control over my motives and aims, even with the aid of a skilled analyst. The ethical imperative suggested by psychoanalysis must therefore run more or less thus: Act in accordance with the results (for the time being) of as honest an inquiry as you can manage (for the time being) into the question of what you are really doing here and now. This, I think, is the imperative Freud is following when he comes down in favor of Eros in *Civilization and Its Discontents*.

Does it follow that if my honest reflection convinces me that I am engaged in child molestation or genocide, I must therefore continue the same with renewed vigor? Of course not. Acting in accordance with a developing self-recognition can mean any number of things, including the cessation of an activity. If Freud, for example, in writing *Civilization and Its Discontents*, had decided on the view of civilization as a temple of death, the result would have been a different sense, on his part, of the character of his own activity in writing, hence a different judgment upon it, hence perhaps an abandonment of the project. It does follow that the ethical principle I have suggested—or more accurately, the ethical *method*—ensures not the slightest degree of predictability in the actions of one who uses it. And it does follow that that method can be used fruitfully only by an individual whose conception of honesty is Nietzschean in its radicality and fastidiousness, radical and fastidious to the point of denying all possibility of conviction or settled understanding. And it follows further that there are never sufficient objective grounds for deciding whether a particular individual is operating ethically in this (let us call it) psychoanalytic sense, or whether that individual is even constitutionally equipped to operate thus.

But I still think it is reasonable to take Freud as an instance of the ethical attitude in question and to take psychoanalysis—we recall the huge project suggested at the end of *The Question of Lay Analysis*—as an advocacy of that attitude for the whole spectrum of intellectual disciplines. We have discussed several examples, in Freud as a person and in his movement, of the opposition not to theory considered as a product, but to theory *as an activity* (an inherently dishonest activity). Just this move of opposition is indispensable in the limitlessly self-doubting ethical method and is generally characteristic of that method. Or we might take a step back and consider the whole shape of psychoanalytic theory and practice, the manner in which the actual analytic procedure, the encounter of analyst and patient, is insulated from the world of theoretical discourse by the exclusion of any nonparticipating witness (e.g., GW 14:211; SE 20:185) and by technical recommendations, like Freud's that no notes be taken (GW 8:378–80; SE 12:113–14). It is as if an element of significant uncertainty were being deliberately introduced into the traffic between theory and practice, that the latter might remain as unencumbered as possible, the former (the unavoidable Witch) as questionable as possible.

We might sum up by saying that psychoanalysis is a fundamentally clinical or case-oriented discipline, in which the particular instance, the detailed interaction between an individual and an analyst, is always capable of disrupting or unbalancing the theory. To be sure, exactly the opposite has been urged against psychoanalysis by its opponents, from the earliest critics of its supposed obsession with sex down to serious feminist thinkers like Monique Wittig.[10] And it is certainly true that theoretical prejudices can influence and damage analytic work—for instance by disrupting the analyst's "evenly-suspended attention" (GW 8:377; SE 12:111). (It is true, similarly, that the method of radical honesty in ethics is easily damaged or contaminated by the temptation to clutch at stability in theoretical principles.) But psychoanalysis as such—no matter how drastically the avoidance of such damage might restrict the class of its practitioners—is still characterized by the irreducible multiplicity of viewpoints ("vocabularies," Rorty would say) that we have discussed above.

And as we might expect, it is in the relation between theory and analytic practice that vocabularies clash most obviously. I have pointed out that serious theoretical difficulties arise if one attempts to think of the id as belonging to an individual. One cannot reasonably speak of "my" or "your" or "his" or "her" id—even though, as we saw, Freud refuses arbitrarily to take the further theoretical step to a collective unconscious. (In the book title "The Ego and the Id," the word "the" means two different things. First it governs a *class* of similar but differing phenomena [egos] by which individuals are characterized; then it governs something close to a *single* "inherited" entity.)[11] But in a real or hypothetical analytic situation, how shall we *avoid* speaking of "the patient's id"? Freud does not even bother trying. In "Analysis Terminable and Interminable" he says that "the analytic situation consists in our allying ourselves with the ego of the person under treatment in order to subdue portions of his id which are uncontrolled" (GW 16:79; SE 23:235); and in the next paragraph, apropos episodes in analysis, we hear of the ego's "task of mediating between its id and the external world" and of the ego's "defensive attitude toward its own id" (GW 16:80). And even inside the topographical scheme, it is the very nature of the controlling super-ego to reduce the id (out of which it is formed!) to something like a manageable organ of the individual. In *Civilization and Its Discontents*, accordingly, we read that the super-ego "assumes that a man's ego ... has unlimited mastery over his id" (GW 14:503; SE 21:143). No attempt is made to avoid the clash of vocabularies. And I think we have grounds for inferring that that clash, as such, belongs to the very nature of psychoanalysis.

Myth and Method

The further we go into Freud, the more we come back to Lessing. What I have called the ethics (or the ethical method) of psychoanalysis, the ethics of radical honesty and limitless self-doubt, is exactly the ethics that arises from Maimonides' reading of Job—which is also Lessing's reading, behind his irony. Elihu confutes the arguments of the three comforters, in large measure, by repeating them. He therefore accuses them not of being *wrong* but of being *dishonest*, of pronouncing their advocacy of moral humility from a perspective of presumed knowledge, which produces the same type of contradiction that would have arisen if Freud had yoked his civilizing work to the idea of civilization as a temple of death. (We think of Nietzsche's recognition of dishonesty in all conviction, hence in every instance of supposed understanding.) When Job, presumably in consonance with Elihu, repents of his dust and ashes (repents of his repentance), he is admitting perfect ignorance concerning right and wrong, hence limitless doubt with respect to the question of what he himself is really doing. And this admission can make sense, can be protected from the trap of becoming itself a moral precept, a Nietzschean conviction, only by his maintaining an unflagging honesty with respect to his own mental situation.

The story of Job, in this reading, can thus be taken as a founding myth of the ethical method of limitless self-doubt and radical honesty, and the story of Lessing's Nathan becomes an instance of that myth. Indecision has no place in either story because indecision is a symptom of the need for certainty, not a result of the adamant renunciation of certainty. And in both stories, the protagonist, although he has suffered and lost much in the past, ends his career in a condition of relative comfort and prosperity. This feature of the myth is strictly symbolic.

Self-denial, self-abasement, nobility in suffering, and the virtue of poverty have no standing in relation to the ethics we are talking about, because self-denial in any of these forms inevitably presupposes the dishonesty of pretended self-knowledge. (Can you deny what you do not know?) The myth does not suggest that practicing the ethics of Job (or of late Lessing, or of psychoanalysis) guarantees prosperity in reality. The *image* of prosperity in the myth signifies the untenability of self-denial—of the ascetic, in Nietzsche's terms—as an ethical move.

Nor do I think it is unjustified to speak of these stories as constituting a "myth" in the strict sense, rather than an allegory or an illustration. The ethics we are talking about is what becomes Nietzsche's ethics of irony, an ethics of pure method, beyond all principle or conviction or understanding. And ethics in this form does not have enough object-quality to admit of being allegorized or illustrated. Again, there is no conceivable way of deciding whether any particular individual's thought or action is ethical in the ironic sense. Making a judgment of that sort is bound to entangle one in an error like Nathan's about Saladin. The story of Job or the story of Nathan is not a story *about* an ethical ironist—it cannot possibly be—but rather, like the doctrine of eternal return in Nietzsche or Lessing, it is a significant verbal gesture in which the ethical ironists for whom it is meant will find themselves reflected, and perhaps for a moment justified. Which is, I take it, the manner in which a myth operates *as myth*.

I do not mean to say that the story of Job *is* the myth of an ethics of irony or of radical honesty. I am not sure what such an assertion would mean. But I do think it is reasonable to say, on the basis of arguments advanced in Chapter 4, that Job operates as a myth of that sort for Lessing and provides background for the story of Nathan as a myth of lonely diasporic wisdom. And on the basis of arguments developed in the present chapter, I think it is reasonable to include psychoanalysis and its implied ethics of nothing-but-method in the fabric of thought engaged by that myth. Freud himself, as far as I know, never makes a connection between Job and psychoanalysis. But Lessing's Nathan is certainly a presence in his thinking. And the well-known "Nathan letter" to Martha, of July 23, 1882, includes an early instance of his opinion on the necessity of diaspora, here still with reference to Judaism only—"the invisible edifice of Judaism became possible only after the collapse of the visible Temple" (Freud *Letters* 7)—not yet with reference to psychoanalysis.

Thus a kind of pattern emerges, a pattern we might be tempted to call "Jewish ethics." Not in the sense that the non-propositional ethics we are trying to lay hold of in the work of Lessing and Freud is, in historical fact, originally or essentially Jewish. The idea of a Jewish ethics, rather, turns out (from our discussion of Lessing and Freud) to be useful for giving a kind of provisional contour to the non-formulable ethics of irony that we associated primarily with Nietzsche in Chapter 2. Like Freud's idea of a single original living substance in *Beyond the Pleasure Principle*, or for that matter like Lessing's idea of a religion of the good for its own sake, it is an idea about which we ourselves cannot tell whether or not, or how much, we believe it. But it seems a useful idea, and would perhaps have been that much more useful if Freud, like Lessing, had found his way to the myth of Job.

The Diaspora of the Wise

But Freud's Job is Moses. And Freud's Moses has in common with Lessing's Job, above all, the quality of absolute solitude. In Lessing's case it is the solitude of wisdom, the solitude to which we see Nathan condemned when the very last words directed at him, from the one man with whom he has sought a true fellowship of understanding, are nothing but an unjust imputation of base motives. It is the solitude of the radical ironist, the Job or the Nietzsche, whose ethical existence is governed by the recognition that all conviction is dishonest, indeed that the very act of understanding is dishonest, and who therefore cannot reach out verbally to others except in an impenetrable disguise. But reach out he does nevertheless, and in cryptic gestures, like the doctrine of the Great Year, seeks contact with others of his kind, with a community of the wise which must be *constituted*, as a community, by the irremediable solitude of each member. Community in the form of an absolute diaspora, whose members are separated not merely by space and time, but by an infinite gulf of incommunicability, which is exactly the wisdom that unites them.

The solitude or isolation of Moses, however, is not that of the wise man but that of the *great* man—which is Freud's word for him and, by implication, it seems, for himself. The third part of the *Moses* book includes a long section on the subject (GW 16:214–19; SE 23:107–11), which asks whether historically "great" individuals really exist and, if so, what makes them great. The answer is easy enough:

> It is a longing for the father felt by everyone from his childhood onwards, for the same father whom the hero of legend boasts he has overcome. And now it may begin to dawn on us that all the characteristics with which we equipped the great man are paternal characteristics, and that the essence of great men for which we vainly searched lies in this conformity. The decisiveness of thought, the strength of will, the energy of action are part of the picture of a father—above all the autonomy and independence of the great man, his divine unconcern which may grow into ruthlessness. (GW 16:217; SE 23:109–10)

But since Freud is talking specifically about the reasons for Moses's historical influence, why start from the idea of the "great man" in general? Is he still thinking of the parallel with himself as the bringer, with psychoanalysis, of mankind's next major step forward? If so, then an obvious question arises: How does the great man's greatness appear *to himself*?

Once we agree that this question is lurking in the background here, we have no trouble answering it. The great man's experience, above all, is one of *aloneness*: for he lives, by definition, in a world that has not yet come fully into being. Moses is the creator of the Jews, but the Jews are not there—Freud stresses the period of "latency"—until long after his death. And in a Europe infested by Nazis, it is certainly clear to Freud that he will die without ever seeing the new humanity with which he imagines psychoanalysis is pregnant.

Exactly how is the solitude of greatness to be differentiated from that of wisdom? The wise man recognizes that all conviction is dishonest, whereas the great man is characterized precisely by the uncompromising firmness of his ideas, by his "decisiveness of thought ... which may grow into ruthlessness." But is the *creative* decisiveness that decrees there shall be Jews—or there shall be a fully secularized rational humanity—the same thing as a conviction or firmly held opinion about how things are? Is the very idea of "how things are," hence the idea of a valid conviction, not contradicted by the possibility of such radically creative paternal decrees, whether Mosaic or Freudian? Does it not follow that even the great man— in the sense of the *Moses* book—lives in a Nietzschean ethical universe where neither conviction nor understanding is compatible with honesty?

The difference between the great man and the wise man, then, is reduced to this: The great man has an effect upon history, the wise man none. But this criterion is meaningless from the point of view of "the man" himself, who is not in a position to make the requisite distinction. Concerning the great man, all we can ask is: Does he *believe* in the ultimate efficacy of his creative decision? If not, then his one governing thought loses the quality of conviction, and the difference between him and the wise man evaporates. They both experience the same absolute isolation in the same conviction-free ethical universe.

About Moses's belief in the future of his chosen people we have no grounds for saying anything. But we do know the actual future of the Jews, in a diaspora which Moses (I mean Freud's Moses, the creator of the Jews) could never have imagined, a condition of unceasing existential struggle against "two thousand years of severe oppression."[12]

And Freud himself? The author of *The Future of an Illusion*, in 1927, may still have believed in the destiny of reason and science. But the author of the *Moses* book, who encodes his historical ambitions and the destiny of psychoanalysis in the phrase "unter meinen neuen Volksgenossen," is in more ways than one a changed man. The vision as such, like Nietzsche's in *The Antichrist*, is megalomaniac: what Moses was for the Jews, suggests Freud, I am for all humanity. But the expression is deeply cryptic and signals that his hope of putting an end to religion is in truth no greater than Nietzsche's hope of destroying Christianity. It is the type of expression, the type of gesture, by which a wise man reaches out, hoping against hope for some scrap of contact with others of his kind.

For Freud with his Moses, then, as for Lessing with his Job, the practice of wisdom and the absolute diaspora of the wise are the intellectual conditions of existence. And the ethics of irony belongs to this complex as well. But once again: Is it a Jewish ethics, and if so, in what sense? As I have said, the main problem in talking about ethics of irony is that one cannot say anything at all specific without missing the point. But its association with the diaspora of the wise suggests an analogy with the diaspora of the Jews. And this real diaspora, in turn, is already a considerable challenge to the understanding. Freud ends *Moses* with an acknowledgment of the still unsolved "problem of how it is that they [the Jews] have been able to retain their originality till the present day" (GW 16:246; SE 23:136–7). Perhaps the progression from the un-understood (but indisputably real) to the inherently un-understandable at least gives a direction to our thought. The real but inexplicable diasporic "we" of the Jews, so to speak, is a step on the way toward the entirely unimaginable diasporic "we" of the wise. Without the "we" of the Jews and its history, the "we" of the wise would be that much fainter, that much closer to being completely inaudible. To this extent, the ethics of irony has what we might call a Jewish aspect or component.

It will not have escaped notice, finally, that I have made no attempt whatever to attenuate the gender bias in the phrases "great man" and "wise man." In Chapter 7, the tables will be turned.

Chapter 6

HABERMAS, RORTY, AND MACHIAVELLI

One of the first distinctions drawn in this study was that between ethics, understood as a *method* for making decisions, and ethical philosophy in the manner of Lévinas or Buber. Ethical philosophy may authorize or reject or even require a specific method, but is never completely reducible to a method, whereas by ethics I mean nothing but the method itself. In the chapters above, accordingly, I describe what I claim are instances of ethical method that can be attached to no principle, no propositional basis whatever. I call this type of method rhetorical ethics; and I claim that it characterizes a long tradition of humanist thought in the West, a tradition which is suppressed by the Kantian move toward propositional ethics but then reemerges in writers like Nietzsche to take its place as a modern ethics of irony.

This is one side of the story I want to tell, one side of what one might consider a contest for modern ethics. It is time, now, to give the other side its due.

Problems for a Modern Ethics

Let us recapitulate the argument so far, in its logical structure. We started from Wittgenstein's recognition of the impossibility of a "book" about ethics, which I take to mean a formulable universal ethics on the Kantian model. The attempt to create such an ethics, according to Wittgenstein, results in a collision with the boundaries of language. And I suggested that the place at which that collision occurs is the word "we," especially when it is used in the common unspecific manner that seeks to include, enfold, anticipate whoever happens to be reading or listening.

If ethics is to be rescued, I reasoned further, its range must be limited, its "we" must be restricted to a specific group. But if an ethics is to operate as an ultimate forum for judgments of good or bad in what I do, judgments of proper or improper, right or wrong, then the "we" governed by it must be such that an individual's membership in it is never open to question. Otherwise a larger ethics will be required to decide the range of the ethics we are proposing, and we will never be satisfied until we arrive at exactly the universal ethics we have recognized is impossible. From this point we were drawn to the idea of an ethics of irony as the only possible alternative to that universal ethics. The question of whether a particular individual belongs to the "we" governed by an ethics of irony is pointless, not really a question, because a reliable affirmative or negative answer cannot be given. True ethical ironists, if they exist at all, live in an extreme diaspora where, despite the cryptic signals that occasionally seem to reach them, they are absolutely denied the experience of belonging among their kind, in some imagined homeland of the intellect. Who would be in a position to question (or even identify) any claimants to that status?

But I have nevertheless conducted discussions of several authors which, in order to make sense, require the supposition that theirs is an ethics of irony. Clearly those discussions are speculative. But for all their speculativeness, they have brought us to a couple of ideas by which the ethics of irony receives contour: radical honesty as a prime virtue, especially honesty with regard to what one is actually doing here and now; and the recognition that radical honesty is incompatible with conviction in any form, therefore incompatible even with understanding. We have been drawn toward eccentric but easily graspable historical notions, such as the Great Year and the collapse of the difference between greatness and wisdom, and toward the Jewish historical experience, the diasporic "we," as perhaps not entirely an accidental analogy.

Still, we cannot possibly be satisfied with the idea of an ethics of irony. We may find that we are stuck with that idea, that it is the best we can do. (I think, in fact, that this is the case.) But it is not a satisfying idea, and we must therefore expect to see attempts to provide a better substitute for Kantian ethics. In Chapter 1 we discussed a number of initiatives that might be regarded as halfway to an ethics of irony, departures in the direction of Nietzsche's or Rorty's or Lessing's or Freud's thought, but which are then pulled up short at some organizing idea (especially "the literary") by which they are meant to be given an intelligible shape and predictable consequences. And precisely this attempt at clarification undermines such initiatives, confuses their ethical focus. Indeed, the attempt to apply any sort of conceptual control over ethics (thus to make a Wittgensteinian "book"?) is likely to be inherently dishonest in Nietzsche's sense of the word. Certainly, we have seen, it is hard to imagine a rigorously honest use of the concept of the "literary."

But many thinkers in the last century or so have also tried to rescue Kantian ethics by modifying it while preserving its propositional character. Jürgen Habermas, in my view, is the best of these thinkers: in his focus on method, and in his willingness to confront the constructionist fallacy, rather than pretend it is not there. I propose to focus on a critique of his work and to exploit his summaries and criticisms of other writers—principally in the essay collections *Moral Consciousness and Communicative Action* and *Remarks on Discourse Ethics*[1]—in order to suggest a broader critique of propositional ethics as such.

Habermas and the Range of Ethical Thought

The essay "Remarks on Discourse Ethics" (JA 19–111; ED 119–226) includes a thematically organized collection of Habermas's critiques of competing ethical thinkers. It begins with a discussion of Bernard Williams's book *Ethics and the Limits of Philosophy* (1985). Habermas argues that this book's focus on the "ethical" process of coming to a satisfactory collective self-understanding, a sense of identity, undervalues the categorically separate normative status of "morality" (JA 24; ED 124). (What Habermas calls "morality" here is what I call "ethics.") In particular, the moral asserts itself here only as an "exercise of abstraction" which "explodes the culture-specific lifeworld horizon within which processes of ethical self-understanding take place" (JA 24; ED 124). Thus, in Habermas's view, Williams sets "limits" to philosophy that are unnecessarily narrow, by failing to recognize that the needful rootedness of morality in the lifeworld does not weaken its categorical difference from ethics (in the same terminology as above) even while it keeps open the possibility of a clarifying role for philosophy on the moral side of the divide. And John Rawls, in a similar manner—according to Habermas—permits his ethical thought to be impaired by the unnecessary "fear of an epistemological assimilation of practical to theoretical reason" (JA 29; ED 130), a fear which could have been allayed by the recognition of a form of philosophical constructivism which engenders—"From physics to morality, from mathematics to art criticism"—"a continuum within the common, though shifting terrain of argumentation in which validity claims are thematized" (JA 30; ED 131).

Habermas thus tends to criticize, in other ethical writers, a kind of timidity, an unwillingness to go far enough in the direction of what he calls "morality" and "moral theory"—what I would call a normative ethical *method*, as opposed to a hovering between ethics and ethical philosophy in the attempt to use each as an excuse for the other. After a discussion of technical matters having to do with the distinction between justification of norms and their application, he takes up Ernst Tugendhat's ethical thinking and its development from an essentially egocentric model based on the idea of self-respect to a recognition of society or community as "the primary phenomenon" (JA 46; ED 150, "Das Erste"). But as we might expect, Tugendhat, in Habermas's view, fails to take a needful further step.

> He is misled by the observation that in the process of socialization, conscience is formed through the internalization of external sanctions to suppose that, even *from the participant perspective* of the conscientious individual who has been socialized in this manner, behind the moral "ought" there is concealed a sanction, the inner sanction of loss of self-respect, instead of the unforced force of the good reasons in terms of which moral insights impress themselves on consciousness as convictions. (JA 47; ED 151)

Tugendhat thus fails to adopt fully the "moral point of view." And basically the same holds, at a much greater historical remove, for G. H. Mead's notion of ideal role taking, which Habermas asserts requires a more thoroughly collective understanding in order to support "public discourse" as "a form of argumentation in the strict sense" (JA 49; ED 154).

We can understand now why Habermas spends as much time as he does on Charles Taylor's *Sources of the Self: The Making of the Modern Identity* (1989). For while Taylor's thought also does not cross the divide from ethics to "morality"—which in the terminology I favor would mean roughly: from ethical speculation to ethics as method—still in his case it is hard to speak of a timid or "truncated" thought process (JA 25; ED 125). Taylor, Habermas concedes, knows exactly what he is doing and knows fully the difficulties in which "his Catholic skepticism toward the potential self-sufficiency of a purely secular, proceduralist ethics" (JA 72; ED 180) places him, difficulties which he attempts to circumvent by an appeal to tradition and to the historical "sources" of the modern self. In Habermas's formulation, "His goal is not merely to describe modern identity by exploiting the resources of the history of ideas but to justify the identity outlined as a formation of fundamental orientations that is ineluctable and authoritative for us (and for all other moderns)" (JA 74; ED 182). But the difficulties remain, and in Habermas's view remain insuperable: especially the problem of how "philosophy should protect us from becoming blind or cynical toward moral phenomena" (JA 75; ED 184); and the indispensability of a highly questionable *aesthetic* component in the persuasive strategy of the modern moral philosopher (JA 74; ED 183).

With the discussion of Taylor, Habermas changes direction. Up to this point, he has sought to show how his "discourse ethics" makes possible the leap from ethical speculation into the more difficult domain of "morality" or ethics as method. But Taylor problematizes this domain to the point where the question "Why be moral?" assumes new urgency and appears to require a full philosophical treatment of the type suggested by Karl-Otto Apel in his idea of "ultimate justification" (JA 75–6; ED 184–5). The task of discourse ethics now becomes not to increase the demands made on ethical speculation, but rather to decrease the demands made upon ethics by philosophy, to counteract "the thesis [supported by Apel] that more must be accomplished by philosophy than is allowed by a crude cognitivist ethical theory" (JA 80; ED 190). The object is now to simplify matters in accordance with the recognition that "An ultimate justification of ethics is neither possible nor necessary" (JA 84; ED 195).

Hence Habermas's eager response to Thomas McCarthy's concern that growing diversity in society and among societies must create situations that become too complicated for discourse ethics to deal with:

> This fact, however, supports rather than undermines the universalistic approach of discourse ethics …. To be sure, the sphere of questions that can be answered rationally from the moral point of view shrinks in the course of the development toward multiculturalism within particular societies and toward a world society at the international level. But finding a solution to these few more sharply focused questions becomes all the more critical to coexistence, and even survival, in a more populous world. (JA 90–1; ED 202)

And then, in the same vein, he argues that the primacy of debate in discourse ethics makes room for the idea of "*a bilingually extended identity*" in debate participants (JA 103; ED 217), hence for what one might call a Davidsonian alleviation of the cross-cultural difficulties suggested in Alasdair MacIntyre's *Whose Justice? Which Rationality?* (1988).

Thus Habermas takes a position at the center of a large spectrum of ethical thought, all of which I would categorize as propositional ethics, ethics oriented toward the production of valid theoretical statements and of methods for recognizing valid practical declarations. Depending on the text he is looking at, he finds, from his own discourse-ethical perspective, either that it imposes unnecessary limits on itself, which prevent the emergence of real problems, or that it insists on problems or difficulties that need not have been worried about. And there is plenty of material in both directions from the position he stakes out. In a different essay on discourse ethics as a program, he begins with a critique of both objectivist and subjectivist ethics (MC 50-7; MkH 60-7)—going as far back as G. E. Moore, and including Stephen Toulmin, Alan R. White, and R. M. Hare—on the grounds that they back away from the problem of "our moral vocabulary" by subordinating it to "experiential sentences, imperatives, or intentional sentences" (MC 55; MkH 65). And he concludes with the critique of a generic skeptic (MC 98-109; MkH 108-19)—Alan Gewirth and Thomas McCarthy are mentioned—on the grounds that skeptical objections overcomplicate the issues they address by "dramatizing" or giving an "overdrawn account" (MC 106; MkH 116) of limitations that discourse ethics can easily concede without damaging its consistency or validity.

It is not necessary to agree with Habermas in all cases in order to see how far the tentacles of his thought reach in the ethical universe. And I propose now to attempt a critique of that thought.

The Ethical Gap

In the Preliminary Remarks, I spoke of a conceptual "gap," in Strawson's thinking and in Habermas's, between "moral sentiments" or "moral feelings" in everyday experience (Strawson's "facts as we know them") and the normative force of a fully developed ethics, which, in order to be derivable from experience, would presuppose a knowable *structure* in those emotional "facts." In Strawson, I argued, this gap is closed by implications of his use of the word "we." If I buy into that word, if I acknowledge that its reference includes me, then *I myself* (regardless of what anyone else might think) have posited a communicable (shared) knowledge of "the facts as we know them," hence a knowable structuration of those facts, hence the possibility of their growing into a valid ethics.

Habermas seems to require a more systematic closing of the gap. He suggests in his discussion of Strawson that "linguistic analysis" might be required. But he does not attempt at that point to make good on his suggestion. Nor, I pointed out, does his idea of grounding ethics in debate include a mechanism for controlling participation in the debates he imagines.

But these criticisms do not get to the center of his ethical project. When he speaks of "morality," he means what I call "ethics," a method for regulating behavior that does not rest on any form of ideal premise or sanction. He insists that ethics must take its origin not in reason or theory or metaphysics but in the "lifeworld," the fabric of unquestioned habits, reactions, feelings, and assumptions in which we live our lives from minute to minute alongside, and in constant contact with, other individuals. He distinguishes between "lifeworld" and "world" thus:

> On one side we have [lifeworld,] the horizon of unquestioned, intersubjectively shared, nonthematized certitudes that participants in communication have "at their backs." On the other side, participants in communication face the communicative contents constituted within a world: objects that they perceive and manipulate, norms that they observe or violate, and lived experiences to which they have privileged access and which they can express. (MC 138; MkH 149)

This is another formulation of what I have called the "ethical gap," between the immediacy of experience on one hand and, on the other, the world of knowable, manipulable, expressible entities in which anything worthy of being called an ethics (or a morality) must be organized. My own inclination is to speak of a gap between experienced immediacy and the world of *theory* in a broad sense, a world where we can *see* what we are faced with and what we are doing.

Habermas would object that my formulation of the ethical gap confuses matters by conflating the notions of "world" and "system." He would not, I think, deny that such a gap exists; but in *The Theory of Communicative Action* he maintains that it exists only in the form of an historical process, "The Uncoupling of System and Lifeworld," which he follows from the level of undeveloped tribal societies down to the full development of modern mass society.[2] Thus the ethical gap is stripped of the simple structural inevitability that I attribute to it (as does Wittgenstein) and is given an historically fluid character by which its transformation or even disappearance is made to seem possible. Whether this objection preserves his position against my argument below will have to be decided on the basis of that argument.

The gap, in whichever form, is the prime ethical problem for Habermas—as we saw in his reading of Strawson—and we can expect a determined effort on his part to close it. The problem as such is by no means a new one. It is, for instance, an integral element of social-contract theory (and of the problems of that theory) in the eighteenth century: the lifeworld is made secure, thus livable, only by means of a contractual sacrifice of liberty on the level of world. And we have observed the ethical gap in operation in the thought of all those whom I have claimed for ethics of irony: in Lessing's Nathan as a vessel of the tension between immediate cultural belonging and the vision of universal humanity; in the experience of Rorty's ironist, torn between commitment to her own "final vocabulary" and her grasp of the unjustifiability of that commitment; in Freud's constant maneuvering between a theory that cannot be permitted its own closure and a practice that cannot be permitted a firm theoretical underpinning; in Nietzsche's struggle with both the theoretical unacceptability and the practical inevitability of understanding. But the ethics of irony has no interest in closing that gap. Precisely the openness of the gap creates a space for irony, a space in which the contradictions that add up to an ironic existence can be lived by one of those few great or wise or uniquely honest individuals who belong to the restricted "we" that makes a modern ethics possible in the first place. Habermas's project, however, his attempt to close the gap, defies the ethics of irony and aims to bring the whole enterprise of modern ethics to a conclusion on more or less Kantian terms.

Kant, Habermas, and the Gap

In one of his clearest ethical expositions, Habermas begins by asking "Does Hegel's Critique of Kant Apply to Discourse Ethics?" Obviously he means to show that to the extent that Hegel's criticism of Kant is valid, it does *not* apply to discourse ethics. But three of the four Hegelian arguments that he identifies are objections to instances in Kant of precisely the ethical gap: that "the categorical imperative requires that the moral agent abstract from the concrete content of duties and maxims"; that "the categorical imperative enjoins separating the universal from the particular"; and that "the categorical imperative enjoins a strict separation of 'is' from 'ought'" (MC 195–6; ED 9–10). He does not simply accept Hegel's views; in the first two cases, his justification of discourse ethics includes a nuanced defense of Kant's position. But in the third case he begins by conceding, "Kant is vulnerable to the objection that his ethics lacks practical impact because it dichotomizes duty and inclination, reason and sense experience" (MC 207; ED 25). Now he must distinguish his own position sharply:

> The same cannot be said of discourse ethics, for it discards the Kantian theory of the two realms .... Discourse ethics also reformulates the concept of autonomy. In Kant, autonomy was conceived as freedom under self-given laws, which involves an element of coercive subordination of subjective nature. In discourse ethics the idea of autonomy is intersubjective. It takes into account that the free actualization of the personality of one individual depends on the actualization of freedom for all.

But how is the discarding or reformulating of ideas supposed to affect a gap that separates the whole realm of ideas from that of facts and practices?

(Let it be noted, by the way, that Habermas's formulation of Hegel's fourth criticism of Kant is highly suggestive in relation to our discussions above. He speaks of "Hegel's objection to the terrorism of *pure conviction [Gesinnung]*" [MC 196; ED 10]. It is true that the meaning of the term "Gesinnung," which is translated here as "conviction," tends more in the direction of "general attitude of mind" than does that of Nietzsche's word "Überzeugung." But his retention of Hegel's strong idea of [French Jacobin] "terrorism" suggests that at least under certain circumstances, Habermas might not be entirely out of sympathy with Nietzsche's dictum "Überzeugungen sind Gefängnisse" [convictions are prisons], hence perhaps not out of sympathy with the ethics of irony. We will come back to this suggestion later.)

To summarize: For Kant, the ethical gap is definitely present, but the power of pure practical reason (in the categorical imperative) renders it inconsequential from the point of view of rational beings; pure practical reason can in fact be understood to *require* that the gap be ignored. Habermas, by contrast, recognizes that the gap cannot be ignored, that it creates crippling problems for a rationalist ethics, problems which cannot be solved by practical reason as a supposedly unified method. Indeed, in a 1991 essay "On the Pragmatic, the Ethical, and the Moral Employments of Practical Reason," he questions the very idea of "practical reason in the singular" and concludes:

> Moral theory must bequeath this question [that of the unity of practical reason] unanswered to the philosophy of law; the unity of practical reason can be realized in an unequivocal manner only within a network of public forms of communication and practices in which the conditions of rational collective will formation have taken on concrete institutional form. (JA 17; ED 117–18)

And exactly this conclusion applies to the problem of the ethical gap. If the virtues of a rational and "universalist" Kantian ethics are to be preserved, the gap must be closed. But it cannot be closed by a purely theoretical move. Without the establishment of suitable institutional conditions in the real world, discourse ethics remains empty theorizing.

In a sense, therefore, there are now two gaps. Nothing can be accomplished ethically until philosophical thought and real institutions have been brought within reach of each other:

> This much is true: any universalist morality is dependent upon a form of life that *meets it halfway*. There has to be a modicum of congruence between morality and the practices of socialization and education .... In addition, there must be a modicum of fit between morality and socio-political institutions. Not just any institutions will do. Morality thrives only in an environment in which postconventional ideas [see MC 156–170; MkH 169–82] about law and morality have already been institutionalized to a certain extent. (MC 207–8; ED 25)

And only under these conditions can the original ethical gap, between the immediacy of experience and valid normative thinking, be dealt with. Only under these conditions can ethics be anchored where it must be anchored, in the lifeworld. Only under these conditions can an ethically fruitful debate unfold, "The process of reaching an understanding between world and lifeworld" (MC 136; MkH 146).

Habermas does not mean that institutional reform must be completed before ethical debate can begin. Obviously the two processes must move together. Without some incipient form of ethical debate, or debate on the theory of ethical debate, political thinking will have no goal by which to orient itself. Without some sense of developing political reform, ethical debate must quickly collapse under an awareness of its isolation from concrete reality. The first of these propositions accounts for the detail with which Habermas expounds the operation of discourse ethics. The second accounts for his activity as an interpretive historian, especially on the history of reason and discussion, beginning with *The Structural Transformation of the Public Sphere*. "Moral universalism," he now claims, "is a *historical result*" (MC 208; ED 25-6) rooted in the eighteenth century and traceable today in "the gradual embodiment of moral principles in concrete forms of life." And finally, his ultimate focus, on closing the ethical gap, is reflected in his occupation with theories of human growth and behavior (e.g., MC 116-33, 141-89; MkH 127-43, 152-200), theories by which the concept "lifeworld"—even while still "decoupled" from "system"—might receive the type and level of contour it requires in order to support serious normative thinking.

Habermas and the Ethics of Irony

Habermas's ethical thinking thus contains a large number of variables, hence a large number of places where it can go wrong. What distinguishes him among modern propositional ethicists, I think, is precisely his willingness to deal with the full complexity of the intellectual situation in which he finds himself.

But what if something does go wrong? Suppose, for example, that he turns out to be mistaken about history. It is true that he does not expect history to do his work for him, or ours for us; he understands that

> the gradual embodiment of moral principles in concrete forms of life is not something that can safely be left to Hegel's absolute spirit. Rather, it is chiefly a function of collective efforts and sacrifices made by sociopolitical movements. (MC 208; ED 26)

But suppose those efforts and sacrifices are hopeless in the end, at least on a large scale. Suppose the "bits and pieces" of an "existing reason" (*existierende Vernunft*) in history are really only the remnants of reason's despair, not a promise of its future growth. Suppose that even among the best Enlightenment thinkers, there was never really any hope for a rational politics.[3]

Or suppose the doubt I suggested earlier about Habermas's idea of the debate process underlying discourse ethics turns out to be insurmountable. Suppose that even the slow development of a friendly political atmosphere does not obviate the need for an extrinsic procedure by which debate participation can be controlled, a procedure which cannot be imposed without violating the very reason for existence of limited, lifeworld-anchored debate.

Or suppose, finally, that the whole idea of anchoring ethical debate in the lifeworld turns out to be unworkable. Even if it is true that ethics cannot be imposed upon life in the form of a theory or system, even if it is true that "the world of moral phenomena can be grasped only in the performative attitude of participants in interaction" (MC 50; MkH 60): still, suppose that that "world of moral phenomena"—which must surely be imagined as an undetached extension of the lifeworld—turns out not to be able to support having an actual normative ethics built upon it. In fact, this supposition seems close to being a certainty. The trouble with the concept of "lifeworld" is that, *as* a concept, it is emptied of precisely those qualities that it seeks to conceptualize. As a concept—as a possible object of knowledge, not of unquestioning certainty—it belongs unequivocally to the domain of world, not lifeworld, in Habermas's terminology. (There are any number of concepts that share this problem, for instance "the particular" as a general idea.)[4] Habermas is of course entitled, in principle, to use the concept "lifeworld" in a theoretical discussion of the nature of ethical thought. But his theoretical arguments cannot be neatly detached from their subject matter. What he is talking about is a complicated gradual process by which ethical theory, institutional reality, and the lifeworld are maneuvered into a pattern of fruitful relations by which the ethical gap will eventually be closed. And his own ethical theory is an integral part of that process! Which means that the ethically needful operation of the actual lifeworld, assuming it can get started, must constantly be confused by having to be coordinated with (or perhaps separated from—but how?) the presence, in his theory, of its corrupt conceptual double.

I think this point contributes substantially to the likelihood that Habermas's ethical ideas are unrealizable. But I do not claim that it settles anything, especially since Habermas himself appears to have anticipated it. He insists, for example,

> In anthropological terms, morality is a safety device compensating for a vulnerability built into the sociocultural form of life .... Creatures that are individuated only through socialization are vulnerable and morally in need of considerateness. Linguistically and behaviorally competent subjects are constituted as individuals by growing into an intersubjectively shared lifeworld, and the lifeworld of a language community is reproduced in its turn through the communicative actions of its members. This explains why the identity of the individual and that of the collective are interdependent; they form and maintain themselves together .... Unless the subject externalizes himself by participating in interpersonal relations through language, he is unable to form that inner center that is his personal identity. This explains the almost constitutional insecurity and chronic fragility of personal identity—an insecurity that is antecedent to cruder threats to the integrity of life and limb. (MC 199; ED 14–15)

There is a good deal of conceptual vulnerability in this argument, especially in the question of exactly how "subject" and "individual" are differentiated in their relation to "identity." But quibbles aside, what Habermas is suggesting here is a unified theory of lifeworld and elemental morality, which indicates quite an exact knowledge of where the sore point is in his thinking.

And it follows now that he is not likely to be unaware of how close to hopeless his whole ethical project is. His situation with respect to the question of how the ethical gap might be closed is therefore similar to Freud's with respect to the question of Eros and civilization. The question does not admit of being answered on anything like objective grounds. One must choose an answer on ethical grounds, which in Habermas's case means he has decided ethically that an ethics beyond the gap *must* be possible. And as in Freud's decision for Eros over death, the ethics (or meta-ethics) driving that decision can be nothing but an ethics of strict honesty with respect to the character of his own present activity. Habermas finds himself operating on the very brink of an ethics of irony—as is also suggested by his retention of the Hegelian idea of a "terrorism of conviction." And his treatment of other philosophers, in the long essays on discourse ethics, suggests further that he brings with him, to that brink of irony, the whole idea of rescuing a propositional ethics in the modern world. But now, finding himself at the brink of irony, he is moved to ask what he is doing there. And his answer takes the form of an ethical (or meta-ethical) move: he has arrived at a point where he must simply say no to irony—just as Freud had found it impossible not to say yes to Eros.

Ethics, Politics, and the Gap

Why does Habermas pull back from irony as decisively as he appears to? Ethics of irony, I have conceded, is an unsatisfactory idea. But is it any more unsatisfactory than the idea of closing a categorical gap without altering the basic Kantian (or "universalist") categories that bring it into being as a problem?

The ethical gap, at its most fundamental, is a gap between experienced immediacy and the theorizing mind or, in Habermas's terms, between lifeworld and world. But the avenue by which that gap comes to be perceived as a problem—in most cases, I think—passes through politics. Rorty, we observed, is made uncomfortable by the impossibility of understanding liberal politics as an ethical imperative. And in Habermas's early concept of an eighteenth-century "public sphere" we can recognize retrospectively the hopeful assertion that an eventual reconciliation with ethics is built into the very origin of modern politics.

At issue here is the question of what precisely the issue is, whether ethical or political. Rorty's liberal politics compels him to posit the goal of a perfectly "nominalist and historicist" cultural situation. But this goal can be arrived at only by way of an ethics of irony, which in itself does not imply, or even support, the liberal politics from which he had started. It does not, for instance, guarantee the non-advocacy of cruelty (Rorty 74). Correspondingly, it is his liberal politics that draws Habermas into the labyrinth of theorizing by which he is eventually brought to the brink of an ethics of irony, to a meta-ethical crossroads where he must, as honestly as he can, determine and then conform to the exact character of his own thinking at exactly that crossroads. Again—as for Freud, or Rorty—there are no objective considerations to guide him, and in a certain sense his decision is exactly the opposite of Rorty's. Rorty maintains the consistency of his ethical thought at the expense of permitting doubts to infect his politics; Habermas insists on an uncompromised politics, but at the expense of permitting confusion to arise in his ethical thought, a confusion that is confronted but not eliminated by the idea of an open ethical debate. Both philosophers enact analogues of Freud's meta-ethical decision in favor of Eros: Rorty finds that he is engaged in a fundamentally ethical project; Habermas finds that the project he is engaged in is fundamentally political.

And yet, despite their opposed ways of deciding, the situations at which Rorty and Habermas arrive are essentially the same. Both are characterized by an irresolvable tension between ethics and politics. (Both writers would disagree here. Rorty tries to square the circle in his final chapter on "Solidarity," where he says that precisely the distinction between public and private "makes it possible for a single person to be both [liberal and ironist]" [198]. But he needs for this point a notion of the "human," which, however nuanced, is as unworkable in the end as Habermas's nuanced notion of debate.) And exactly where does that tension originate? Is it built into the very nature of ethics and politics? Or is it accidental, a consequence of the particular starting points in Rorty's and in Habermas's thinking?

Lessing's position on this question is interesting. In *Ernst und Falk: Gespräche für Freymäurer* (Conversations for Freemasons), the two interlocutors agree that the basic ethical purpose of the state, to ensure each individual his or her full share of happiness (LM 13:352), conflicts unalterably with the actual constitution and operation of states in the world. Even the best possible political constitution, they agree, cannot bring people together without also separating them and creating advantage and disadvantage (LM 13:354–9), thus impairing the happiness of at least some. But it is also suggested that no purpose is served by open discussion of this truth, that it might better be consigned to silence (LM 13:352–3), that the business of dealing with the conflict between ethics and politics (since it cannot be handled politically) were best left to an international secret society of individuals who "did not believe that everything had to be good and true that they recognized as good and true" (LM 13:360: nicht glaubten, daß alles nothwendig gut und wahr seyn müsse, was sie für gut und wahr erkennen). Individuals, in other words, capable of *knowing* something (*erkennen*) while yet not *believing* it. Individuals, therefore, whose cryptic or Masonic "we" would be that of an ethics of irony. Lessing is thus led to the same choice that is faced by Habermas and Rorty, but he does not yet confront it as a choice. The task of the Freemasons, he suggests, is not to decide one way or the other, but rather to deal somehow with the tension between ethics and politics as a whole, to find ways of "making its consequences as undamaging as possible" (LM 13:360). Where does this view of the matter place him historically?

Machiavelli and the Location of Ethics

At the present juncture, as at many others in this book, I will attempt to clarify my view by discussing a particular case. And the figure to whom our attention is now drawn is Niccolò Machiavelli, whose work is characterized by what seems an enormous separation between ethics and politics—especially in the ruthless political thought of *The Prince*—yet not by any sense of tension. Even in the *Discourses on Livy*, where the focus on republican politics accords better with modern political preferences which tend to be ethically grounded (most often in theories of human rights), ethical considerations are absent for the most part. Therefore it seems fair to ask: where is Machiavelli's ethics located? Or shall we decide that he has no ethics—which seems hardly conceivable, despite the number of readers who have reached essentially that conclusion?

My opinion is that ethics, for Machiavelli, is located strictly outside of the discourse practices of politics, in the same manner that morals and metaphysics, for Leibniz, are each located strictly outside the discourse of the other. It does not follow that ethics and politics, in the real world, never come into direct contact or conflict. But I infer from Machiavelli's practice the assumption that in the arena of theoretical or speculative discourse, any attempt at a combined treatment of the two subjects would produce mere confusion. I will suggest that Machiavelli and Leibniz both observe the same overarching meta-ethical imperative: that one *not pretend* (as Kant would later) to embrace all fields of inquiry in a single form of discourse, that one accept the insufficiency of language-as-such and bow to the necessity of using radically different languages for different areas of concern. (This imperative in a sense reappears, in the ethics of irony, as the meta-ethical imperative of radical honesty. The two imperatives—the pre-Kantian and the ironic or post-Kantian—have in common that both enjoin careful attentiveness to the exact character of what one is doing, in discourse, here and now.)

Even within the single domain of politics, in fact, Machiavelli appears to distinguish separate and incompatible discursive practices. Hans Baron opens his chapter on Machiavelli by calling attention to a perennial "puzzle": "how could the faithful secretary of the Florentine republic, the author of the *Discourses on the First Ten Books of Titus Livy*, also be the author of *The Prince*?" (Baron 2:101). But I do not think a solution to this puzzle requires a demonstration of how Machiavelli could have been first a *sincere* theorist of tyranny and then a *sincere* republican. (The solution Baron settles on, like those offered by many others, is biographical in this sense. My point is not that such arguments are always wrong, but that they are unnecessary.) What needs to be shown is the manner in which Machiavelli chooses, on different occasions, to write in at least two different languages, and why one language is not enough.

It is not hard to find instances to show that the idiom of the *Discourses* is fundamentally different from that of *The Prince*. Baron (2:109–10) calls attention to Book Three, Chapter 42 of the *Discourses*, where Machiavelli refers to an argument he had made in Chapter 18 of *The Prince*. The writing in this chapter of *The Prince* is remarkably arbitrary in character. We read first that although it is unquestionably "laudable" for a prince to be true to his word and "to live with integrity rather than cunning," still, "in our times," princes who have flouted these virtues have done great things and have gotten the better of those who build on trust and loyalty.[5] (Exactly what does "laudable" *[laudabile]* mean therefore?) Then, as if in explanation of these facts, we are told that there are two basic types of combat, legal and physical ("with laws" and "with force"),[6] the former being proper to man, the latter to beasts, and that since the former is often insufficient (for what? we are tempted to ask), even men must have recourse to the latter.

(What does this point have to do with the matter of keeping one's word?) But now the author mounts and rides his own metaphor, telling us that when a prince uses the beast's way, he must choose which beasts to emulate, and that he is best served by choosing the lion and the fox. (Thus, under the rubric of "force," the fox returns our attention to the idea of unscrupulous cunning—although cunning is equally suitable, or more so, for "legal" combat!) And although the metaphor is now dropped, the rest of the chapter is devoted to praise of those princes (showing them, surely, to be "laudable") in whom the vulpine qualities are most developed.

The writing of the *Discourses* has an entirely different flavor. Chapter 42 of Book Three is headed, "That promises made under compulsion should not be observed"; and this proposition has the political corollary "that forced promises regarding public matters, when the force is no longer there, are always broken, and with no shame to him who breaks them." But then Machiavelli changes the subject. He has been talking about the *patria*, the state considered as the fatherland of its citizens, not as the domain of a prince, and in particular about the need to defend the *patria* at all costs, "whether with disgrace or with glory" (Ch. 41).[7] Now, however, he continues,

> And among princes, not only are forced promises broken when the force is gone, but all their other promises are broken when the reasons for having made them are gone. Whether or not this is a laudable thing *[cosa laudabile]*, and whether or not such measures should be followed by a prince, is the subject of broad discussion in my treatise *The Prince*. I shall therefore now pass over it in silence. (Ch. 42)

The claim about "broad discussion" in *The Prince* is inaccurate. For "discuss" Machiavelli uses here the verb *disputare*, which, especially with the adverb "broadly" (*largamente*), suggests that both sides of the issue had been presented in detail. But in Chapter 18 of *The Prince*, the question of "laudability" is disposed of in one sentence—of course it is laudable in princes to be true to their word—and the balance of the chapter is devoted to asserting, *not* arguing, that no prince with any brains wants to be laudable in that sense.

What Machiavelli describes in *Discourses* 3.42 is what Chapter 18 of *The Prince* would have looked like *if* it had been written in the relatively judicious and balanced idiom of the *Discourses*—in a less peremptory, less high-handed, or, let us say, less princely and more republican language. Thus he calls our attention indirectly to the difference in language between the two works. And I maintain that it is a difference between *languages* that we observe here, not simply a difference in style. For it is undergirded by a difference in the very nature of truth or truthfulness that operates in each case. Throughout the *Discourses*, the central value of *patria* stabilizes the idea of truth and makes possible cogent arguments of considerable length. In *The Prince*, truth has no stability at all. To return to Chapter 18: it is true (morally) that keeping your word is laudable; it is true (empirically) that keeping your word does not help you as a prince; it is true (in the order of nature) that legal fighting is proper to man, physical fighting to beasts, but it is also true that this truth does not in truth describe human behavior; it is true (politically) that moral truth must often be disregarded; and it is true (psychologically) that a successful prince is in effect never morally bad after all, since his methods will be judged honorable and laudable by everyone (*da ciascuno laudati*).

Machiavelli makes no attempt to conceal the multiplicity of idioms in his work. In the notorious Chapter 15 of *The Prince*, which takes up the general question of whether princes should prefer good actions over bad, he opens his presentation by saying that

> in consequence of my intention to write something useful for those who understand it, it has seemed to me more fitting to go straight to the effectual [actual? practical?] truth of the matter [*alla verità effettuale della cosa*] than to go to an imagined version of it.

In other words, we assume, he intends to talk about politics the way it really is, and not about the republics and principalities that people have "imagined," but which "have never been seen or known to exist in truth [*essere in vero*]." But the concept of truth—as opposed, for example, to that of reality or practicality—gives another dimension to this passage. The notion of an "effectual truth" suggests the possibility of *other* truths, one of which is immediately brought up by the question of whether or not a particular thing exists "in truth." And truth in this latter sense does not admit the possibility of alternatives. It is unitary and exclusive; everything, without exception, either exists or does not exist. This exclusivity also characterizes ideal truth, which is presumably what governs the imagining of nonexistent political models. Thus the difference is insisted upon: between language here and the language of the *Discourses*—or of what will become the *Discourses*, depending on how one dates various pieces of text. It is the difference between language in which truth operates as a single organizing force (*Discourses*) and language in which truth is subject to doubt, ambiguity, volatility (*Prince*).

Machiavelli and the Disjunction of Languages

In order for the use of different languages to operate as a meta-ethical acknowledgment of the inherent limitedness of discourse, however, the languages in question must be more than just different. They must be *disjoint*. They may not share a common boundary across which they could make contact; for even if it took the form of pure opposition, such contact would still be available as substance for a larger discourse that would embrace them and undermine their separateness. In particular, the languages cannot be of the same *type*. (This is true of the languages of metaphysics and of ethics in Leibniz. The language of metaphysics—in its dependence on a strict notion of unity—operates by being constantly at odds with its own discursive medium, in which, for example, the possibility of repetition is indispensable. The language of ethics, by contrast, operates precisely by embracing the discursive medium even in its most egregious metaphysical inaccuracies and inconsistencies. Even if the need for a language of ethics can be deduced metaphysically, still that deduction does not form a direct bridge to it. Or we think of Rorty's "final vocabularies," which, if they are truly "final," cannot be different without being irreconcilable.)

In Machiavelli's work, we shall probably search in vain for a language of ethics—or, for that matter, for a language of metaphysics. But his insistence on two disjoint political idioms is itself already ethical or meta-ethical in character, in the sense suggested above. And the disjunction between those two idioms is emphatic. The language of *The Prince* defines itself by its object, which it calls *la verità effettuale della cosa*. Assuming that the *cosa* is politics, what exactly is meant by its "effectual truth"? By denying the usefulness of any form of "imagined" political model, the context makes clear that the argument will somehow entirely avoid the theoretical. And the notion of an "effectual *truth*" (not merely facts) suggests that the non-theoretical will have here the quality of a principle, hence that it must be understood in the strictest possible sense. But how does one treat brute facts or simple particulars in discourse without embedding them in a conceptual system? We have already discussed, with reference to *Prince* 18, an extreme example of how a language might set itself this goal. It must be a language that profoundly distrusts its own continuous or connected or structured quality as logic or even merely as description—a language that changes direction constantly, using unconnected factual references and unmotivated rhetorical moves (the animal metaphor in chapter 18) to disrupt its conceptual or descriptive operation. Nor does it follow that such a language must become incoherent. The object of interest in *The Prince*, the *cosa*, is never lost sight of for a moment; politics is always in the center, however various or quickly changing the directions from which it is approached. Indeed, the volatile and elusive language, as such, says more about practical politics, more about the difficulty of mastering it systematically, than any specific statements in the text.

I have supported my view of *The Prince* as language, so far, only by a short discussion of chapter 18, and a comprehensive demonstration of my view would not fit here. But there is an interesting instance of how that language works in the first paragraph of chapter 15, the same paragraph that names *la verità effettuale della cosa*. It concerns uses of the verb *dovere*:

> E molti si sono immaginati republiche e principati, che non si sono mai visti né conosciuti essere in vero; perché elli è tanto discosto da come si vive a come si doverrebbe vivere, che colui che lascia quello che si fa per quello che si doverrebbe fare, impara più tosto la ruina che la preservazione sua; perché uno uomo, che voglia fare in tutte le parte professione di buono, conviene ruini infra tanti che non sono buoni.

> [And many have imagined republics and princedoms that have never been seen or known to exist in truth; because there is such a large discrepancy between how people live and how they might be supposed (?) to live that he who eschews what is done in favor of what might be supposed (?) to be done reaps more likely

his ruin than his preservation; because a man who, in everything he does, wants to make profession of the good, will inevitably come to grief among so many people who are not good.]

Generally, *dovere* with an infinitive means: to be supposed or expected to do something, either in accordance with some form of necessity or in accordance with morality. And the context, the idea of "imagined" political models, suggests that the first clause containing "doverrebbe" be understood: because there is such a large discrepancy between how people live and how they might be expected to live (according to the rules and incentives which, *in various theoretical models*, are "imagined" to govern political behavior). But the clause immediately following must certainly be read: he who eschews what is done in favor of that which might be supposed to be done (in the sense of that which *morality* might demand). How could an individual possibly deviate from common practice ("quello che si fa") out of a wish to act in accordance with the theory that supposedly describes that practice? From the point of view of someone ("colui") inside the polity, in this second clause, only morality, not political theory, can provide the standard for *dovere*.

Thus an ambiguity is created by which the concepts of morality and political theory become confused, which reflects a recognition that the two are not really different, that morality is merely political theory in disguise. And that ambiguity is reinforced by the locution "fare ... professione di buono" in the next clause. Surely one can "make profession of the good"—that is, claim or pretend to be good—without actually being good; and surely such a profession will be made commonly by the Machiavellian fox and will often be useful to him in *avoiding* ruin. It appears, therefore, that we have to read "fare ... professione di buono" as meaning something closer to: make a fetish of the good, insist on the existence of the good, *fail* to recognize that "the good" is a politically relative category. But then how shall we read the rest of chapter 15, which seems to insist on an absolute notion of the good, even going to the extent of listing eleven pairs of qualities to illustrate the difference between good and not good? (It is true that the order in which the opposed qualities are named is reversed repeatedly: good first in 1, 2, 6, 8, 10, 11; not good first in 3, 4, 5, 7, 9.) And how can you learn, as Machiavelli says you must, how to be able to be not good ("potere essere non buono") and how to use that ability, if you do not know what good is in the first place?

The linguistic or rhetorical ground thus shifts constantly beneath our feet, without, however, distracting us for an instant from the "effectual" point, the maintenance of political advantage. But the same sort of shifting is not at all prominent in the *Discourses on Livy*, where the language is of an entirely different type. Here the language is defined not by its object (not by something like *la verità effettuale della cosa*) but by *an axiomatic proposition*: that the only reasonable method in practical politics is the use of the history of classical antiquity, especially ancient Rome, as a source of models for imitation. If one's language is defined in this manner (no matter what the actual proposition is, as long as it makes sense), then since the definition is now situated within the linguistic medium itself, as a verbally formulable proposition, nothing prevents the language from being shaped into extensive self-sustaining arguments. This is not to say that the *Discorsi* attempt to demonstrate the validity of the proposition that founds their language. Such a demonstration could not be carried out logically except in a meta-language founded upon some presumably deeper ground, whereas the Preface to Book One of the *Discorsi* simply states that proposition insistently and, in various ways, tries to persuade us that it expresses a reasonable basic attitude for one who wishes to talk about politics.

Indeed, in the "Proemio" to Book Two, it seems as if Machiavelli has begun to worry about not having made sufficiently clear that his guiding proposition must be regarded as an arbitrary assertion of principle, not a topic for discussion. He begins that Preface with a short argument about why people tend to prefer the past to the present, and especially about the reasons why such preference is often deluded. We read, for instance, that since people's desires always exceed what they possess, they are automatically dissatisfied with the present and compensate with an exaggeratedly rosy idea of the past. Then he continues:

> I do not know, therefore, if I shall deserve to be counted among those who fool themselves, if in these discourses of mine I praise too much the times of ancient Rome and condemn ours. And truly, if the virtue that ruled then and the vice that rules now were not clearer than the sun, I would adopt more caution in speaking for fear of falling into the same error that I accuse others of. But since the matter is plain enough for all to see, I shall be bold in saying plainly what I understand of those times and these, so that the minds of young readers might be able to flee the latter and to prepare themselves to imitate the former whenever fortune gives them the opportunity.

Thus the quality of the preference for antiquity as an arbitrary assertion—in the face of very good reasons to question it—is dramatized, and we are obliged to recognize that the guiding proposition of the *Discorsi* has exactly the same function as the arbitrarily chosen object ("effectual" truth) for *The Prince*: not to show or say anything, but rather to establish peremptorily the language, the discourse, the idiom, in which all subsequent showing or saying must take place. And as I have said, the two idioms in question are therefore entirely disjoint, because they are the result of different *manners* of definition.

"Languages," Wittgenstein, History

I do not mean to show uniqueness in Machiavelli. On the contrary, I present his thought (along with Leibniz's) as representative of the ethical attitude that characterizes a long succession of European intellectual elites from the Middle Ages through the eighteenth century. I focus upon Leibniz and Machiavelli because the argument for my view is uncommonly easy to make in these two cases. And with Machiavelli it is made even easier by the existence of a little piece called the "Discorso intorno alla nostra lingua" (Discourse Concerning Our Language). There is some question about whether Machiavelli is really its author. But I will take his authorship as given, even though my argument might in a way be strengthened if the author were shown to be someone else, which would imply a sharing by others of what I claim is his basic intellectual method.

The center of the "Discorso" is Machiavelli's fictional dialogue with Dante, in which he takes issue with the latter's development, in Book One, chapters 16–19 of *De vulgari eloquentia*, of the idea of a single "illustrious, centrally operative, courtly, and curial" Italian language ("illustre, cardinale, aulicum et curiale") to which all the local and regional dialects are subordinate. That language, argues Machiavelli, is in truth only a figment of Dante's unjustifiably violent resentment against his home city and against the excellent Florentine dialect that he actually spoke and wrote—and which, indeed, receives much of its excellence from his writing in it. This argument parallels neatly what I have suggested about Machiavelli's view of the "languages" in which politics is discussed. Force and cogency—"nature," as opposed to mere "art"[8]—are found only in the individual dialect, so to speak. Any attempt to establish a single master idiom subsuming the dialects must suffer the fate of the Italian language at the court in Rome,

> a place where speaking takes as many forms as nations are represented, and where no rule can be applied to it, and (I marvel that you wish to cite it as an example) where nothing laudable or good is done. For where the customs are perverse, the language will inevitably be perverse, and will have the same effeminate lubricity as those who speak it. ("Discorso" 54–5)

The ease with which the leap is made here from linguistic practice to ethics indicates an habitual understanding of the ethical problems in any pretended master discourse—an understanding, incidentally, which Dante certainly shared in general, if not with respect to the plurality of Italian dialects.[9]

Once this point is accepted, for however great or small a range of instances, it brings us back to the vicinity of our starting point, Wittgenstein's lecture on ethics. A book on ethics (meaning a comprehensive book) is impossible, whence it follows that we are ethically prevented, by our honesty, from claiming to produce such a book. And it follows further that we are ethically prevented from claiming to have found a single language in which the whole scope of any subject matter with an ethical dimension (e.g., politics) might be adequately represented. It is because Machiavelli (in a pre-Kantian manner) accepts this ethical limitation that his writing avoids the unresolvable (post-Kantian) tension between ethics and politics, which characterizes, in different ways, the thought of both Rorty and Habermas.

But we are still left with a number of questions. First, is it necessary, in order to practice rhetorical ethics in the pre-Kantian manner of Leibniz or Machiavelli, that one operate in at least two different intellectual idioms? The answer is no. If Machiavelli had written only *The Prince*, or only the *Discourses*, careful analysis would still have enabled us to understand his ethics of rhetorical self-limitation.

That we have both texts, and are in a position to compare them, only makes that analysis easier, just as the existence of Leibniz's monadological treatises makes it easier to approach the rhetoric of the *Theodicy*.

Second, if Machiavelli's rhetorical ethics, as I have described it, is really characteristic of a significant slice of the intellectual life of pre-Kantian Europe, how does it happen that in that same pre-Kantian Europe, he is considered by so many prominent intellectuals to have no ethics at all? This question is bothersome only so long as one assumes that prominent intellectuals are not likely to misunderstand one another. (Machiavelli himself has no trouble misunderstanding Dante.) And it becomes even less bothersome when one reflects upon the slowness (thanks in large part to the Church) with which Machiavelli's actual writings were propagated in Europe as a whole and even in Italy.

Then finally, why should something like Machiavelli's rhetorical ethics of self-limitation not be available to post-Kantian writers, say to Rorty or Habermas, or for that matter to Nietzsche? In a sense, of course, the ethics of irony *is* a form of self-limitation. But it involves an element of communicative despair (with a corresponding defiance, "It is none of your business") that would have been entirely foreign to the character of a Leibniz or a Machiavelli. What keeps later writers from accepting the insufficiency of language-as-such with the same equanimity as their forebears? The mere fact that Kant devises for the *Critiques* a new and supposedly universal philosophical language, encompassing metaphysics and morals and everything in between, does not account for the historical difference between intellectual attitudes and rhetorical practices that I have marked with his name. People took Kant seriously, it is true, but not that seriously.

We have to recognize a broad epochal difference that establishes itself at more or less the same time as Kant's "critical" project. One cannot write like a Machiavelli or a Leibniz without having confidence in the existence of a large self-defining class of intellectual readers upon whom the ethical implications of one's rhetorical self-positioning will not be lost. Once that confidence vanishes, the ethics of rhetorical self-limitation, if it continues to operate at all, has automatically become ethics of irony, the condition of speaking cryptically into a diasporic void. But in the course of the eighteenth century, especially toward its end—with the fear of an enormous expansion of "knowledge" in the form of printed artifacts, with the regularization and regimentation of intellectuals in the form of university faculties, with the replacement of individual ethical self-limitation by institutional limitation in what came to be known as "disciplines"—the space in which a Leibnizian or Machiavellian temper might have developed was reduced to nothing.

Kant of course plays a considerable role in this historical process. Chad Wellmon points out with respect to knowledge in general—as John H. Smith had with respect to religion[10]—that Kant's project is fundamentally "ethical." But it is ethical only in a sense that is irreconcilably inimical to the rhetorical ethics that I claim had been practiced by the cream of European intellect in earlier centuries. His method is still a type of self-limitation, the saving of philosophy from a swamp of verbiage "by forming disciplined thinkers committed to the project of critique" (Wellmon 124). But self-limitation no longer means acceptance of the inevitable rhetorical relativizing of one's thought. It now means exactly the opposite, an uncompromising resistance *against* rhetoric, for "true philosophy, as Kant envisioned it, shunned the ornaments and excesses of rhetoric and relied instead on the immediacy of pure 'insight'" (131). Kant's "solution" to the problem of philosophy—"to detach his system from the printed text and tie it to reason itself, which he considered unencumbered by technologies and even space and time" (135)—was, strictly speaking, impossible. But the direction in which this ambition drove him was a clear indication of the advent of a new age, and an important element in the creation of that age.

And in that new age, in that atmosphere of new forms of intellectual qualification and new universities—not to mention the new political reality of developing modern nation-states—any lingering vestiges of old-style intellectuality would automatically take the form of ethics of irony. In Goethe, for example, who ironically claims to find "irony" even in Kant.[11] The only conceivable alternative to ethics of irony would be the organization of an actual society (necessarily a secret society) of old-style intellectuals, which is how Lessing, as far as we can tell, imagines his version of the Freemasons. But Lessing himself, we have seen, is already, in defiance of chronology, a practitioner of post-Kantian ironic ethics, which raises questions about exactly how we must understand his Masonic speculations.

Finally Machiavelli

The radical difference between languages in his political writings makes it relatively easy to analyze Machiavelli's rhetoric. But can we give any positive reason for his choosing, in the first place, to write at least two of his political works in disjoint languages? The corresponding question with respect to Leibniz is easily answered, since the impossibility of a single language for both metaphysics and morals is an integral element in his thought. But *The Prince* and the *Discourses* both treat the same basic subject matter. Why does Machiavelli not choose a single idiom for that subject?

In order to answer this question, we need to think about the real Machiavelli, as opposed to the rhetorical persona. It seems fairly clear, first of all—from the dedication of *The Prince* to Lorenzo de' Medici (the grandson, Duke of Urbino); from chapter 7 of that treatise, on Cesare Borgia, and the final impassioned chapter 26; and from other documents such as the "Discorso intorno alla nostra lingua"—that what Machiavelli desired personally in the political domain, above all, was a unified Italy free from all instances of subservience to foreign powers. If we take into account, further, the general republican tendency of the *Discourses*, plus the specific points made, for example, in Book One, chapters 10 (on founders and emperors) and 34 (on the Roman institution of the dictator), we might conjecture that he hoped for a strongman who would free Italy by force and then cede power to a republican government. And if we consider, finally, that from 1513 to 1519, Lorenzo was ruler of Florence while his uncle Giovanni de' Medici held power in

Rome as Pope Leo X, we might suspect Machiavelli of wishing that Lorenzo, by exploiting the Florence-Rome axis, would make himself that strongman.[12]

That dream did not come true; nor was there much chance of its coming true. In fact there is a passage by Machiavelli's friend Francesco Guicciardini, in a commentary on the *Discourses*, I.10, that reads like a mockery of his hopes for a strongman with a republican conscience:

> Of those [who have inherited tyrannical rule, let alone those who have imposed it] there are very few, perhaps none, who have let it go except under compulsion, which is not surprising because he who grows up in a tyranny has no eyes for recognizing what glory is to be attained by liberating the *patria* ... and no other reason can ever persuade him to abandon tyranny.[13]

At the end of the same article, Guicciardini makes the reference to Machiavelli even clearer by parodying the vocabulary of chapter 15 of *The Prince*. "Such ideas as this," he says, "that tyrants should give up tyranny ... are more easily depicted in books and in the imaginations of men than they are executed in reality" (Guicciardini 1:628).

Assuming that Guicciardini was right, we are once again faced with a puzzle. How could Machiavelli, the hard-headed political realist, possibly have nurtured such unrealizable hopes for the future? To answer this question, we must return to the idea that the price of cogency in any argument is recognition of strict limits upon the range of the idiom in which one is arguing. And we will also have to refine our notions of "realism" and "hope."

It is true that some facts are rhetorically invariant, retaining exactly the same truth value and exactly the same logical force no matter what idiom they are expressed in. For instance, pigs can't fly. But the proposition Guicciardini advances is of a different type: Even if Lorenzo de' Medici had freed and unified Italy by force of arms, it was still impossible that he should then be willing to cede power to a republican government, because people don't do things like that. This is not a simple statement of fact. It is a theorem, presumably derived from experience. But the validity of a theorem is always conditioned by the idiom in which it is stated. A theorem that is true in idiom X need not even have a meaningful equivalent in idiom Y. And my contention is that the idioms of *The Prince* and the *Discourses* are chosen in such a way that what Guicciardini later states as a theorem is valid in neither of them, and that the possibility of a Medici-dominated, Florentine-speaking republic of Italy is thus preserved in a kind of tacit suspension between them.

In *The Prince*, the idea of *la verità effettuale della cosa* implies the possibility of competing truths, which in a strong sense violates the very concept of truth, in much the same way that the volatility of the style thwarts any expectation we might have of an orderly unfolding of concepts. These qualities of the text create problems for a reader. But precisely in doing so, they also serve the important expressive purpose of suggesting an inherent disorderliness in the *cosa*, in politics, suggesting in fact the idea that everything is possible, that in the political domain there is nothing that cannot happen.

In other words—as modern fact-oriented people like us would put it—Machiavelli knows that his vision of a new Italy is impossible; or more precisely, he recognizes his inability to find or devise an idiom in which that vision can be made plausible. Therefore he proposes to Lorenzo the unification of Italy by force of arms in an idiom in which it at least cannot be shown to be impossible, an idiom which thus constitutes in its very nature an opportunity, an opening for action, which he hopes will be recognized. And by the time he is finished, he becomes enamored of his own procedure to the extent that, in chapter 26, he cannot resist simply laying most of his cards on the table.

But what about the second part of his vision, the foundation of an Italian republic, which is, if anything, even less possible than the first? Clearly the idiom of the *Discourses* comes into play here, an idiom in which, as in that of *The Prince*, the theoretical question of possibility is excluded. With respect to any proposed course in present-day politics, the only question that matters is whether a valid positive precedent for that course can be found in classical antiquity. There is still plenty of room for disagreement. Not only is the hermeneutic issue always present: is the ancient precedent being understood correctly? In addition, the very existence of the idiom is based on an assumption, that the ancient world is fundamentally superior to the modern world, which the Preface to Book Two admits is highly questionable. But no matter how much doubt or disagreement may arise, it remains the case that there is no rhetorical space available for a theoretical assertion of impossibility like the "*considerazione*" of Guicciardini mentioned above.

And if we ask how the construction of this second idiom is supposed to be of practical value in the realization of Machiavelli's hopes, it is clear—not only from the dedication of the *Discourses* to a couple of intellectual friends—that the aim is now not to influence directly the thinking of a future dictator. The *Discourses* are much more a learned work than *The Prince*; and it seems to me that their aim can only be to encourage the establishment of the idiom in which they are written as an accepted intellectual medium of communication, as a kind of general rhetorical atmosphere in which the future dictator must find himself when thinking about the possible uses of his power.

There is plenty of material in the *Discourses* that can be interpreted as specific advice for the eventual founder of an Italian republic. I have mentioned chapters 10 and 34 of Book One. Other obvious instances include: 1.6 (deciding on specific republican forms), 1.9 (one man as sole founder of a republic),1.18 (establishing freedom amid corruption), 1.55 (lack of equality an impediment to republics, especially in parts of Italy), 2.4 (how republics expand), 3.1 (republics' connection to their origins), 3.8 (importance of circumstances in shaping republican forms), 3.44 (the usefulness of sudden decision in achieving difficult ends). But more important to Machiavelli than these specifics is the establishment of a political idiom in which the notion of strict practical impossibility cannot arise, and in which the precedents for activity at once both republican and glorious are ineradicably present for all who participate.

Thus, finally, by considering the examples of Leibniz and Machiavelli together, we can form a sense for the range of possibilities encompassed by the idea of a pre-Kantian ethics of rhetorical self-limitation: from idioms or rhetorical systems that arise directly from metaphysical considerations to such as are conditioned entirely by transient political projects.

Chapter 7

WOOLF, BACHMANN, WITTIG: TOWARD A FEMINIST ETHICS

The idea of disjoint languages, hence possibly new-made languages, is suggestive for feminist theory, which recognizes that the asymmetrical power relation between genders in society and culture is entrenched in language, especially in European languages. A vague awareness of this perception moves people nowadays to say "Ms." instead of "Mrs." or "Miss," to avoid the term "man" in the meaning of "humanity," to say "he or she" or (at the height of barbarity) to use the genderless "they" as a singular. Nothing is accomplished by these gestures, except to show that one would be happy to do something useful if only one could. For the problems in language, from a feminist perspective, are much deeper-seated. Monique Wittig argues, for example, that the non-relativized speaker of modern European languages, the sole claimant to the powerful status of "total subject," is gendered male (*Straight Mind* 81). Thus Nietzsche's argument on the grammatical conditioning of life is given a feminist dimension—or is shown always to have had that dimension.[1] And thus feminism is faced with the problem of finding or creating language in a fundamentally new form. (I will discuss below the extent to which Wittig's use of the pronoun "elles" in *Les Guérillères* [see *Straight Mind* 84–7] manages this problem.)

Sex and Gender

Let us begin, on a simpler level, by being clear about what we mean by the terms "sex" and "gender" and by the concepts "sex difference" and "gender difference." Simone de Beauvoir says,

> One is not born, but rather becomes, woman. No biological, psychic, or economic destiny defines the figure that the human female takes on in society; it is civilization as a whole that elaborates this intermediary product between the male and the eunuch that is called feminine. Only the mediation of another can constitute an individual as an *Other*. (283)

What Beauvoir calls the civilized "elaboration" of one's *sex* at birth is what we designate as *gender*—or at least I will shape my terminology by this assumption.

But the distinction in this form does not work as neatly as one might wish. We can be fairly certain about assigning to sex, not gender, things like the type of reproductive organs and the arrangement of chromosomes possessed by a given individual. But how certain can we be about denying the influence of millennia of civilization upon secondary sexual characteristics, especially if we move beyond the physical to the psychic? The question of nature and nurture, among others, is raised here. Are my feelings about the sex of people who arouse my desire, and the sex to which I belong, strictly natural? One need not be either an advocate or an enemy of the imagined "homosexual agenda" to have doubts about whether the same-sex attraction that arises unprompted in many people might not have a long history, which at various points interacts with the history of civilization. And given the types of surgical and chemical intervention now available, there is good reason to question how stable the category of "sex" actually is, and to question the determinative power in our lives of a strict binary on the level of sex.

But on the level of gender, the strict binary male/female or masculine/feminine is present everywhere. We speak of variable "gender identity" in a social or cultural context. But in that context we have to mean: variable with respect to the male/female binary. When we speak of "gender-bending" we mean the distorting of just that binary. Indeed, once we step outside the domain of sex in the strict sense, once we have begun talking about culture or society in broad terms, how shall we even know that we are talking about "gender" in the first place if our discussion is not associated with the masculine/feminine binary? Gender, as opposed to sex, simply means that binary.

And gender difference is important because it is the location of a crucial structure of power relations, especially in Western societies. If I am a woman, I am not discriminated against because of the condition of my sex organs or my hormones or chromosomes. I am discriminated against because I have been assigned to a particular class, "woman," in the scheme of gender difference. Of course gay males are also objects of discrimination. But even here the binary male/female operates, because such discrimination is based either on a person's perceived failure to satisfy a specific cultural definition of "normal male" or else, in some cases, on a sense that the whole masculine/feminine power structure is being challenged.

And when I say "structure" I mean structure. The asymmetrical influence of gender difference upon the real lives of people in society is made possible by a structural peculiarity of that difference, which we can perhaps best understand by way of an analogy. The difference between "red" and "green" arises within the general category "color," which enables it to be understood with great clarity, and without which it cannot be understood at all. Gender difference, correspondingly, since it belongs to the domain of human civilization, tends to be thought of as arising within the general category "human." But "human" is not a general category in the same sense that "color" is; it does not occupy a position categorically superior to "masculine" and "feminine," as "color" does with respect to "red" and "green." For unless the evidence of etymology in European languages is completely misleading, the concept "human" is itself subject to gender difference, being gendered masculine. It follows that there is no strictly neutral or superior category within which to understand gender difference, or in other words: *gender difference is in a strong sense not available to the understanding.*

(One might perhaps speculate about whether a fully developed matriarchal society would produce a structure of gender-thinking tilted correspondingly by a feminine gendering of the concept "human." Or perhaps the whole category of gender would be missing in such a civilization. After all, nothing excludes the possibility of a perfectly serviceable language in which no noun, pronoun, or adjective bears a grammatical mark of gender.)

A great deal depends on how seriously one takes the genderedness of the "human." One might argue, at one end of the spectrum of possibilities, that the history of the word need have no effect on the *concept* of the human, that a perfectly neutral version of this concept arises from impartial observation of the well-defined class of creatures known as human beings. It is here that the distinction between sex and gender comes into play. For while it seems clear that the concept of the species is neutral with respect to the sexes, the corresponding proposition concerning the human and its genders is of a fundamentally different type. One cannot simply remake the concept of the human from observation, because there is no sufficiently detached point of view (as there is in the case of physical differences), no nonhuman point of view, from which to conduct one's observation. The concept of the human cannot be abstracted from its history, which is anything but neutral with respect to gender.

The response to this objection, let us say at the midpoint of the spectrum, is to accept history as a positive factor. In earlier centuries the human was confused with the masculine; but now our awareness of this confusion will have the effect, over time, of clearing it up, whereupon a purified and neutralized concept of the human must emerge. I do not see any way to refute this position directly. But if it were true that our concept of the human is becoming more complete, less gender-tilted, then it would follow that gender difference is in the process of becoming less resistant to the understanding, hence that practical measures necessary to correct the social imbalances caused by gender difference are becoming more clearly identifiable. And it does not seem to me that this is the case. It does not seem to me, for instance, that any progress at all has been made in the debate about whether or not feminism's ultimate goal should be simple equality for women in an existing power structure that has always favored men, or perhaps in some modified version of that power structure. Or what form that ultimate goal could possibly take if the existing power structure must simply be rejected.

In other words, I think gender difference is as unavailable to the understanding as it has ever been. And if I were forced to take a position, it would have to be that that condition is permanent, that the concept "human" is irreversibly gendered and consequently useless from a feminist point of view. (People who use "the human" as an ethical guide, in my view, however benign their views on specific feminist concerns, have not yet made the move that would qualify them as feminists.) This is the opposite end of the spectrum from where we started and is perhaps thus an extreme view. But what could a more moderate position possibly look like? Gender difference—unless I am completely mistaken about the conceptual structure in which it arises—is not merely misunderstood. It is altogether unavailable to the understanding, because the process by which such understanding would have to be achieved—the development of a "human" perspective upon it—is always itself enmeshed in it, always in its midst. Which means there is no path by which an understanding of it, and a mastery of its problems, might be arrived at. The only conceivable way to solve this problem—if one can even think of it as a problem—would be to establish a completely different form of gender difference, which would presuppose a complete remaking of civilization, or at the very least a language radically disjoined from all European languages in their present form.

Thus we have returned to our starting point, the importance for feminism of the idea of disjoint languages. And we have also returned to the question of the usefulness of the notion of the "human." In Chapter 1, we saw that an insistence on the "human" represents a retreat from crucial issues in discussing the possibility and the shape of a modern ethics. The same, it appears, is true with respect to the organizing of feminist thought. And as in the earlier case, we will approach the matter of feminism by discussing texts.

Have You Read *Orlando*?

The hook on which I propose to hang Virginia Woolf's contribution to feminist ethics is *Orlando*—in spite of its quality as a "joke" (*Diary* 3:177, March 22, 1928). And I will start with Woolf's "Preface" to the book and with the list of names it contains, fifty-three of living people if we include Leonard Woolf and the dedicatee Vita Sackville-West. The list, Woolf says, is of "friends" who "have helped [her] in writing this book" (*Orlando* 5) But from my point of view as a later or even a contemporary reader (even on October 11, 1928), it is a list of probably most of the people who have immediate access to the relatively intimate personal information that is alluded to in the "biography" proper, people, therefore, who in this sense (unlike me) can read the book understandingly. In order to approach their way of reading, I must use an annotated edition, which means that my reading is not "reading" at all, but a constant flipping back and forth between text and notes. Even if I take the trouble to study all that information until I can recognize it instantly when I come upon it in the text, still it remains for me mere information, not the direct knowledge or experience I imagine it must be for that privileged fifty or so.[2]

I can, of course, ignore the personal information that I would not normally have access to and content myself with as much of the needful general information, historical and otherwise, as I happen to possess. And having made this decision, I can read the text as a novel, by translating as much of it as I can into the kind of experience, the kind of generalized privacy, that most novel readers look for when they read. The experience that underlies and inhabits and informs the writing would thus become, as far as I am concerned, *my* experience, and would enable me to develop, in the strict sense, an aesthetic judgment of the text.

But *Orlando* strongly resists this kind of treatment by a reader. Its numerous Shandyesque structural elements—Laurence Sterne, though not among the living, is one of the "friends" cited in the Preface—make readerly empathy difficult. Especially the photographs, including the presumably sixteenth- or seventeenth-century photograph of a Russian princess (not of a painting of her), block the normal readerly process of internal quasi-visualization. The suspension of normal constraints upon time and human life provides more grist for the intellect than it does food for the imagination. And most important, Orlando's change of gender—not sex but *gender*, in the intense cultural complexity of this document—conflicts with even the bare minimum of world-like continuity normally required by a novel reader.

Gender difference, I have argued, is not available to the understanding. If I say, "I am a man, not an animal," what I mean, strictly speaking, is that I *am* after all an animal and so in a position to measure the qualities that make me human. When I say, "I am a man, not a god," I mean I am aware of what is godlike in me and so able to measure the insufficiencies that make me human. But when I say, "I am a man, not a woman," the idea that I am a woman has no place in my meaning; the "not" marks a gulf of emptiness beyond mere logical negation. (The same structure arises, but with a different emphasis, a kind of defiance, if I say, "I am a woman, not a man.") Orlando, however, seems exempt from this constraint. After the three sisters, Purity, Chastity, and Modesty, have been driven from the room by Truth, we read,

> Orlando had become a woman—there is no denying it. But in every other respect, Orlando remained precisely as he had been. The change of sex, though it altered their future, did nothing whatever to alter their identity. Their faces remained, as their portraits prove, practically the same. His memory—but in future we must, for convention's sake, say "her" for "his," and "she" for "he"—her memory then, went back through all the events of her past life without encountering any obstacle. (102–3)

Superficially this passage seems to contradict my point about the gulf of gender difference, but actually it confirms that point. The absence of any possibility of measuring (on the level of gender) the difference between being a man and being a woman is here represented by the simple and absurd absence of any difference. Woolf's text, on the wings of the plural "their," flutters aloft for a moment into the Unthinkable, and then returns resolutely to earth. Nothing *can* be said about the difference (in gender) between being a man and being a woman, and therefore nothing *shall* be said.

But wait a moment. Is it not precisely the business of the novel, at least since the nineteenth century, to say what cannot be said, to show what cannot be shown, to know what cannot be known? To throw open before us, to see from the inside, a subjectivity that is not our own? To master the simultaneous and to offer its elements to us in the form of immediate experience? Or else to offer something like the diametrical opposite of both simultaneity and experience, as in the section "Time Passes" of *To the Lighthouse*. At all events, to offer not reality itself, but an "essence of reality," always one step beyond the sayable, the visible, the knowable.[3]

That is my point exactly. The moment in which Orlando changes gender, and in which Woolf's text accepts the representational unavailability of gender difference, is the moment in which that text declares itself, once and for all, *not* a novel. Not a novel, but a biography, a biography, first of all, of Vita Sackville-West. And in the case of a biography, the division of readers into two classes, those who know or knew directly the person described and those who only learn about that person from the book, is perfectly normal. There is no need to imagine or perhaps somehow create a single generalized Reader who receives the text as personal experience and in doing so represents, ideally, every actual reader.[4] But when the biography is as cryptic as *Orlando* is, and when the fifty or so people who presumably possess the key to it are actually listed in the Preface, an ordinary or later reader may very likely, and very justifiably, have a sense of being excluded. Is there a way around this difficulty, or should we all simply give up on reading the book?

Understanding Orlando

The plot of *Orlando*—even biographies have plots—was summarized twenty-one years after its publication by a woman who had probably read it but was probably not thinking of it. I refer to Simone de Beauvoir and to a sentence of hers that I have already quoted, "One is not born, but rather becomes, woman." But whereas Beauvoir means what she says in a negative sense—one born as a member of the female sex is soon marked, or stigmatized or branded, as belonging to the feminine gender—Orlando's change of gender seems at least as much a liberation as an entrapment.

The plot of *Orlando* is: one is born a man, one only becomes a woman. The book has nothing to do with androgyny, and in its plot, the change of sex is a metaphor for change of gender, in the sense discussed above. One is born masculine, which is to say, the world into which one is born is gendered masculine (culturally and politically); and with a certain maturity, say at age 30 (*Orlando* 103), one becomes the representative of an alternative world that is gendered feminine—or in many cases, doubtless, one fails to become such. This is the shape of Orlando's life. It is also, I will suggest, Woolf's idea of the shape of European intellectual and literary history. And if we can assume that Orlando's son—of whom we hear nothing but that he is born—is an incarnation of (whom else?) Vita Sackville-West, then her life too is made to fit the pattern (born man, becomes woman) of gender change. (Much of *Orlando*, like much of *Tristram Shandy*, is thus taken up with preparing for the main character's birth, or one of her births.)[5]

The trouble with that alternative feminine-gendered world, which Woolf speaks of at some length in *A Room of One's Own*, is that one can never say exactly how it is constituted. If one pretended to define it, or dared to associate it with specific elements of personality or behavior, one would thereby have undertaken to put women in their place and so would have marked oneself clearly—even a woman would have marked herself clearly—as a representative of the masculine world of one's birth, as one who has never "become a woman" and so was never qualified to speak on the matter anyway.

Woolf herself, for all her eloquence, is not satisfied with the result of her attempt in *A Room* to illuminate an alternative feminine-gendered world. Even at the outset she distances herself from her own thinking—first by one and then by two Mary's. Apropos the more or less fictional novelist Mary Carmichael, she now writes,

> For if Chloe likes Olivia and Mary Carmichael knows how to express it she will light a torch in that vast chamber where nobody has yet been. It is all half lights and profound shadows like those serpentine caves where one goes with a candle peering up and down, not knowing where one is stepping. And I began to read the book again, and read how Chloe watched Olivia put a jar on a shelf and say how it was time to go home to her children. That is a sight that has never been seen since the world began, I exclaimed. And I watched too, very curiously. For I wanted to see how Mary Carmichael set to work to catch those unrecorded gestures, those unsaid or half-said words, which form themselves, no more palpably than the shadows of moths on the ceiling, when women are alone, unlit by the capricious and coloured light of the other sex. (*A Room of One's Own* 84)

But at the end of this passage—in which Olivia is also described as an "organism that has been under the shadow of the rock these million years" and now "feels the light fall on it" (85)—there is suddenly a retreat: "But alas, I had done what I had determined not to do; I had slipped unthinkingly into praise of my own sex." Assuming this sentence is not meant ironically, I think it is inaccurate. If the technical vocabulary had been available to her, Woolf would have accused herself here, correctly, of substituting sex (which characterizes individuals) for gender (which characterizes institutions). For although she has made some rather definite remarks on sex—for instance, "that a man is terribly hampered and partial in his knowledge of women, as a woman in her knowledge of men" (83)—still, in her final chapter, she is concerned almost exclusively with what she calls "the unity of the mind" (97), with the recognition that masculine and feminine, man and woman, do not exclude each other in the individual, that in the individual, in fact, they are combined "in a natural fusion" (98). When she insists on opposition between man and woman, or masculine and feminine, she is therefore talking gender, not sex.

Mary Carmichael's "vast chamber where nobody has yet been," therefore, that serpentine cave or alternative world, arises in the domain not of sex difference but of gender difference, where no words are adequate to describe it, or where the words that try to do so lose their footing and slip off the edge into the relative simplicity of sex difference. Here, in the strictly bifurcated domain of gender, is where in truth "whole flights of words would need to wing their way illegitimately into existence" (87) before a clear general description could be given of the feminine alternative. To put it more prosaically, such a description will never be given: for description itself, in the sense required here, belongs to the masculine world. Which means not the world of that half of the population that is born male, but rather a specific cultural situation in which "virility has ... become self-conscious" (101) to the point of insisting upon its dominance as gender. (We think perhaps of Nietzsche's ancient gods, who laugh themselves to death because one of them claims to be the only God.)[6]

Curiously enough, one of the major pre-twentieth-century British poets whom Woolf does *not* refer to somewhere in *A Room of One's Own* is the one who comes closest to naming the quality that distinguishes the world as gendered feminine. I mean William Blake and his assertion, beyond all possibility of justification, that "To Generalize is to be an Idiot To Particularize is the Alone Distinction of Merit—General Knowledges are those Knowledges that Idiots possess" (Blake 641). The world as gendered feminine is a world without the masculine power move of generalization, a world in which life is focused entirely on the "minute particulars" we hear of in *Jerusalem* (Blake 185, 205), or on those "Particulars" in which "Wisdom consists & Happiness too" (Blake 560).

But if this is the case, how shall we possibly hope to understand *Orlando*? Surely there can be no understanding without generalization. Surely X is not understood until its relation to some more firmly settled Y is described in terms supplied by a larger, more general category. The only type of writing that we might suppose is understood by a different process, a process closer in kind to one's own personal experience, one's experience of strict "particulars," is probably the novel. But *Orlando* is not a novel, and our predicament remains. And unless I am seriously mistaken, it is Woolf's predicament as well. For the Cambridge lectures that grew into *A Room of One's Own* were given very close to the birthing of *Orlando*, within a couple of weeks of "the present" on that book's last page. For this reason, and for reasons belonging to the texts, I cannot see how the concern with the problem of gender, and of the inaccessible world-as-gendered-feminine, in *A Room of One's Own*, is not Woolf's attempt to get at the material of *Orlando* from a different direction—in a manner less likely to be confused with fiction, albeit still, by the interposed Mary Beton, wedged away from the domain of simple theory.

I will not say that *A Room of One's Own* tries to understand *Orlando*. That gender difference is inaccessible to the understanding is certainly clear to Woolf, if perhaps not in the form of a theorem. And Orlando's change, again, is a change of gender, not sex. A spontaneous change of sex while asleep would cause consternation for anyone, even Orlando. But Orlando does not change sex. She slips, rather, from one world into another, from the world as gendered masculine into the world as gendered feminine. And since (apart from gender prejudice) there is after all only one world, the transition is gentle and untroubling. Our predicament, it is true, has not been resolved. Neither we nor Orlando can see the difference between worlds: for to "see" would be to understand, and the difference in question is not available to the understanding. Therefore, in *Orlando* itself, where the transition simply happens, there is no predicament. A second book is needed, and is supplied in *A Room of One's Own*, to bring into some sort of focus the predicament that *Orlando* had left behind in the very process (involving Purity, Chastity, Modesty, and Truth [99–102]) of arriving at it.

But what about the predicament itself? If understanding is not available as an option, how shall we position ourselves in dealing with *Orlando*? The obvious answer is that we need to follow Orlando and "become woman." But how do we proceed in detail? I think we can deal with this question more or less as we did with a comparable question raised in the work of late Nietzsche, where the option of understanding was also denied us: by asking after the implied "we." How shall we imagine the group of people who have found an adequate relation to *Orlando*? Obviously we cannot make use of generalization here. There can be no common characteristics by which we recognize such people. They can be joined by no common attitude or idea or "conviction" (in Nietzsche's sense). In fact, they cannot be known at all except one by one, by their proper names, which brings us back to the list in the Preface, which we now recognize forms a kind of gateway to the world as gendered feminine.

In principle of course, since what is required of us is a strict focus on particularity, any other list of proper names would have done just as well. But as soon as we permit this thought to enter our heads, the list itself has been supplanted by the principle of the list, and the gateway disappears. What is required of us, really, is a special kind of discipline, by which the generalizations that arise constantly in our mental life are constantly suppressed. A discipline like Nietzsche's ethical "method," a method which is nothing but itself, subject to no form of principle or regulation. An ethics that is what it is not by saying what it is, not by taking a position but by taking no position, by not saying, not knowing, not understanding, an ethics of irony.

But what does ethics in this form have to do with feminism? Is it a feminist ethics or is it simply the form taken for Woolf by a typical post-Kantian ethics? Specifically, where does the readerly discipline required by *Orlando* belong in history? Gender difference, as a cultural and institutional structure, is subject to historical change. But if gender difference as imagined in *Orlando* is historically variable, it becomes that much harder to deal with in detail.

The History of Writing

At least one way to approach these matters is by way of the hypothesis that *Orlando* and *A Room of One's Own* are sister texts. For much is implied about the history of writing (and by extension, it turns out, the history of gender) in *A Room*. Woolf says there of Jane Austen:

> Here was a woman about the year 1800 writing without hate, without bitterness, without fear, without protest, without preaching. That was how Shakespeare wrote, I thought, looking at *Antony and Cleopatra*; and when people compare

> Shakespeare and Jane Austen, they may mean that the minds of both had consumed all impediments; and for that reason we do not know Jane Austen and we do not know Shakespeare, and for that reason Jane Austen pervades every word that she wrote, and so does Shakespeare. (68)

But this consuming of all impediments happens differently in Shakespeare and in Austen. Woolf finds in Shakespeare an "incandescent" quality of mind (56–7), whereas Austen, she says, simply "devised a perfectly natural, shapely sentence proper for her own use and never departed from it. Thus, with less genius for writing than Charlotte Brontë, she got infinitely more said" (77).

And the manner in which she compassed her achievement, according to Woolf, did after all involve a kind of genius—genius, however, not as brilliance but as steadfastness and, above all, as "integrity." Innumerable nineteenth-century women's novels, says Woolf, were permitted to rot like so many apples by their authors' "deference to the opinion of others," meaning the opinion of men.

> But how impossible it must have been for them not to budge either to the right or to the left. What genius, what integrity it must have required in face of all that criticism, in the midst of that purely patriarchal society, to hold fast to the thing as they saw it without shrinking. Only Jane Austen did it and Emily Brontë. It is another feather, perhaps the finest, in their caps. They wrote as women write, not as men write. (74–5)

Still, "integrity" in this sense is not a specifically feminine quality. Woolf had in fact introduced the concept in connection with Tolstoy:

> Thus [by showing "the relation of human being to human being"] a novel starts in us all sorts of antagonistic and opposed emotions. Life conflicts with something that is not life .... The wonder is that any book so composed holds together for more than a year or two, or can possibly mean to the English reader what it means for the Russian or Chinese. But they do hold together occasionally very remarkably. And what holds them together in these rare instances of survival (I was thinking of *War and Peace*) is something that one calls integrity .... What one means by integrity, in the case of the novelist, is the conviction that he gives one that this is the truth .... One holds every phrase, every scene to the light as one reads—for Nature seems, very oddly, to have provided us with an inner light by which to judge of the novelist's integrity or disintegrity. (71–2)

Writing "as women write," therefore, means, in Jane Austen and Emily Brontë, a specifically feminine form of integrity, of creating the conviction that "this is the truth." And given the parallel with Nietzsche's ethical method suggested above, it is reasonable to see something like Nietzsche's "honesty" in Woolf's "integrity," the honesty of writing as who or what you are, "as women write" (in one case) or as a man of Tolstoy's background and experience must write (in the other).

In the age of Austen and Tolstoy, however, incandescence is nowhere to be found. Woolf does not say so explicitly, but it appears that what had been the highest possible virtue for a writer in Shakespeare's time is now no longer even a possibility, that its place has been taken by a quality, "integrity," which is much more widely shared, which can be found equally in the work of a woman without broad exposure to the world, without even much "genius for writing," and in the later work of "a young man living freely with this gipsy or with that great lady [like early Orlando!]; going to the wars; picking up unhindered and uncensored all that varied experience of human life" (71). Clearly something of great significance has changed between the two historical times. Clearly this historical change includes the coming into its own of the modern realist novel. And the connection with gender issues is made when Woolf discusses "the sentence that was current [among men] at the beginning of the nineteenth century" (76)—she gives an example from Hazlitt[7]—and then says,

> There is no reason to think that the form of the epic or of the poetic play suits a woman any more than the sentence suits her. But all the older forms of literature were hardened and set by the time she became a writer. The novel alone was young enough to be soft in her hands—another reason, perhaps, why she wrote novels. Yet who shall say ... that even this most pliable of all forms is rightly shaped for her use? No doubt we shall find her knocking that into shape for herself when she has the free use of her limbs; and providing some new vehicle, not necessarily in verse, for the poetry in her. (77)

Thus the development of the novel goes hand in hand with the arrival of women writers. And the "new vehicle" Woolf speaks of may even be a veiled reference to *Orlando*.

The gendered aspect of this historical development is brought out further by Woolf's parable of Shakespeare's "wonderfully gifted" hypothetical sister Judith (46). She had everything William had, says Woolf, except the male sex and a male's access to education. But nowhere is it suggested that there was anything feminine about her genius, that if she had been able to, she would have written "as women write." If she had managed somehow to educate herself—and if she had then perhaps masqueraded as a man and so evaded the clutches of Nick Greene (48), whom we know from *Orlando*—there is no reason to suppose that her work would not have had exactly the same "incandescent" quality as her brother's. How, in any case, could she possibly have written "as women write" in an age when practically no women wrote, or at least no women's writing was widely known?

What can we say, then, about Woolf's view of the history of writing, and about how that history is reflected or allegorized in the large historical life led by Orlando? And why is Orlando's change of gender situated where it is, vaguely enough, somewhere in the reign of Charles II? As far as I can make out, there was no uprising or invasion in Constantinople that might enable us to locate the event exactly. But if we are looking for an allegory of the history of writing, there is one extremely important event that happens in this period, around 1670: the beginning of Aphra Behn's career as a published and performed writer. Woolf pays homage to her in *A Room*.

> All women together ought to let flowers fall upon the tomb of Aphra Behn which is, most scandalously but rather appropriately, in Westminster Abbey, for it was she who earned them the right to speak their minds. (66)

Surely "to speak their minds" means to write "as women write." And surely the institution of this possibility in the practice of writing is an event not in the history of the sexes but in the history of gender, and is at least a crucial element of what is represented in Orlando's transformation. What is meant by masculine and feminine in culture is now profoundly altered. That opposition now unfolds in the entirely new arena of writing.

Ethics, Gender, and the Individual

Aphra Behn, for Woolf, is a marker in the history of writing just as Kant, in my argument, is a marker in the history of ethics. Neither of these figures affects history single-handedly; their work illuminates large historical processes in which they participated. But exactly what is the relation among the processes in question here? Are the history of writing, the history of ethics, and the history of gender simply three parallel developments in the shaping of modern Euro-America? Or are they intertwined with one another to an extent that would permit us to understand modern ethics of irony as a feminist ethics—by way of the example of Woolf's ethics of the particular—at least as plausibly as we might call it a Jewish ethics?

We cannot expect a simple direct answer to these questions. Here, as above, we are reduced to talking about specific instances in the form of texts. Our problem is similar in structure to the problem of gender difference. There is no separate elevated perspective from which to organize all the material that interests us. We seek rather, in the forest or mosaic or labyrinth of existing thought—that is, in the whole world that is given to us as writers and readers, the whole terrain of meaning as a possibility—a few specific pathways by which to think our way through some difficult problems, such as the impossibility of an adequate propositional ethics or the unavailability of gender difference to the understanding.

But let us begin by being clear about the general historical region we are looking at. Kant and Aphra Behn are not strictly parallel. Behn, in Woolf's view, stands at the beginning of an historical movement that reaches fruition only much later, in Jane Austen and Emily Brontë. Kant's work, on the other hand, as a fully developed propositional ethics based on reason alone, is itself the fruition of an historical movement which had begun long before, at least as early as Descartes: the establishment in philosophy of the modern "free" individual as the irreducible unit or atom of human existence—that individual who is constituted in experience by solitary reflection (later called "consciousness") and who is known technically as a "subject," the vessel, in turn, of "subjectivity." The period we are interested in thus includes most of the seventeenth century, all of the eighteenth, and extends into the nineteenth, that period in which the human individual is newly imagined as so thoroughly independent an entity that, for instance, his forming of societies can only be explained by positing a free contractual agreement on his part. (I say "his" advisedly—not "her" in the specific historical situation.)

Just this new free individual is the principal customer for a complete propositional ethics. How, without such an ethics, can he hope to regulate successfully his relations with others, since he can have no reason for confidence, other than propositional reasoning, that the ethical results of his own strictly private ruminations will find an echo in other minds? And conversely, it is only the individual in this new form who has any use for propositional ethics. At least this is so if my suggestion is accepted that in pre-Kantian intellectual Europe, the prevailing first move of rhetorical ethics is to recognize as fundamentally deficient any particular form of discourse, which implies in turn an intuition of precisely the ethical impossibility of a system of valid ethical propositions. I do not mean that specific ethical principles are not enunciated, or specific ethical questions not debated, before Kant. But for a writer like, say, Machiavelli or Leibniz, ethics presents itself as a task not so much for the individual as for the whole intellectual collective, in its conventions and practices and tacit understandings. It is less a problem for reason than a form for discussion, less matter than manners.

But what shall we say of the history of gender in this connection? Unless the etymological evidence is completely misleading, the asymmetrical structure of gender difference is much older than the eighteenth century, indeed so old that it seems impossible to assign its origin to any historical period. And yet, there is after all an important event in the history of gender that is associated with the coming of the new independent individual, an event which also belongs to the history of sex. I mean the shift, traced most comprehensively by Thomas Laqueur, from a one-sex to a two-sex model of human anatomy, the process by which

> the old model, in which men and women were arrayed according to their degree of metaphysical perfection, their vital heat, along an axis whose telos was male, gave way by the late eighteenth century to a new model of radical dimorphism, of biological divergence. An anatomy and physiology of divergence replaced a metaphysics of hierarchy in the representation of woman in relation to man. (Laqueur 5–6)

Prior to the period we are interested in, according to Laqueur, the female human body was regarded as an imperfect version of the fully realized human body, which is male. Now, in a change of attitude that has obvious resonances with the idea of the strictly independent individual, every human body has its own sex, either male or female, which is not subsumable under the other (now called "opposite") sex.

The crucial point here is that under the old model, gender difference and sex difference had exactly the same structure. The general human type (either etymological or anatomical) was understood as male, whereas the female was regarded as only subordinately or partially human. It follows that there was no reason to doubt one's ability to understand gender difference. One had simply to look at the human body, to see in the anatomical structure of sex difference a sufficient cause for the structure and nature of gender difference. But once the idea of sexual dimorphism takes hold, gender difference, as it were, is cut loose from sex difference and must be thought of (and justified, if at all) as a free-standing logical structure representing the cultural dimension of precisely that sex difference with whose basic shape it no longer has anything in common.

Nor would it be reasonable to expect the shape of gender difference to change, to adapt itself to the shape of sexual dimorphism. For gender difference, in its old asymmetrical form, is a principal intellectual justification, in Europe and elsewhere, for the whole culture of power relations, favoring men, in which we live to this day. The accepted idea of gender difference will therefore be much more resistant to overturning than that of sex difference, especially since, in the dawning age of independent individuals, there arrive large numbers of new ways for large swathes of the male population to enjoy their masculine privileges—as voters, for example, and property-owners. The result, as I have pointed out, is that we are now left with an idea of gender difference that is unavailable to the understanding, at least to the extent that understanding presupposes a point of view not governed by the difference needing to be understood—a point of view of the sort that had been provided earlier by the supposed irrefutable factualness of a convenient idea of sex difference.

And the importance of this change in how gender difference is regarded must not be underestimated. Without it, the whole idea of becoming woman—in Woolf's and Orlando's positive sense, not in Beauvoir's sense—could never have arisen. And becoming woman, in this sense, is the only possible alternative to "understanding" as an inaugural move in feminist thinking, hence the only possible inaugural move that does not undercut the whole project by presupposing an idea of the "human" that is gendered masculine. The same historical period in which the new individual or subject is born, and in which rhetorical ethics grows toward the possibility of an ethics of irony—under the pressure of an opposed movement toward propositional ethics, culminating in Kant—is therefore also the period in which modern feminism first becomes available as an intellectual commitment for individuals of either sex. Not that "becoming woman" is a matter of simple choice. It involves an inherently unconceptualizable abandonment or suppression of thinking by generalization, an embracing, somehow, of strict particularity. But it could not even have arisen in our intellectual horizon without the changes in sex and gender difference in the period we are talking about.

How deeply connected, then, are these more or less contemporary historical developments? And how deeply connected are they to the history of writing, especially as Woolf understands it, marked by the advent of the novel as a form, by the emergence of writing "as women write," and by the arrival, apparently, of "integrity," in place of "incandescence," as the perfection that writing aspires to?

Individuality, Writing, and Gender: The Case of Defoe

Again, these questions do not admit answers except in the form of instances. The instance I have in mind now is that of Defoe's last two novels, *Moll Flanders* and *Roxana*, as seen through the lens of a significant argument in Nancy Armstrong's *How Novels Think*. With an eye to Althusser's critique of Rousseau, Armstrong presents the idea of the modern independent individual in the form of a problem: "the modern state creates a contradiction within the subject between the ideology of free subjectivity and the fact of social subjection."[8] And this contradiction is insoluble unless one or both of its arguments—individual freedom and social authority—is drastically attenuated. Armstrong suggests:

> Bourgeois morality accomplishes this sleight of hand .... [It] distinguishes those passions and drives that serve the general good from those more likely to disrupt the social order. For the expressive individual [whose freedom, strictly construed, would make him a "bad subject"] to become a good subject, his desires must not only be strictly his; they must ultimately serve the general interest as well. (33)

But the assumptions needed to reconcile "strictly his" and not uniquely "his"— assumptions best understood, for Armstrong, in Althusser's critique of Rousseau— require endless, and endlessly tenuous rejustification.

There are basically two ways of approaching the problem. Rousseau's way, and that of a great many eighteenth- and nineteenth-century novels, is based on manipulation of the concept of "the human," about which we have learned to be skeptical. The other way, developed mainly in German idealist philosophy, involves a resolute surpassing of the concept of the human. How is individual freedom in the strictest possible sense to be reconciled with order or authority? The trick is supposedly accomplished by one of three concepts: reason, existence, or history. The free individual, for Kant, is at once both absolutely liberated and strictly governed by a moral regime, known as the categorical imperative, which resides not in his labile humanity but in reason itself. For Fichte, the very existence of the individual in a world requires the positing of a radically free act, essentially his act, of strict self-limitation. And for Hegel, the problem of the free individual is the motor and shaper of the whole history of mind (which is world history) and is resolved only at its culmination in a state of absolute knowledge.

But solutions of this type do not satisfy most of us any more than a doctrinaire Rousseauism would, or the sentimentalized idea of humanity in most ordinary novels. Thus our original dilemma, between freedom and authority, has been supplanted by a second: between philosophical ideas which we cannot genuinely believe in and novelistic fictions which receive whatever they have of genuineness only from the gesture of belief that we are induced (by other readers, as a rule) to make toward them.

This is where Defoe comes in. Crusoe, Armstrong points out, is a clear instance of the misfit or "bad subject" whose inclinations and impulses are disruptive with respect to any form of social authority. But his assertive individuality is also the source of the energy with which he mobilizes a "distinctive form of literacy" (35)—his ability as a planner, builder, administrator, politician—for the creation of an orderly commonwealth. Thus the problem of the individual might seem to have been solved.

> But such are the wages of his success in crossing over from the one category to the other that Crusoe loses the moral energy of the misfit as he becomes the exemplary citizen, so that his successful negotiation of contractual logic is his downfall in rhetorical terms. (36)

Actually, more is at stake here than just rhetoric. Crusoe and his island, we might say, turn out to be a kind of laboratory for demonstrating the strict insolubility of the problem that produces them. You can have either the misfit or the citizen, but not both at once.

Moll Flanders and *Roxana*, however, take the problem itself to a new level. The female autobiographers "identify the entrepreneurial energy of the bad subject with sexual energy: the power both to attract and to satisfy customers" (37). But unlike Crusoe, they thus "set themselves on a course that leads not to citizenship but in the other direction, to criminality and social exclusion." And the problem of the individual, in this form, has become not so much different as more fully itself, no longer subject to being outshone by the triumph of a misfit's taming. Moll and Roxana can never be anything but misfits, a fairly obvious fact to which Armstrong adds a dimension that is not obvious at all:

> Because neither heroine can incorporate the very features that got her to the point where she can offer the reader such a retrospective [the written text before us], neither achieves the wholeness and autonomy of a citizen subject. In each case, the narrative subject, or desirous individual, is completely at odds with the narrating subject, or citizen subject. (40-1)

Thus the basic problem of the individual is not only made more fully itself by being focused on women, but is also moved in the direction of *writing* as a problem.

And here Armstrong arrives at the main point of her presentation of Defoe, where the perfected form of the problem, in a sense, becomes its own solution. For,

> if, instead of sexuality, we think of writing as the addition that transforms her [Moll, but Roxana fits here as well] from a docile body into a misfit whose upward mobility, as marked by literacy, we can admire, then it suddenly becomes possible to imagine turning such a misfit into a self-governing subject. Writing can serve both purposes: to express the aspects of individuality that an unsatisfactory social position would suppress and to limit those excesses once they have found a satisfactory situation. (41-2)

This solution to the problem of the individual—if it is such—does not apply to the masculine narrative of *Robinson Crusoe*, where the protagonist's "distinctive form of literacy" (35) is already required *inside the fiction* in the building of his commonwealth. *Moll Flanders* and *Roxana*, by contrast, display the simple fact that no true solution to the dilemma of the free individual can ever be offered inside a cohesive fiction. In these books, the only possibility for leaping "the ontological gulf separating the bad subject from the exemplary citizen" (37) involves the strictly extra-fictional fact of the written text before us.

Is there really a solution here to the contradiction of free individuality? If there is, then it is certainly a solution that depends on gender. Mindful of Woolf, we are even tempted to suggest that Defoe's last two novels evince something like a definition of writing "as women write." Men's writing—represented for Woolf by an example from Hazlitt—is characterized by self-assurance and stability, which, in Armstrong's terms, means consonance between the narrative subject and the narrating subject—their combination, perhaps, in the absolute or total subject theorized by Wittig (*Straight Mind* 80–1). Where the one subject is "completely at odds" with the other, we might expect to find writing "as women write." Of course this expectation does not answer the question of whether a narrative subject *can*, in a strict sense, be "completely at odds" with its narrating subject.

But even without answers to our theoretical questions, we might still be inclined to recognize, in Defoe's choice of protagonists over time, an instance of "becoming woman" in the sense in which this idea is derivable from Woolf and *Orlando*. Becoming woman—abandoning a supposedly universal "we" in favor of a limited "we" less hampered in its quest for "integrity"—would then be yet another way of describing the achievement of a union of true freedom with valid authority. We would be thinking of something like an intellectual culture of strict particularity, subject to only one imperative: that the generalizing move of Aristotelian logic be either avoided or revoked at every turn.

Can it be argued, then, that only the concept of gender is of real use to us in finding our way beyond the contradiction of the free individual? Neither Woolf nor Armstrong would accept such an argument. Neither would I, if only for the reason that it could not help but be, itself, an argument in and on generalizations. But making an argument of that type has never been my intention. I am trying only to make more plausible, by way of the case of Defoe, my suggestion that the history of gender (the decoupling of sex difference and gender difference), the history of writing (including especially the advent of the novel), and the history of ethics (as driven toward the propositional, hence also toward irony, by the problem of free individuality) are all intertwined in a single historical unfolding. The question of whether or how the problem of free individuality is solved is probably in itself an idle question anyway.

An Ethics of Becoming: One Is Not Born a Jew

If we agree, provisionally, that the history of gender and the history of ethics belong together, that the same historical space is occupied by both the emergence of modern feminism as a possibility (in that gender difference is decoupled and catapulted beyond understanding) and the emergence of modern ethics of irony as a necessity (in that a long tradition of rhetorical ethics is driven underground), then we can form a fairly clear idea of what might be meant by a feminist ethics. Like the ethics of Nietzsche or Freud, it will be characterized by restriction to a specific but not theorizable "we," a "we," in this case, that is formed by the process of "becoming woman" as I have tried to read it out of *Orlando*.

The same problems arise here that we encountered in discussing other types of a modern ethical "we." There is, above all, no way of adjudicating anyone's claim to belong to a feminist "we," any claim to have "become woman" in the Orlandian sense—or, in other words, to have grown up historically—because the condition in question is subject to no form of general definition, reducible to nothing that for Nietzsche would be a conviction, for Freud a theoretical closure. We can perhaps come close to describing it by invoking the idea of strict particularity—as if this were not itself a general idea. In fact, the difference between the general and the particular is inaccessible to the understanding in exactly the same manner as gender difference. Any category under which that difference might be understood would have to be characterized precisely by generality and hence disqualified as a measure of difference.

But the feminist aspect of a modern post-rhetorical, non-propositional ethics, in the form of the idea of becoming woman, draws our attention to certain features of that ethics which might otherwise be lost sight of. First, the ethics in question is realized not in what one says or does, but entirely in what one *is*: in the present case "woman," in a sense that is never anything but historical, therefore plural, never a predicate of this or that individual. We recall Nietzsche's insistence that "*we ourselves,* we free spirits, are already a 'Revaluation of All Values,' an *incarnate* declaration of war and victory on all old concepts of 'true' and 'untrue'" (KSA 6:179). And the consequences of the idea of a Jewish ethics of absolute diaspora are basically the same. One's ethical situation is expressed solely in what one *is*, in the condition of perfect abandonment. But that condition does not operate as an individual's predicate. It cannot define an individual, which would create a context and so revoke the individual's abandonment. It exists solely as the property of an unreachable but still undeniable collective.

Or we might go yet a step further and ask whether the ethical condition—as free spirit or Jew or woman—can ever actually be achieved, whether it is not rather always at best in the situation of being approached, of "becoming." This question appears most clearly in Nietzsche's need to say, "we spirits who have *become free* ['wir *freigewordenen* Geister']" (KSA 6:208). For even if understanding is the ultimate impediment to freedom, still we cannot be free spirits simply by being empty-headed, by never having understood anything at all. The condition beyond understanding can never be anything but an object of unending approach. And if I am correct in suggesting that "woman," in *Orlando*, must operate historically, not as an individual predicate, then it follows, again, that my personal situation with respect to woman, regardless of my sex, can never be any more than "becoming."

Perhaps, in fact, we might want to speak in broad terms of the shaping of a modern ethics as a contest between the attempt to rescue propositional ethics and the acceptance of an *ethics of becoming*. Post-rhetorical non-propositional ethics is expressed not in what one says or does, but in what one is; it is an ethics of condition, not of action or opinion or conviction. But the condition in question—free spirit, Jew, woman—refuses to hold still for identification. If this were not so, then the ethics in question would be reducible to propositional form. This point is probably most difficult to grasp in the case of the Jews. The uniqueness of the Jews, their quality as an historical conundrum—in both Lessing's view and Freud's—is precisely their persistence, their identifiability as a people, in the diaspora. And both Lessing and Freud, accordingly, imagine an intermediate form of ethical operation for the Jews: for Lessing, the encouragement of a firm but critical commitment to one's particular cultural situation; for Freud, the prefiguring of a new type of intellectual class of lay analysts. But for both, ultimately—in Lessing's Nathan and Freud's Moses—the condition of being a Jew is aimed at the condition of absolute diaspora, hence at the practically unimaginable solitude of the wise or the great, a solitude that supersedes being or identity in the same way that the quality of the Jews as a people is superseded by the recognition now that, ethically, one is not born a Jew.

Doubt

The idea of "becoming woman" thus occupies a central place in the pattern of possibilities for a non-propositional modern ethics. And if the pattern itself is now about as complete as one could expect it to be, then the only task remaining is to show in more detail that that idea—becoming woman, in the positive sense—is as important in modern thought as I have suggested.

Woolf's version of the idea does not seem sufficient by itself. Becoming woman, for her—to judge from *A Room of One's Own*—means above all learning to *write* "as women write" (*Room* 74–5), which means learning to write not on the model of either Shakespeare's con fuoco (56–7) or Hazlitt's andante (76), but rather with "integrity" (72). That this quality, however, is no sooner named than it is found as applicable to male writers (Tolstoy) as to female writers (Austen, by implication from the negative remarks on Charlotte Brontë [73]) need not trouble us; the distinction between sex difference and gender difference leaves plenty of room for men here. But then we read further in *A Room*, to Chapter 6, where the sight of two people meeting and getting into a taxicab moves Mary Beton to begin thinking of "the unity of the mind" (97) and to speculate,

> If one is a man, still the woman part of the brain must have effect; and a woman also must have intercourse with the man in her. Coleridge perhaps meant this when he said that a great mind is androgynous. It is when this fusion takes place that the mind is fully fertilised and uses all its faculties. Perhaps a mind that is purely masculine cannot create, any more than a mind that is purely feminine, I thought. (98)

What has happened now to the idea of writing "as women write" or to the whole idea of becoming woman?

There is one fairly obvious way to rescue the cohesion of Woolf's thought here, at least on its surface. We must understand "becoming woman" not as an absolute desideratum but as a unique and unrepeatable historical move. Writing is a form of power; and as long as writing is men's sole province, woman is disfigured into "an odd monster ... made up by reading the historians first and the poets afterwards—a worm winged like an eagle; the spirit of life and beauty in a kitchen chopping up suet" (44). But now, in 1929, now that a tradition of women writers has finally established itself—in the wake, ultimately, of Aphra Behn—two separate centers of writerly power must be distinguished, masculine and feminine, and this situation can have consequences tending in opposite directions. On the one hand, "No age can ever have been as stridently sex-conscious as our own" (99); women's writing and men's writing tend each to become self-conscious and focused on maintaining distance from the other. But on the other hand, something like the "fusion" Woolf imagines in individual thinking has perhaps also become possible on a large cultural scale. The assumption of this possibility enables Woolf (no longer Mary Beton) to conclude by advising her listeners,

> that it is much more important to be oneself than anything else. Do not dream of influencing other people, I would say, if I knew how to make it sound exalted. Think of things in themselves. (111)

Power, after all, inevitably distorts perception. And if the operation of power (in writing) is inevitable, then only the fusion of opposing powers (masculine and feminine) can ever produce that condition of equilibrium in which we might, at last, think of "things in themselves."

The historical mission of writing "as women write" thus appears to be completed, for Woolf, by just that equilibrium. And if this is really how we have to read *A Room of One's Own*—if the absence of a more direct explanation of the history of writing does not signal some deep irony—then we have cause for disappointment. Becoming woman, in this case, would have nothing like the ethical significance of the interminable and indeterminate condition of becoming a free spirit or becoming a Jew; it would be merely a stage on the way to utopia. Indeed, we might have reason to doubt whether modern ethics includes a feminist component in the first place, however neat the pattern such a component might make.

If we wish to deal with this doubt, and in the process perhaps reassure ourselves about the integrity of the historical vision we thought we had derived from *Orlando*, we must proceed, as usual, by discussing instances.

Monique Wittig and the Limit of Revolution

Simone de Beauvoir's statement that "One is not born, but rather becomes, woman" offers an inadvertent but exact summary of the plot of *Orlando*—except that in

Woolf's book, becoming woman seems a liberation, not the relentless constraint Beauvoir is thinking of. And if Woolf is thus positioned in one possible direction from Beauvoir, Monique Wittig takes exactly the opposite direction. Beauvoir never questions the idea that the reproductive function defines women as a "natural group"[9] within the species. (And Woolf has said to women, "You must, of course, go on bearing children" [*Room* 113].) But Wittig, in the essay "One Is Not Born a Woman," her response to Beauvoir, invokes a "materialist feminist approach" (9) to argue that exactly the naturalness of women as a group is an ideological or social construct. Nor is this merely a theoretical point:

> A lesbian society pragmatically reveals that the division from men of which women have been the object is a political one and shows that we have been ideologically rebuilt into a "natural group." In the case of women, ideology goes far since our bodies as well as our minds are the product of this manipulation. We have been compelled in our bodies and in our minds to correspond, feature by feature, with the *idea* of nature that has been established for us. (9)

Why should the ability to reproduce be more suited as the definition of a "natural group," Wittig suggests, than, for example, the ability to wiggle one's ears?

"Lesbian society," for Wittig, is an effective answer to the oppression of women because it undermines society as a whole by attacking a bedrock notion, the supposedly natural heterosexual principle:

> For the category of sex is the product of a heterosexual society which imposes on women the rigid obligation of the reproduction of the "species," that is, the reproduction of heterosexual society. The compulsory reproduction of the "species" by women is the system of exploitation on which heterosexuality is economically based. (6)

The aim of lesbian society, and its effect, is thus not liberation but revolution.

> What is woman? Panic, general alarm for an active defense. Frankly, it is a problem that the lesbians do not have because of a change of perspective, and it would be incorrect to say that lesbians associate, make love, live with women, for "woman" has meaning only in heterosexual systems of thought and heterosexual economic systems. Lesbians are not women. (32)

The "panic" ignited by the question "What is woman?" is a result of what I have argued is the inaccessibility of gender difference to the understanding, or what would be the result if "straight" society actually paid attention. For gender difference as such, by refusing to be the same kind of difference as sex difference, is already an undermining of heterosexuality in its cultural dimensions. The revolutionary lesbian move thus rescues the integrity of the understanding by simply tearing down the whole heterosexual framework within which gender difference first arises as an object of interest.

But the lesbian revolution can never be fully successful. Lesbian society can never become society as a whole—Wittig acknowledges this point in a footnote (102)—if for no other reason than because a society whose heterosexual component has been completely eliminated cannot persist beyond one generation. The very idea of revolution thus generates an inherent limit for itself when its lesbian version is developed. And if we agree that the problem of the oppression of women is equivalent, in our culture, to the intractable problem of gender difference—which the understanding cannot even confront, let alone solve—then it follows, for Wittig, that nothing less than the lesbian revolution (against heterosexuality) can achieve women's liberty. Thus the oppression of women drives the very idea of revolution to an absolute limit, which is to say, the oppression of women represents a more fundamental social challenge than the condition of any other group.

The lesbian revolution is thus a great deal more than just a response to the question of reproduction. Nor is that question, as such (in Wittig's view), a unique determining factor with respect to the basic shape of heterosexual society, where it operates mainly as a device for controlling women politically and economically. "Lesbians," says Wittig, "are not women." Lesbian society requires more than that women, by having sex exclusively with women, exempt themselves from the obligation to reproduce. That lifestyle choice alone cannot possibly liberate women from all the other controlling mechanisms in heterosexual society.

But then what, or who, *are* lesbians in the revolutionary sense? And how, exactly, are they not women? As far as I can see, Wittig never raises this question in this form. But she does ask, "What then is heterosexuality?" (41). And the answer she offers has more to do with the history of philosophy than with the biology of reproduction. A lesbian reflection "on women's situation in history" requires that one "interrogate dialectics ... back to its originating locus ... back to Aristotle and Plato to comprehend how the categories of opposition that have shaped us were born" (49). For the heterosexual opposition masculine/feminine is not merely one opposition among others, not merely one instance of the universal dialectical character of Western thought. Wittig credits Claude Lévi-Strauss, writing on the exchange of women in *The Elementary Structures of Kinship*, with recognizing "heterosexuality not only as an institution but as *the* social contract" (43), with recognizing, therefore, that heterosexuality "has sneaked into dialectical thought (or thought of differences) as its main category." And where does this leave the lesbian revolutionary? If heterosexuality is as ingrained in our thinking as Aristotelian logic, then it follows that "even if they [women], if we, do not consent, we cannot think outside the mental categories of heterosexuality."

The lesbian revolution is thus not only uncompletable; it is inconceivable, because the very process of mental conception excludes it. But Wittig continues nevertheless:

> I will say that only by running away from their class can women achieve the social contract (that is, a new one), even if they have to do it like the fugitive serfs, one by one. We are doing it. Lesbians are runaways, fugitive slaves ....

> Is this mere utopia? Then I will stay with Socrates's view and also Glaucon's: If ultimately we are denied a new social order, which therefore can exist only in words, I will find it in myself. (45)[10]

Is this defiant assertion at all different from Rorty's recognition that we can never hope to manage the clash between politics and irony except as individuals, one by one, and his insistence that how I do it is "none of your business" (Rorty 91)? And what prevents us, then, from regarding Wittig's revolutionary lesbianism as an instance of ethics of irony? Our inability to say exactly who lesbians are is the same problem we have encountered repeatedly in discussing the ironic ethical "we," which is formed one individual at a time "like the fugitive serfs" and renounces all claim to universality. And surely "lesbian" for Wittig, in the sense of lesbian revolutionary—like "woman" in general for the Woolf of *Orlando*—can never designate what one is, but only what one becomes.

That move of defiance in the face of strict impossibility or self-contradiction is typical of Wittig. In "The Mark of Gender," she talks at considerable length about how, in her book *Les Guérillères*, the feminine plural pronoun *elles*, used insistently without antecedent, "establishes itself as a sovereign subject" (85). Which borders on nonsense, because the "shock" or "assault" on our sensibilities by which this purpose is meant to be carried out depends for its effect precisely on our assumption that the sovereign or "absolute" or "total" subject (80-1), whether grammatical or philosophical, is gendered masculine.

Subjectivity, in any case, is always a problem for revolutionary lesbianism, especially to the extent that it is recognized as arising in the Lacanian "symbolic order," the domain of language:

> Alas for us, the symbolic order partakes of the same reality as the political and economic order. There is a continuum in their reality [reality as asserted by "the straight mind"], a continuum where abstraction is imposed upon materiality and can shape the body as well as the mind of those it oppresses. (58)

It follows that the militant lesbian has no choice but to adopt a materialist position—as Wittig does in "One Is Not Born a Woman," juggling historical materialism (Marxism) and strict philosophical materialism—a position which denies outright the substantiality of the subject in its oppressive verbal matrix. But how can one possibly be a militant, how can one fight, without the ability to "constitute oneself as a subject (as opposed to an object of oppression)" (16)? Hence the contradiction:

> It is we who historically must undertake the task of defining the individual subject in materialist terms. This certainly seems to be an impossibility since materialism and subjectivity have always been mutually exclusive. Nevertheless, and rather than despairing of ever understanding, we must recognize the *need* to reach subjectivity. (19)

But exactly how any particular individual satisfies this need is obviously not predictable and, in any case, none of our business.

Secret Conversations

Wittig's version of feminist ethics seems both more extreme and more consistent than Woolf's. She admits the possibility that her thinking is utopian, but declares that if so, she will find her utopia strictly "in herself"—not in any hopeful interpretation of historical conditions like Woolf's apparent idea of a balance between masculine and feminine writing and the arrival of an age where at last we can "Think of things in themselves" (*Room* 111).

Or perhaps we should reconsider our reading of that passage in Woolf. She provides no explanation of the historical view she seems to be suggesting. We are left with nothing but the idea of thinking of things "in themselves," which is both an extremely simple and an extremely difficult idea. It had in fact already occurred earlier in the book, where Mary Beton reflects upon how her five hundred a year has dissolved her emotional narrowness:

> And ... by degrees fear and bitterness modified themselves into pity and toleration; and then in a year or two, pity and toleration went, and the greatest release of all came, which is freedom to think of things in themselves. That building, for example, do I like it or not? Is that picture beautiful or not? Is that in my opinion a good book or a bad? (39)

Things "in themselves," it is suggested here, are nothing but things that one views without considering the judgments, or prejudgments, of others. But how is the locution "things in themselves" justified by this definition, or those examples? Is the pleasure or displeasure given me by the sight of a building somehow "in" the building? Is beauty "in" the picture? Is my opinion "in" the book? Woolf is after all a writer. If she means the freedom to apply one's own tastes and prejudices in judging things, why does she not say so?

Or more generally, is it not true that to "think of" a thing means inescapably to measure that thing against categories that are not inherent in it, which produces a contradiction with the idea of "things in themselves"? Therefore the idea of "freedom to think of things in themselves" is meaningless—unless Woolf's choice of just those words is motivated by something more complex than meaning in the sense of reference: perhaps by something "exalted," as she herself suggests (111); perhaps by a materialism so extreme that it simply refuses to accept a categorical separation between the verbal medium and the material world it refers to, so that thinking of things "in themselves" would mean recognizing that thought is never anywhere but "in" its objects to begin with. Materialism in this form would perfect the contradiction with "subjectivity" that Wittig speaks of. Could it be just this contradiction, this impossibility, that is working in Woolf's mind when—at the climactic valedictory moment of her talk—she recommends thinking of "things in themselves" immediately after insisting on the value of subjectivity: "that it is much more important to be oneself than anything else" (111)?

As far as I can see, there is no way to develop these suggestions into an interpretive argument. An interpretive argument is probably out of the question anyway, since the thinking we would be trying to pin down is a thinking beyond the range of meaning, a thinking which Woolf, who is less militant than Wittig, does not attempt to approach more explicitly than by producing a disorienting absence of meaning in the clause "Think of things in themselves."

Wittig, on the other hand, with the benefit of a larger technical vocabulary, attempts to lay hold of the supersedure of meaning directly, at least from a negative direction:

> Every philosopher ... will tell us that without these precise categories of opposition (of difference), one cannot reason or think or, even better, that outside of them meaning cannot shape itself. (52)

But that "outside," outside the possibility of meaning, is exactly where Wittig positions the militant lesbian. Or again,

> In this ["straight"] thought, to reject the obligation of coitus ... would mean to reject the possibility of the constitution of the other and to reject the "symbolic order," to make the constitution of meaning impossible, without which no one can maintain an internal coherence. (28)

Which of course does *not* suggest erecting some form of lesbian thought in opposition to "straight" thought. The very category of opposition—which is presupposed by all meaning, by the whole "symbolic order"—belongs to straight thought. Lesbian thought, if it exists, operates beyond meaning, hence beyond opposition.

It is entirely possible, therefore, that Woolf and Wittig—without either one's knowing it—are conducting a kind of silent conversation over our heads, a conversation of the sort, for instance, that characterizes the diaspora of the wise. And there are other suggestive resonances between the two. I have commented on the manner in which the list of proper names in the Preface to *Orlando* affects our reading of the text. The same type of commentary—if different in content—is required by the separate pages containing lists of proper names that are inserted at random (as far as one can tell) among the pages of Wittig's *Les Guérillères*, lists of female given names, all printed in capitals, which appear to have no connection at all with the running narrative that their presence interrupts. Clearly those lists are connected in some manner to the "sovereign subject" *elles* which is insisted upon in the main text, perhaps by particularizing the reference of that pronoun but without embedding the particular individuals in the narrative, where the inevitable operation of meaning would confine them within an oppositional structure of predicates.[11] Woolf and Wittig thus share an attentiveness to the problem of the proper name and its usefulness in disrupting literary conventions.

And as with the idea of a supersedure of meaning, this recognition is important, but without actually helping in what might reasonably be called the interpretation of either writer.

Secret conversations such as we might surmise between Woolf and Wittig, with a feminist component, are important as signs of a feminist ethics which, like the other versions of modern ethics we have looked at, cannot be realized as propositions without losing precisely its ethical character. These conversations and this ethics, we might add, are not restricted to the twentieth century and beyond, nor are they the exclusive province of writers who happen to be women.[12] But feminist ethics does seem to be the form of modern ethics that has developed the closest relation to concrete social and political issues in the present day. For this reason—plus the difficulty of taking up Woolf's suggestions and tracing the historical awakening of feminist ethics in detail, which I leave for another day—I will conclude with the discussion of one further instance, a text which I think converses with both Woolf and Wittig in perhaps an unexpected manner.

Healing the World

The departure from genre conventions in Ingeborg Bachmann's *Malina* is not as obvious as in *Orlando* or *Les Guérillères*. The novel has a reasonably clear plot, unlike Wittig's book, and the events in the plot remain more or less plausible, at least until the very end. The narrator is an Austrian woman who has achieved enough stature as an author to be subjected to extended newspaper interviews. She shares an apartment in Vienna with a man named Malina, with whom she has apparently never had a sexual relationship, although it appears in the course of the narrative that he knows a great deal about her earlier life, including her sex life, in detail. The first main part of the story, "Happy with Ivan," is devoted mainly to her love affair with a Hungarian gentleman who works in the financial sector. And in the story as a whole, her life is suspended, so to speak, in a force field created by three male figures, Malina, Ivan, and her dead father, by whom she had been raped as a child, probably in reality but conceivably in her fantasy alone. This triangular structure is emphasized by the title of the second part, "The Third Man," which refers to the father and uses the allusion to the Graham Greene film to suggest the idea of an evil man presumed dead but in truth still living—in the narrator's mental and emotional life.

The plot, as I say, remains plausible throughout most of the book. But it repeatedly approaches implausibility in regard to the relation between Ivan and Malina—or rather the absence of a relation, the absence of any direct encounter at all, even though much of the narrator's affair with Ivan is conducted in her apartment, where Malina also lives. Malina certainly knows of Ivan. Not only must he constantly notice remnants of Ivan's visits—a second whiskey glass, an unfinished chess game, and so on—but he also has to put up with the stink of two cats now in residence,[13] which belong to Ivan's children and for the time being cannot stay with his estranged wife. And Ivan, for his part, is aware of Malina—how can he not be?—but as far as we can tell, only just barely aware. The one point in the book where he pronounces the name "Malina" (unless I have missed something) occurs during one of his chess games with the narrator, where we read:

> Ivan asks, out of the blue: Who is Malina?
> I can't answer that, we play on in silence, with wrinkled foreheads. (45/25)

It is almost as if Malina were an imaginary cotenant, not a real one; it is as if, for Ivan, Malina were nothing but an unattached name.

This possibility, to the extent that we entertain it as such, is reinforced by the narrator's account, in the novel's introductory section, of how she had become acquainted with Malina.

> Certainly I was *subordinate* to him from the beginning, and I must have known early on that he was destined to be my doom, that Malina's place was already occupied by Malina even before he entered my life. (14/15)

For years he had been a kind of ghostly presence for her: at an often used streetcar stop; at a lecture in Munich, where she had actually bumped into him, yet then had quickly lost sight of him (15–16/6); in the newspapers, where he is mentioned in accounts of his famous actress sister's funeral (16/6–7: but how does the narrator know at that point that the mysterious stranger's name is "Malina"?); as the topic of a "notorious, droll story concerning Malina and Frau Jordan" (18/7–8). At least two possibilities suggest themselves: that Malina does not exist at all, or that he is really the actress's brother, with whom the narrator forms an imaginary relationship. Especially the contrast with Ivan—whose lovemaking the narrator calls "injections of reality" (76/45 *et passim*)—brings out his imaginary quality, a quality that persists despite her invocation of "Malina for me today, no longer the product of rumors, but redeemed, sitting next to me or walking with me around the city" (18/8).

But on the other hand, there are any number of elements in the narrative that make it impossible to dismiss Malina as some kind of figment. To take only two examples, one purely physical, the other plot related: At one point, in the narrator's apartment, Ivan's children, Béla and András (the real results of his "injections of reality" deposited elsewhere!) "have now found Malina's and my shoes in the hall [and] stick their little feet inside and come wobbling in" (150–1/94), and later, when the narrator can no longer tolerate the friends she is staying with near Salzburg, she wires Malina and gets him to send her a fake emergency telegram calling her back to Vienna (174/109). How can we make any sense at all of what we are reading here if we do not assume Malina's reality?

Thus the narrative hovers uncomfortably between Malina as figment and Malina as reality. I do not mean that the narrated world is undermined or unbalanced by the question of whether or not Malina is real—which is the kind of thing that happens, say, in E. T. A. Hoffmann. The point is that in Bachmann's novel there is no single narrated "world" to begin with. There is, we might say, an unlimited multiplicity of worldlets, in which Malina exhibits conflicting degrees and modes of reality or phantasmality, and which succeed or supplant one another repeatedly as the narration moves forward. It is not a question of how the world is seen—by this or that character, or by us, through whatever fictional eyes—but rather we, as readers, never receive anything other than incompatible world fragments in the first place. What we might otherwise think of as "the" world is here simply broken into pieces. In a late conversation between the narrator and Malina, this point is acknowledged explicitly:

> Me: I'm still always wanting to spread myself too thin, to lose my self, to lose my way.
> Malina: What you want doesn't count any more. In the proper place you will have nothing more to want. There you will be yourself so much you'll be able to give up your self. It will be the first place where someone has healed the world. (330/208)

The narrator, after all, has always known that "the world is sick and doesn't want a healthy force to prevail" (35/18).

And the healing of the world that Malina speaks of is the content of the book's last scene. It is his day off from work, and the narrator, after clearing off the supper table, slips into the other room, collects all the letters and messages she has ever received from Ivan, and hides the bundle in the bottom drawer of her desk, which she locks stealthily. Then she returns to Malina.

> I sit down in the living room opposite Malina, he shuts his book and looks at me inquisitively.
> Are you finished?
> I nod, for I am finished. (352/222)[14]

Malina now demands coffee, which the narrator prepares and serves. Then,

> I stare at Malina resolutely, but he doesn't look up. I stand up, thinking that if he doesn't say something immediately, if he doesn't stop me, it will be murder, and since I can no longer say this I walk away .... I have walked over to the wall, I walk into the wall, holding my breath. I should have written a note: It wasn't Malina. But the wall opens, I am inside the wall, and Malina can only see the fissure we've been looking at for such a long time. He'll think I've left the room. (354/223)

But he thinks nothing of the kind. The phone rings and, while picking up the receiver, he begins destroying systematically every trace of the narrator's existence. "Hello!" he says into the phone, and then "coldly, impatiently, you've dialed the wrong number" (354/224).

The narrator is now inside the wall, "a very old wall, a very strong wall, from which no one can fall, which no one can break open, from which nothing can ever be heard again" (356/225). She not only ceases to exist, but Malina is now seeing to it that she ceases to *have* existed. The phone has rung a second time; we, Malina, and the narrator all know it is Ivan calling; and we have heard Malina's end of the conversation:

> I'm sorry?
> No?
> Then I didn't express myself clearly.
> There must be some mistake.
> The number is 723144.
> Yes, Ungargasse 6.
> No, there isn't.
> There is no woman here.
> I'm telling you, there was never anyone here by that name.
> No one else is here.
> My number is 723144.
> My name?
> Malina. (355–6/224)

This is the act, this destruction of her whole existence, including her past, that the narrator names "murder" in the book's last line (356/225).

But that murder is also a healing, most obviously with respect to Malina, who has now at last directly encountered and dismissed his rival Ivan. His ontologically uncertain condition, hovering between the real and the phantasmal, is now a thing of the past. He is now a single whole person; and his world, now freed from the narrator's constant clumsy self-questioning—or for that matter *our* world, now that we have finished reading the novel—has correspondingly been healed, closed its gaps (like the apartment wall, or like the now closed book), organized itself once more into a single coherent system worthy of the title "world." At most a crack, a "fissure" of doubt remains. But we have been watching that crack, dealing with that doubt, for years anyway, and it no longer worries us seriously.

Beyond Meaning

Of more interest to critical readers, however, is the relation between this still largely fictional state of affairs and the status of the actual text we have been dealing with. What happens at the novel's conclusion is the exact opposite of what is called the "naturalizing" of a fictional text. When we read an epistolary novel, the text we have in our hands is substantially identical to a document that exists inside the fictional world and so forms a bridge, a "natural relation," between that world and our own. But at the end of *Malina*, the real world—which we share, presumably, with Ivan and with Malina, each now the sole proprietor of his apartment—has been healed, which means that all contact with the world of the fictional text we have been reading has been severed. An impenetrable barrier has been erected between the two worlds. A fictional barrier, it is true, but one that corresponds, after all, to the difference between what we imagine while reading and what our physical senses receive as reality.

And the insistence upon this barrier, in turn, denies to the fictional text what we would ordinarily understand as its *meaning*. Even if we restrict ourselves to the purely emotional, to the idea of meaning as an involuntary positive or negative feeling with respect to this or that suggestion in the text, we are still imagining a form of direct commerce between that text and the real world in which we are doing our reading. And how much richer must that commerce be if it involves social or philosophical ideas about our world—that commerce which the end of *Malina* insists has been broken off, rendered impossible? Again, the insistence in question is itself fictional, hence an instance of exactly the kind of meaning it denies. And it is true that no one can in any reasonable sense have "read" the book without attaching meaning to the text. But what the end of the novel actually does is point us toward a drastic critique of this reading process, toward the question of whether the presupposed commerce of meaning, between text and world, ever really happens. And it is clear that if such questioning is pursued far enough, if it insists strongly enough upon the categorical difference between the notions of "world" and "text," the answer will be no.

The impenetrable barrier created by the narrator's "murder" therefore does after all exist in reality; and in reality, therefore, the whole text we have been reading is exposed as meaningless, or meaning-free. At two significant points in the novel, the motif of a writer's wastebasket is introduced. Early on, we read of an "artistic" mess in the narrator's wastebasket (111/69), which suggests the jumble of different forms of text through which we have been reading. And at the story's end, that same wastebasket is where Malina gets rid of the narrator's whole existence, including her very eyes (355/224). The suggested inference is that the entire book might be dismissed as the contents of a wastebasket, that what we have been reading (and supposedly understanding) are not really connected words, not words producing a meaning, but rather discarded words, words connected to nothing, words as mere objects. Indeed, once again, a strong argument could be made that mere objects (ink-traces) are what the book's words actually are in truth, an argument toward which the narrated fiction gestures strongly and so, like its narrator, gestures itself out of existence.

This production of a meaning-free text, finally—or perhaps more exactly, this use of literary meaning to strive beyond meaning—is both the vehicle and the substance of what I claim can be understood as Bachmann's secret conversation with Woolf and Wittig, a conversation involving the fictional operation of *Malina*, the surreptitiously cryptic sentence "Think of things in themselves," and the radicality of *Les Guérillères* as viewed through the lens of Wittig's essays. And even in Bachmann's case, I think we can say that it is a feminist conversation. The healed world at the end of *Malina*—*our* world, as I have said, outside the now closed covers of the book—is a man's world. It is Ivan's world (as it has always been, for his anagrammatical naïveté), and it is a world able to contain Malina's newly completed reality. That the center of this world is formed by a conflict—between, say, the "naïve" (German *naiv* = Ivan) on one hand and the "animal" or "malign" on the other—need not trouble us. Precisely conflict, clarity of opposition (we recall Wittig on this point), characterizes the heterosexual or essentially masculine world, as opposed to that nowhere where an infinitely self-critical feminine intellect strives to lay hold of things in themselves.

Nor does the ethical character of this conversation appear to be lost on Bachmann. We know that the narrator of *Malina* holds a doctorate in philosophy, summa cum laude, and we hear over and over again about the books in her personal library and their loss or destruction. The last such reference, the last visible pinnacle of a sinking ship, immediately following a quotation from Kant's *Critique of Pure Reason*,[15] reads, "I'm also sulking because I no longer have all my books, whether it be the moral sense of Hutcheson or even of Shaftesbury" (340/214), which brings us back to our own beginning, with Strawson's nostalgia for eighteenth-century moral sentiments. But the ship finishes sinking. Moral sentiments will no longer do the job. If ethics is to continue at all, it will do so only in the form of Wittgensteinian or Nietzschean irony or in the form of a feminist reaching beyond the knowable, beyond the thinkable, beyond meaning.

CONCLUSION

Is a "Conclusion" to this book appropriate? I have said that what I am talking about cannot be gotten at except by way of the instances I have discussed in detail. But still, the interpretive arguments I have made can all be used to support a conclusion something like this: *European intellectual history since the Middle Ages has produced, from generation to generation, an elite group of thinkers whose basic ethical stance is that of strict rhetorical relativism, the recognition—ingrained in their practice, not set forth in propositions—that language-as-such is inherently insufficient, that one has no choice but to employ* disjoint languages *for different areas of concern; thus the recognition that there can never be a single master discourse of the intellect. In the post-Enlightenment age, however, in which mass education, mass communications, parliamentary government, social sciences, and school philosophy all rest on the presumption of a master discourse—whence the need for an ethics of propositions—there has been no acknowledged public place for that relativist elite. Its ethical stance, consequently, to the extent that it still exists, takes the form of an ethics of irony.*

But does this conclusion make any difference? Surely that ethics of irony, if it exists at all, is doomed henceforward to obscurity and eventually to extinction. And yet, if the argument of Chapter 7 holds, there is a corollary conclusion that may make a great deal of difference: *That feminism—far from being the new departure in philosophical and social thought which many of its strongest advocates consider it—is in truth a culminating instance of the long history of rhetorical ethics in the West; that feminism will likely occasion a uniquely significant intersection of rhetorical ethics with public life in the twenty-first century; that feminism, in this sense, may perhaps be regarded as the destiny of Western ethics.*

One problem with these ideas—and with a possible comparable situating of diasporic Jewish ethics—is that they have not been supported by nearly enough textual material. But there is another problem, which cannot be met by simply writing more books. The conclusions I have suggested require, in order to be stated, a point of view from which the question of rhetorical relativism can be surveyed, hence a non-relativized point of view which presupposes a master discourse and so in effect denies validity to precisely the ethical attitude for whose sake it has been adopted. In one of Kafka's well-known stories, "Investigations of a Dog," the canine narrator spends his life working on the unanswered questions of dogdom. Every human reader of the story quickly discovers the key to all those dog-puzzles: dogs doing balancing tricks which seem to produce music out of nowhere; physically unimposing dogs who fly through the air; especially the appearance of food, sometimes on the ground, sometimes coming down from above. Evidently the narrator, perhaps along with his fellow dogs, has developed a perceptive mechanism by which human beings are simply erased, those human beings who play the circus music, who carry some pampered dogs in their arms, and who supply the food, either by leaving it or by tossing or handing it down. Taking seriously the conclusion I suggested above places readers in exactly the dog narrator's situation. In the very act of professing interest in an ethics of irony, or of strict particularity, they will in a sense have excluded exactly that ethics from the range of conceivable intellectual practices.[1]

I cannot see any logical way out of this paradox. And I cannot see any way of refuting the suggestion that its presence might well affect my argument as a whole. I conceded earlier, in Chapter 6, that ethics of irony is unsatisfactory as an idea, and I may now have to make a similar concession about the conclusion formulated above. But as I said with respect to the idea of an ethics of irony, I still think that that conclusion, along with the interpretive arguments on which it is based, is the best we can do, or at least a good candidate for the best we can do. One clear implication of Wittgenstein's lecture, in any case, is that a fully satisfactory argument on ethical matters is too much to hope for.

Still, even the instances I have adduced, considered strictly as instances, create problems. In order to make it probable that certain texts exemplify ethics of irony, I have conducted a number of "close readings"—probably better described as *deep readings*—readings that attempt to penetrate beneath what the surface of the text might be expected to offer a relatively casual reader. And at this point a critical reader could suspect my procedure of *petitio principii*. For a deep reading cannot be undertaken without presupposing that its text operates on a level "beneath" the surface, which is to say that it operates ironically. The method of reading thus presupposes the conclusion at which the reading is aimed, at least in some important cases.

I will not pretend to refute this objection. But I think the matter requires clarification, because what is actually being done in close (or deep) reading is not generally understood. Close reading is often associated with New Criticism. And since both of these critical practices are associated strongly with the United States, their detractors (including their American detractors) typically find that they lack breadth and sophistication. New Criticism is often accused of being ahistorical and politically naïve.[2] And Franco Moretti, the prophet of "distant reading," has this to say about close reading:

> The United States is the country of close reading, so I don't expect this idea to be particularly popular [in the U.S.]. But the trouble with close reading (in all of its incarnations, from the new criticism to deconstruction) is that it necessarily depends on an extremely small canon. This may have become an unconscious and invisible premise by now, but it is an iron one nonetheless: you invest so

much in individual texts *only* if you think that very few of them really matter. Otherwise it doesn't make sense .... At bottom, it's a theological exercise—very solemn treatment of very few texts taken very seriously. (Moretti 48)

At the risk of sounding American, I think Moretti is wrong. Close reading is neither quasi-theological exegesis nor *explication de texte*. In fact, paradoxical as it may sound, the identity of the particular text under scrutiny in close reading does not matter much.

Close reading, at its best, is always *an experiment with the acknowledged conventions of reading*. You cannot even begin to read until you agree to observe a system of conventions, according to which you exclude certain features of the text from consideration (e.g., usually, the size of the type) and always take account of certain other features (e.g., ordinarily, the dictionary meaning of words). The complete system of such conventions at any particular time in any given culture is very extensive and complex. But it is worth thinking about, because it produces a measure of precision concerning what is meant by a text's "surface." This idea, in actual practice, refers not to any more or less objective feature of the text, but rather to a *reading* of the text in which, as far as possible, all applicable conventions are strictly observed. A deep reading or close reading, by contrast, means in my view a reading *that experiments with the nonobservance of certain conventions elsewhere considered indispensable*. Such readings are necessarily experimental, for the nonobservance of an important convention will usually produce gibberish. But wherever such a reduction to gibberish does *not* occur, it follows that the convention itself has been subjected to a valid critique, that it has been shown to be nonessential. And this showing, in my opinion, when it is made successfully, is the *raison d'être* of close reading.

One obvious instance of the nonobservance of a reading convention, the instance that will occur to most Americans, is the one codified by Wimsatt and Beardsley in "The Intentional Fallacy." Moves had been made earlier toward challenging the idea that in reading we must always be guided by a plausible understanding (if possible, by a documentable understanding) of the author's personal intention in writing. Schleiermacher's hermeneutics, and Dilthey's, are already willing to dispense with intention as a touchstone. But American thinking in the immediate postwar period, and the practice of the American New Critics, does most to establish this challenge as a principle—a principle upon which, for instance, all subsequent deconstructive and ideological criticism is founded. Without this principle, in fact, it would be hard to imagine the development of those habits of mind—of a general willingness to "focus on units that are much smaller or much larger than the text: devices, themes, tropes—or genres and systems" (Moretti 48-9)—that make it possible for precisely the idea of "distant reading" to resonate in the literary community.

Close reading and its supposed opposite, "distant reading," are therefore natural allies in the intellectual world, if not indeed two sides of the same coin. The present book provides an instance for this suggestion. In the close readings I have carried out, one convention that is challenged (by being experimentally dispensed with) can be formulated thus: In reading two or more texts that are closely related by history or culture, and especially in reading different texts of a single author, we are entitled to assume that on some level those texts share a common idiom, a common intellectual language. I have tried to show, by producing readings that make sense, that that convention can be dispensed with.

But even if it is granted, this point does not necessarily imply that the convention in question *is* dispensed with in the cases we are speaking of, or in other words, that the texts are characterized by strict rhetorical relativism. (My readings may make sense, but they could still be wrong.) And still less are we compelled logically to accept my historical suggestion: that in European intellectual history through the eighteenth century, strict rhetorical relativism, the firm denial of any claim to the standing of a master discourse in matters with a philosophical dimension, is the insignia of a relatively constant intellectual elite. But this suggestion does establish a relation to the domain of distant reading, because it is conceivable that a statistical method could be devised to measure degrees of disjunction between the idioms employed in different texts and so to produce a map showing, for a large number of writers, the extent to which a master discourse is or is not presupposed in the work of each. My argument as a whole could be strongly supported by such a procedure. Or alternatively, the existence of the elite I have spoken of could be rendered highly doubtful, forcing me to change my mind—which, heaven knows, as someone who is prone to making ambitious claims, I have had to do often enough in my time.

But even in the unfortunate latter case, the point I am making now would still stand: that close reading is indispensable in the serious study of texts, that it is not merely a luxury which enables us to wallow aesthetically in a secular substitute for religion. The question of the presence or absence of a master discourse is more than just an aesthetic matter. And how would we ever even get to that question without close reading, without an experiment in the nonobservance of post-Kantian reading conventions?

It is true that none of what I have said here refutes the objection that irony, or something akin to it, is always presupposed by the technique of close reading, and that my argument therefore cannot claim to demonstrate conclusively the operation of an ethics of irony in any author or text. But at least I am now relieved of what might have been seen as an obligation to avoid close reading. And the attention of present readers can now be focused on whether the pattern of parallels and echoes and "secret conversations" I have insisted upon is sufficiently persuasive to carry the rest of my argument.

The only questions that remain, as far as I can see, concern real-world implications of the ideas I have proposed. On the matter of politics, we might start with another story of Kafka, "The Judgment," which consists mainly of a verbal duel between Georg Bendemann and his father, a duel which the father wins by talking nonsense and contradictions while Georg struggles to arrive at basic facts and to conduct a reasonable discussion of them. The story was written in 1912. If it had been written twenty-one or twenty-two years later, we should have had no trouble recognizing in it an allegory of the operation of totalitarian propaganda, which, in both the Nazi and the Soviet version, revels in contradictions and in the denial of well-known facts, and exploits precisely the relative rationality of its audience as a device by which to exercise control, as the father controls Georg's final suicidal actions.

The exact mechanism behind such control is still a matter of dispute. But it is a matter to which I have devoted some effort;[3] and my view, in the terminology of the present book, runs thus: Your susceptibility to totalitarian propaganda, hence your availability as part of an acquiescent populace under totalitarian rule, depends on the extent to which you are invested in the idea of a master discourse, the extent to which you are convinced that such a discourse either obtains or is achievable, or is at least desirable. The question of understanding is crucial. A strict rhetorical relativist, accustomed to operating amid an unsurveyable diversity of disjoint languages, will find the very notion of understanding infected with irremediable doubt. But a strong investment in the idea of a master discourse ordinarily brings with it a strong positive conception of understanding, because if a master discourse is assumed, there can be in principle no insuperable impediment to the understanding by any individual of any utterance. The method of Schleiermacher's hermeneutics, for instance, while it can be laborious and depends on a certain "art" in its user, must inevitably approach ever more closely the condition of knowing everything there is to know about its target utterance. And the implicitly postulated master discourse in Kant's "critical" thought has the effect of supporting a demonstration, if not of actual communication, at least of our right to assume the full communicability of certain crucial feelings and thoughts.[4]

The question of whether a master discourse exists or obtains in actuality is inherently undecidable. And the question of whether it pays to be invested in the idea of a master discourse might therefore seem to lack any special reason for being asked. But the association of the idea of a master discourse with a commitment to understanding changes the equation. For in a world characterized by mass communications media and a more or less participatory politics, understanding has the tendency to become in public what it is for Nietzsche in private, a trap. The need to understand is greatest when we are confronted with utterances that have a claim to authority, paternal utterances in Kafka, government and political-party utterances in the public realm. (Even the statements and actions of a party or regime one rejects need first to be understood in order to be dealt with.) And totalitarian propaganda, by arbitrarily thwarting the understanding at every turn, creates an intellectual confusion that threatens to make unwilling and often unwitting allies of even the originally most liberal partisans of a master discourse; they are trapped by the unfulfillable need to understand. The situation is more complicated than this sketch of it; the history of aesthetics, for instance, needs to be considered.[5] But it is still clear that ethics of irony, as the heir to a humanist tradition of strict rhetorical relativism, is an important element of resistance against the totalitarian tendency in our civilization that Hannah Arendt, especially, calls attention to.

Finally, what about the sphere of private personal actions in one's relations with other people, the sphere we normally think of as that of ethics? If the possibility of a propositional ethics is excluded, then it follows that every serious ethical decision must be made *ad hoc*, that having decided one way today does not oblige me to decide the same way tomorrow in a similar situation—or even in an apparently identical situation, since the difference between today and tomorrow is never negligible. We have recognized, I think, only one possible criterion that is generally applicable in the decisions of an ethical ironist: the criterion of strict honesty with respect to what one oneself is actually doing in making one's decision. This does not mean honesty about what one feels, or what one instinctively prefers. (Ethics, again, is a method; it requires discipline, not self-indulgence. Strawson's moral sentiments will play no determining role in the decisions of an ethical ironist.) The honesty we are talking about involves not only both ruthless criticism (to expunge all self-flattery) and iron resolve (without which one is not "doing" anything to begin with), but lacks, in addition, any extrinsic guide by which to orient itself. We have observed one case in which two thinkers arrive at exactly the same ethical crossroads and, using exactly the same criterion of strict self-honesty, make opposite decisions, Rorty's in favor of ethical consistency, Habermas's in favor of political consistency.

There is no general framework within which to organize our expectations with respect to ethics of irony, or any form of rhetorical or non-propositional ethics. The project on which such an ethics is founded can be as expansive and fluid as Leibniz's universal conversation, or as rigid and specific as Machiavelli's political goal. The ethical attitude can be frankly megalomaniac like Nietzsche's, covertly megalomaniac like Freud's, or, we might say, modestly megalomaniac like Wittig's. Or simply modest, like Bachmann's. Or perhaps complicatedly modest in the case of Woolf, whose admonition to her listeners we may have to reinterpret yet once more:

> that it is much more important to be oneself than anything else. Do not dream of influencing other people, I would say, if I knew how to make it sound exalted. Think of things in themselves. (*Room* 111)

Perhaps being oneself has nothing to do with subjectivity. Perhaps it means nothing but being strictly honest about what one is actually doing, which requires above all discipline and method, discipline and method perhaps to the point where one has ceased altogether to be a Kantian subject and things have no alternative but to be in themselves after all.

NOTES

Preliminary Remarks

1 Further citations give the translation page and the original page only, as "47/57."
2 For a recent discussion of this method, see the following essays in the ADE and ADFL bulletins: John Guillory, "Close Reading: Prologue and Epilogue," *ADE Bulletin* 149 (2010), 8–14; Jane Gallop, "Close Reading in 2009," 15–19; Jonathan Culler, "The Closeness of Close Reading," 20–5. The same essays appear, in reverse order, in *ADFL Bulletin* 41, no. 3 (2011), 8–25. A more or less canonical treatment of the matter of paraphrase is Cleanth Brooks, "The Heresy of Paraphrase," in his *The Well Wrought Urn: Studies in the Structure of Poetry* (New York: Harcourt, Brace, 1947), 192–214.

Chapter 1

1 Martin Blumenthal-Barby, *Inconceivable Effects: Ethics through Twentieth-Century German Literature, Thought, and Film* (Ithaca, NY: Cornell UP, 2013), especially the "Prologue," ix–xxxi.
2 The three quoted phrases in this sentence are all from Attridge as cited by Blumenthal-Barby. The first is from Derek Attridge, "Miller's Tale," in *The J. Hillis Miller Reader*, ed. Julian Wolfreys (Stanford, CA: Stanford UP, 2005), 80; the second and third are from Attridge, "Ethical Modernism: Servants as Others in J.M. Coetzee's Early Fiction," *Poetics Today* 25, no. 4 (2004), 669, 654.
3 See also Attridge, "Ethical Modernism," 655, 669, 670.
4 For a fairly complete discussion of this question, see my *The Dark Side of Literacy: Literature and Learning Not to Read* (New York: Fordham UP, 2008), 12–17. Stanley Corngold argues cogently "that we never read for a first time" in his essay "The Curtain Half Drawn: Prereading in Flaubert and Kafka," in *The Comparative Perspective on Literature: Approaches to Theory and Practice*, eds. Clayton Koelb and Susan Noakes (Ithaca, NY: Cornell UP, 1988), 263.
5 See Julia Kristeva, Σημειωτική: *Recherches pour une sémanalyse* (Paris: Seuil, 1969), 84–5 and the references on p. 316.
6 On aesthetics and totalitarian politics, see my *Aesthetics as Secular Millennialism: Its Trail from Baumgarten and Kant to Walt Disney and Hitler* (Lewisburg, PA: Bucknell UP, 2013), which starts out from Arendt's view of totalitarianism.
7 This historical development, I trust, is not hard to recognize in a general way, although of all the people who use the word "literature" to describe their life's work, not one has bothered to investigate its provenance in full detail. I have made some suggestions toward such a study, in my *Goethe as Woman: The Undoing of Literature* (Detroit, MI: Wayne State UP, 2001), in chapter 2 of my *All Theater Is Revolutionary Theater* (Ithaca, NY: Cornell UP, 2005), 27–53, and in various other places including my essays "Freud and the Denationalization of Literature," *artUS* (2010/11), 50–7,

and "It's a Word! It's a Claim! …: Modernism and Related Instances of an Inherently Discredited Conceptual Type," *artUS*, Special Issue 5/6 (January, February, 2005), 10–15. The distinction between "bipolar" and "bimodal" views of artistic illusion is due to Marian Hobson, *The Object of Art: The Theory of Illusion in Eighteenth-Century France* (Cambridge: Cambridge UP, 1982) and is worked out in detail with respect to literary culture in my *Aesthetics as Secular Millennialism*, 202–8.

8 See Alexander Gottlieb Baumgarten, *Meditationes philosophicae de nonnullis ad poema pertinentibus* (1735), translated as *Reflections on Poetry*, trans. Karl Aschenbrenner and William B. Holther (Berkeley: U. of California Press, 1954). For a detailed discussion of Baumgarten, including the reasons to suspect him of outright charlatanry, see my *Aesthetics as Secular Millennialism*, 38–47.

9 The opening quotation is from Heiner Müller, *"Jenseits der Nation": Heiner Müller im Interview mit Frank M. Raddatz* (Berlin: Rotbuch, 1991), 43. What follows is Blumenthal-Barby's summary of Müller's remarks, mainly on Brecht's "Fatzer" material, in Heiner Müller, *Werke*, ed. Frank Hörnigk, 12 vols. (Frankfurt/Main: Suhrkamp, 1998–2008), 9:244–6.

10 Devin Fore, *Realism after Modernism: The Rehumanization of Art and Literature* (Cambridge, MA: MIT Press, 2012), 2, 3. *La deshumanización del arte e Ideas sobre la novella* (1925) (The dehumanization of art and ideas about the novel) is a book by José Ortega y Gasset.

11 Habermas, *Moralbewußtsein*, 68, 86, translated in his *Moral Consciousness*, 58, 76. References are located by page in translation followed by page in the original, e.g., (58/68), as in the Preliminary Remarks.

12 A related difficulty, involving the question of appropriateness of the norm to the situation being confronted by it, is brought up by Habermas himself in section 4 of his "Remarks on Discourse Ethics," in his *Justification and Application: Remarks on Discourse Ethics*, trans. Ciaran Cronin (Cambridge, MA: MIT Press, 1993), 35–9. The original German essay "Erläuterungen zur Diskursethik" is found in his *Erläuterungen zur Diskursethik* (Frankfurt/Main: Suhrkamp, 1991), 137–42.

13 This is the title of an essay by Monique Wittig, in her *The Straight Mind and Other Essays* (Boston, MA: Beacon Press, 1992), 9–20. It abbreviates the sentence "One is not born, but rather becomes, woman," from Simone de Beauvoir, *The Second Sex*, trans. Constance Borde and Sheila Malovany-Chevallier (New York: Vintage, 2011), 283.

Chapter 2

1 Nietzsche, *Werke*, 1:102. References are marked "KSA" as above. The translation I use here is Friedrich Nietzsche, *The Birth of Tragedy and The Genealogy of Morals*, trans. Francis Golffing (New York: Doubleday Anchor, 1956), 95. References to this book are marked "BoT" below.

2 On this matter, see my article, "Nietzsche's Idea of Myth: The Birth of Tragedy from the Spirit of Eighteenth-Century Aesthetics," *PMLA* 94 (1979), 420–33, which takes issue with Paul de Man, among others.

3 The translation uses the same word, "conflict," to describe the opposition that produces tragedy's "suicide" and the opposition between the Dionysian and the

Socratic. But Nietzsche's original uses "Conflict" in the first case, "Gegensatz" in the second. I have added the adjective "inner" to mark this difference.

4 In his very first sentence, Nietzsche characterizes his field of inquiry as "aesthetische Wisssenschaft," for which the translation has simply "esthetics" (BoT 19).
5 See Richard Rorty, *Contingency, Irony, and Solidarity* (Cambridge: Cambridge UP, 1989), ch. 4, esp. 73. Rorty does not appear to require as deep a commitment to one's "final vocabulary" as Nietzsche does, but the structure of the thinking is the same in both cases.
6 Johann Joachim Winckelmann, *Kleine Schriften. Vorreden. Entwürfe*, ed. Walther Rehm (Berlin: de Gruyter, 1968), 29. See also my *Dark Side of Literacy*, 57–73, where this paradox is discussed in detail and developed in its historical context.
7 The translation is from Nietzsche, *On the Genealogy of Morals, Ecce Homo*, trans. Walter Kaufmann and R. J. Hollingdale (New York: Vintage, 1989), 25–6. References to this book are marked "GoM" below.
8 See KSA 5: 273, 288, 341, 386, 390; GoM 39, 54, 99, 138, 141.
9 On the question of what actually constitutes the "aphorism" in question, see John T. Wilcox, "What Aphorism Does Nietzsche Explicate in *Genealogy of Morals*, Essay III?" *Journal of the History of Philosophy* 35 (1997), 593–610.
10 In the first edition of the *Genealogy*, of 1887, the reverse of the title page bears the note: "Dem letztveröffentlichten 'Jenseits von Gut und Böse' zur Ergänzung und Verdeutlichung beigegeben." Colli and Montinari include this note neither in the KSA nor even in the larger "Kritische Gesamtausgabe," 6. Abt., 2. Bd. (Berlin, 1968); and as far as I can see, they never justify this omission.
11 This basic idea, that all understanding is false, is not nearly so outlandish as it might at first appear. Nor, in saying this, am I thinking only of the basic theorem of critical hermeneutics, which my terminology (representing Nietzsche's thought) drastically overstates. No less an intellect than Dante, for example, in *Purgatory* 21.73–75, argues that understanding always provides me with a pleasure that makes me an interested party and so clouds my judgment concerning the validity or value of my supposed understanding. On this passage in Dante, see my *Dark Side of Literacy*, 107.

Chapter 3

1 See Aristotle, *Nicomachean Ethics*, 1094a, Kant, *Grundlegung zur Metaphysik der Sitten*, in *Kants Werke: Akademie-Textausgabe*, 9 vols. (Berlin: de Gruyter, 1968; rpt. of 1902ff.), 4:393.
2 Kant, *Werke*, 4:393. The translation is from Immanuel Kant, *Kant's Foundations of Ethics*, trans. Leo Rauch (Millis, MA: Agora, 1995), 13. This translation is abbreviated "F" below.
3 The modern notion of will has interesting consequences even in the field of grammar. See, e.g., my "The Future of the Infinitive," *The Serif* 8, no. 3 (September 1971), 14–19.
4 See *Die Religion innerhalb der Grenzen der bloßen Vernunft*, in *Kants Werke*, 6:1–202. John H. Smith captures the difficulties here in the chapter, "Kant: The Turn to Ethics as *Logos*," in his *Dialogues between Faith and Reason: The Death and Return of God in Modern German Thought* (Ithaca, NY: Cornell UP, 2011), 68–94. For the basic argument on "radical evil," see Kant, *Werke*, 6:19–53.

5 The translation is from Immanuel Kant, *Religion within the Boundaries of Mere Reason and Other Writings*, trans. and ed. Allen Wood and George Di Giovanni (Cambridge: Cambridge UP, 1998), 164. Further references to this book are marked "R."
6 The unnamed editor of G. W. Leibniz, *Theodicy* (Teddington, Middlesex: The Echo Library, 2008), says on p. 34, "Leibniz now [1702] conceived the idea of putting together all the passages in Bayle's works which interested him, and writing a systematic answer to them. Before he had leisure to finish the task, Bayle died. The work nevertheless appeared in 1710 as the Essays in *Theodicy*."
7 References to the *Theodicy* are located by section number either in the "Discours preliminaire" (DP) or in the "Essais" proper (E), plus page number in the translation described in note 8 above. The present reference is to DP 9, 57.
8 The passage, quoted in E 358, is from a review of William King, *De Origine Mali* (1704) in the *Journal des Sçavans* of March 16, 1705. It is found on pp. 277–8 of the *Journal*, where the reviewer is about to recommend that his reader seek further enlightenment in the writings of Malebranche!
9 For the original see Gottfried Wilhelm Leibniz, *Die philosophischen Schriften*, 7 vols., ed. C. J. Gerhardt (Berlin: Weidmannsche Buchhandlung, 1875ff.), 6:29.

Chapter 4

1 *Gotthold Ephraim Lessing: Sämtliche Werke*, 17 vols., ed. Karl Lachmann and Franz Muncker (Berlin: de Gruyter, 1979), 13:415. This edition is a reprint of the first sixteen volumes of Lachmann/Muncker (eds.), *Gotthold Ephraim Lessings sämtliche Schriften*, 23 vols., 3rd ed. (Stuttgart: Metzler, 1886–1924); the seventeenth volume of the reprint is a "Nachtragsband." Further quotations from *Die Erziehung des Menschengeschlechts* are located simply by section number (§); quotations from *Nathan der Weise*, in vol. 3 of the edition where Lachmann/Muncker give line numbers for each act, are located by act and scene plus line numbers. Other Lessing quotations are located by "LM" plus volume and page number; volumes seventeen and higher are quoted from the old edition.
2 "Apologie oder Schutzschrift für die vernünftigen Verehrer Gottes" is the title Reimarus proposed to give to the work from which (actually from an early version of which) Lessing chose the "Fragments of an Unnamed Author."
3 For Lessing's claim to be a supporter of the Lutheran Church, see LM 13:101. The reported quotation is from Friedrich Heinrich Jacobi's *Über die Lehre des Spinoza*, in Jacobi, *Werke*, 6 vols. (Leipzig, 1812 ff.), 4:54.
4 See, e.g., R. K. Angress, "Lessing's Criticism of Cronegk: *Nathan in Ovo?*" *Lessing Yearbook* 4 (1972), 29. And recently, see Ned Curthoys, "A Diasporic Reading of Nathan the Wise," *Comparative Literature Studies* 47 (2010), 70–95, who speaks of the "wise" and "noble-minded" Saladin (71). For a fully developed argument that *Nathan* is primarily a "ein proislamisches Stück," which presents only "ein schwaches Bild vom Judentum," that in fact Lessing shows Islam as a "natural" (i.e., fundamentally rational) religion, more so than either Christianity or Judaism, see Friedrich Niewöhner, "Das muslimische Familientreffen. Gotthold Ephraim Lessing und die Ringparabel, oder: Der Islam als natürliche Religion," *Frankfurter Allgemeine Zeitung*, June 6, 1996, no. 129, p. N6. Niewöhner's argument about Lessing in general,

here and in his book, *Veritas sive Varietas: Lessings Toleranzparabel und das Buch Von den drei Betrügern* (Heidelberg: Lambert Schneider, 1988), is sound and very significant. But it remains true nonetheless that in *Nathan*, Saladin and his Jerusalem are both given a strong barbaric quality, and that the ultimate focus is much more centrally Jewish. I will argue in fact that in the final scene, Nathan's wisdom is profiled specifically by contrast with a corresponding *lack* in Saladin's character. Aamir R. Mufti, *Enlightenment in the Colony: The Jewish Question and the Crisis of Postcolonial Culture* (Princeton, NJ: Princeton UP, 2007), 46, calls Saladin in *Nathan* a "Frederick the Great figure, as it were." This comparison may be correct, as long as it includes an acknowledgment of the actual barbarity in many of Frederick's policies and practices.
5 Compare Augustine's discussion of the Trinity in *De Civitate Dei*, 11.26. The epigraph of the *Erziehung* is from Augustine.
6 See the summary of relevant material in Jochen Schulte-Sasse (ed.), *Lessing/Mendelssohn/Nicolai: Briefwechsel über das Trauerspiel* (München: Winkler, 1972), 164–5.
7 For a good summary of the debate on this point, see Monika Fick, *Lessing-Handbuch: Leben—Werk—Wirkung* (Stuttgart: Metzler, 2000), 428–9; H. B. Nisbet, "The Hybrid Discourse of Lessing's *Erziehung des Menschengeschlechts*," *PEGS* 80 (2011), 69–77, dismisses most of this debate on the grounds that "it does not greatly matter whether the two passages contradict each other or not," since "the main purpose of [Lessing's] complex strategy is to make it impossible for any 'real' or 'true' opinion as to the relative truth of religion to be extracted from his work" (74–5). I agree in general with the last part of this statement, but I still think there has to be a specific reason for creating the obvious contradiction between §§ 4 and 77.
8 On the relation between self and role in *Nathan*, see Armin Volkmar Wernsing, "Nathan der Spieler," *Wirkendes Wort* 20 (1970), 52–9.
9 There is another way of looking at the radically indeterminate quality of the thinking in *Nathan*, a way that avoids the whole idea of God. I refer to Robert S. Leventhal, *The Disciplines of Interpretation: Lessing, Herder, Schlegel and Hermeneutics in Germany 1750–1800* (Berlin: de Gruyter, 1994), 107–39, which includes what is still, in my view, the best treatment of Nathan's parable as such. Leventhal argues that the parable "moves beyond the boundaries of a purely religious or political *Streitgespräch* and into the questions of secular understanding and the interpretation of texts and history" (123), that what erupts in *Nathan*, understood *historically*, is thus a hermeneutic indeterminacy in the modern sense that develops all the way to Dilthey, Heidegger, and Gadamer. My insistence on the idea of an ironic God has to do with my focus—starting with Nietzsche and Rorty—on the problem of the *individual* ironist.
10 Let it be noted, to avoid confusion, that we are taking the "sons" in the parable to represent both religions and individual adherents of particular religions. The allegorical *form* of the parable, by its freedom from realistic limitations, allows this. On the parable as a form and Lessing's use of it, but not on this particular aspect, see Leventhal, and also Heinz Politzer, "Lessings Parabel von den drei Ringen," in his *Das Schweigen der Sirenen* (Stuttgart: Metzler, 1968), 339–72.
11 Compare Peter Heller, *Dialectics and Nihilism* (n.p.: U. Mass., 1966), 44, who says that "even the undeceiving produces a new phase of deceptions" in *Nathan*. But Heller is still of the opinion that "Lessing … believed quite simply and uncritically in an ultimate providential scheme of infinite progress toward the ultimate absolute truth" (45).

12 See, e.g., KSA 4:179–81, 198–200. The translation I will use is Nietzsche, *Thus Spoke Zarathustra*, trans. R. J. Hollingdale (London: Penguin, 2003). The passages just mentioned are found on pp. 161–3, 177–8.
13 Diaspora is a tricky idea, even when its discussion is restricted to the experience of the Jews. See, e.g., Ella Shohat, *Taboo Memories, Diasporic Voices* (Durham, NC: Duke UP, 2006), esp. the essays "Taboo Memories, Diasporic Visions: Columbus, Palestine, and Arab-Jews" (201–32) and "Rupture and Return: Zionist Discourse and the Study of Arab-Jews" (330–58). The favored Zionist concept of *galut*, which emphasizes the suffering of homelessness, imagines "All Jews ... as closer to each other than to the cultures of which they have been a part" (Shohat 215), which is a clear distortion of historical fact. But it is a very powerful distortion, so much so that even Ned Curthoys (see note 4)—who reads Lessing's *Nathan* as "an enthusiastic commentary on the pluralistic and polyglot societies of the Levant and Moorish Spain" (70–1), where Jews participated easily enough—concludes by seeing Nathan as "the Wandering Jew who mediates between different cultures ... but is never reconciled to his adopted home" (92–3). Which is the true Nathan, the integrated citizen or the isolated wanderer? I think it is fair to say: both, integrated as a Jew, isolated as a wise man (an ironist). Thus both sides of his contradictory advocacy (integration in one's immediate community vs. humanistic detachment) are contained in his own situation. In any case, I have argued elsewhere that Lessing and after him Goethe understand Jewish homelessness as a powerful allegory of their own situation as German writers. See my *Beyond Theory: Eighteenth-Century German Literature and the Poetics of Irony* (Ithaca, NY: Cornell UP, 1993), 10, 60–3, 318–26, 334–8.
14 I do not mean to suggest that Lessing employs an ironic approach only in his late works. In fact, the theologically controversial situation of his last years forces him to apply to ethics an ironic method that he had earlier cultivated mainly in aesthetic matters. See my *Beyond Theory*, 116–61, and my *Aesthetics as Secular Millennialism*, 51–3, 89–93.
15 For Lessing and Maimonides see Niewöhner, *Veritas sive Varietas*, passim but esp. 133–8, 399–403. References to Maimonides are to his *The Guide for the Perplexed*, 2nd ed., trans. M. Friedländer (New York: Dover, 1956; orig. 1904).
16 Compare the King James version: "Wherefore I abhor myself, and repent in dust and ashes," and similarly the New International Version. Maimonides, by contrast, sees the newly wise Job repenting himself *of* his earlier abjectly repentant attitude, regretting his mistaken idea that by repenting, a human might become morally "upright" before God, presumably by anticipating divine judgments of right and wrong.

Chapter 5

1 Reuben Klingsberg (ed.), *Freudiana: From the Collections of the Jewish National and University Library* (Jerusalem, 1973), viii. This pamphlet prints the letter in English and Hebrew but not in the presumably original German. It is true that the same pamphlet contains a letter of Freud's from 1935 to a financial official of the World Zionist Organization, which reads, "I well know how great and blessed an instrument this foundation has become in its endeavour to establish a new home in the ancient land of our fathers. It is a sign of our invincible will to survive which has, until now, successfully defied two thousand years of severe oppression! Our youth will continue

the struggle" (ix). But it should be noted that, with the Nazi danger in mind, Freud here regards the settling of Jews in Palestine not as the arrival at a goal, but as only one move in the *continuing* struggle (to be carried on by "our youth") of precarious diasporic existence.
2 Sigmund Freud, *Gesammelte Werke: Chronologisch geordnet*, 18 vols. plus *Nachtragsband* (Frankfurt/Main: Fischer, 1999), 10:45. This edition is cited henceforth as "GW." The English translation is from *The Standard Edition of the Complete Psychological Works of Sigmund Freud*, ed. and trans. James Strachey et al., 24 vols. (London: Hogarth Press, 1953–74), 14:8. References to this edition are marked "SE" henceforth. SE regularly spells "psycho-analysis" and "psycho-analytic" with a hyphen, which I will do too when quoting directly from it.
3 For an answer to this question different from the one I will propose here, but equally valid, see my "Freud and the Denationalization of Literature," esp. 56.
4 There is an enormous amount of literature on the subject of Freud's relation to Jews and Jewishness. But in the present chapter we will be concerned mainly with his sense, from fairly early on, of an analogy between the Jewish diaspora and the psychoanalytic diaspora, and with his long struggle with the figure of Moses. Three excellent books are especially helpful on these matters: Dennis B. Klein, *Jewish Origins of the Psychoanalytic Movement* (Chicago, IL: U. of Chicago, 1985), Yosef Hayim Yerushalmi, *Freud's Moses: Judaism Terminable and Interminable* (New Haven, CT: Yale UP, 1991), and Moshe Gresser, *Dual Allegiance: Freud as a Modern Jew* (Albany, NY: SUNY, 1994).
5 One of the great virtues of the Standard Edition is that it translates Freud's "Geistigkeit" as "intellectuality" (and "geistig" as "intellectual"), which is strictly correct, and not as "spirituality," which is seriously misleading. See GW 16:219–31; SE 23:111–23. And compare the insistent mistranslation in Sigmund Freud, *Moses and Monotheism*, trans. Katherine Jones (New York: Vintage, 1955), 142–58. Yerushalmi, 51, disagrees and prefers "spirituality."
6 Compare Benjamin's implied distinction, in introducing the "Kunstwerk" essay, between concepts as means of supposedly referring to given facts or conditions and concepts or theses used as a "weapon." See Walter Benjamin, "The Work of Art in the Age of Mechanical Reproduction," in his *Illuminations*, trans. Harry Zohn (New York: Schocken, 1985), 218.
7 The reference, in Freud's footnote, is to Lipps's lecture "Der Begriff des Unbewußten in der Psychologie" at the *Third International Congress for Psychology* in Munich (1897).
8 The relevant material in *Beyond the Pleasure Principle* is found in GW 13:23–9; SE 18:24–9. "A Note upon the 'Mystic Writing-Pad'" is found in GW 14:1–8; SE 19:227–32.
9 On Dante and an idea of the falseness of understanding that he has in part from Thomas Aquinas, see Ch. 2, note 11.
10 See especially Monique Wittig, "The Straight Mind," in *The Straight Mind*, esp. 22–4, where she argues that psychoanalysis reduces "the psyche" to a single invariant object, to whose theorized structures individual patients are forced to conform.
11 We think perhaps of Freud's wrestling, in *Beyond the Pleasure Principle* (GW 13:48–53; SE 18:45–9), with August Weismann's theory of mortal "soma" and immortal germ-plasm. He notes an "unexpected analogy" with his developing dualistic theory of instincts. But there is perhaps an even more suggestive analogy with the duality of the mortal ego and the phylogenetically surviving id.
12 See note 1 above.

Chapter 6

1. I will use the following abbreviations below: MC = *Moral Consciousness and Communicative Action*; JA = *Justification and Application: Remarks on Discourse Ethics*; MkH = *Moralbewußtsein und kommunikatives Handeln*; ED = *Erläuterungen zur Diskursethik*.
2. See Jürgen Habermas, *The Theory of Communicative Action*, 2 vols., trans. Thomas McCarthy (Boston: Beacon Press, 1984), 2:153–97. The original is found in Jürgen Habermas, *Theorie des kommunikativen Handelns*, 2 vols. (Frankfurt/Main: Suhrkamp, 1981), 2:229–93.
3. Jonathan Hess, *Reconstituting the Body Politic: Enlightenment, Public Culture and the Invention of Aesthetic Autonomy* (Detroit, MI: Wayne State UP, 1999) argues that aesthetics owes its very existence as a discipline to the deep-seated recognition of an unbridgeable gap between reason and politics. See also the larger argument on aesthetics in my *Aesthetics as Secular Millennialism*, and the response to Hess and Habermas on pp. 9–10 of that book.
4. For an instance of this difficulty, and of the lengths one must sometimes go to deal with it, see ch. 3 of my *Aesthetics as Secular Millennialism*, 57–78.
5. All references to *The Prince* and the *Discourses* are to Niccolò Machiavelli, *Opere politiche*, ed. Mario Puppo (Florence: Le Monnier, 1967). The translations are mine.
6. This passage is annotated in Machiavelli, *Opere*, 8 vols. (Milan: Feltrinelli, 1960), 1:72 to the effect that "con le leggi" should be understood to mean "con l'osservanza delle leggi morali"; and most translations seem to accept this definition. But it seems to me that "combattere ... con le leggi" can really only mean to contend legally, in court. Otherwise Machiavelli would be distinguishing between two ways of fighting with force, one that follows the "laws" and one that does not. And what "laws" could he possibly have in mind here?
7. William J. Landon, *Politics, Patriotism and Language: Niccolò Machiavelli's "Secular Patria" and the Creation of an Italian National Identity* (New York: Peter Lang, 2005), lists all seventy-nine occurrences of the concept *patria* in the *Discourses*, and all eight occurrences in *The Prince*. And even these eight occurrences say nothing specific about princely politics. Two (in Ch. 6) have to do with the founding of nations in antiquity; two (Chs. 8, 9) have to do with the citizen of a *patria* who then becomes a prince; one (Ch. 8) has to do with a free city that submits to a prince; two (Chs. 8, 9) have to do with occasions on which a prince needs the support of citizens, or of what without him would be a free *patria*; and one, finally (Ch. 26), the best known, refers to Italy as a free *patria* still needing to be created.
8. Niccolò Machiavelli, *Discorso intorno alla nostra lingua*, ed. Paolo Trovato (Padua: Antenore, 1982), 57. Landon's book (see note 10) offers a text and translation of the "Discorso" and discusses in detail questions of authorship and dating.
9. Dante is a special case in this regard. He understands the ethical inadmissibility of master discourses; but he also deliberately assumes the ethical burden, the culpability, involved. From the very beginning of the *Commedia*, for instance, he insists on saying straight out all the things that Paul had said it is not lawful for a man to utter (2 Cor. 12:4). And in *Paradiso* 13 he is warned by Thomas Aquinas about the danger in making exactly the kind of peremptory judgments about individuals' salvation that form the whole material of his poem. For a discussion of these matters, see the more or less self-contained Dante chapter in my *Dark Side of Literacy*, 85–140. My point

there is that the ethical danger associated with an excessively ambitious discourse belongs inherently to Dante's claim to have established an inaugural instance of Christian poetry, comparable to the inauguration of poetic types by the other five poets in *Inferno* 4.

10 See Chad Wellmon, *Organizing Enlightenment: Information Overload and the Invention of the Modern Research University* (Baltimore, MD: Johns Hopkins UP, 2015) and John H. Smith, *Dialogues between Faith and Reason*, 68–94.
11 Goethe, "Anschauende Urtheilskraft" (WA, pt. 2, 11:54–5).
12 This is Landon's view, and he gives a complete summary of the history of arguments for and against it.
13 Francesco Guicciardini, *Opere*, 3 vols., ed. Emanuella Lugnani Scarano (Turin: UTET, 1970), 1:627. Landon, 229, quotes this passage in Italian in a note.

Chapter 7

1 See especially *Zur Genealogie der Moral*, 1.13 (KSA 5:278–81). Also *Jenseits von Gut und Böse*, 12 (on the atomic theory of the soul) and 20 (on the determination of basic philosophical concepts by grammatical convention) (KSA 5:26–7, 34–5). For the aphorism made famous by Fredric Jameson, *The Prison-House of Language*, see KSA 12:193–4.
2 This, I suppose, is what Maria DiBattista means by readers' disappointment with Woolf's "reactionary swerve into coterie art," in her "Introduction" to *Orlando*, xli.
3 For the novel's impossible knowledge of subjectivity, see Dorrit Cohn, *Transparent Minds: Narrative Modes for Presenting Consciousness in Fiction* (Princeton, NY: Princeton UP, 1978). On simultaneity in the novel, see Benedict Anderson, *Imagined Communities: Reflections on the Origin and Spread of Nationalism*, rev. ed. (London: Verso, 2006), esp. 24–36. The phrase "essence of reality" is from Woolfe, *Diary*, 3:113.
4 For a discussion of this Reader, see my *Dark Side of Literacy*.
5 I don't know why Orlando's son should be born on Thursday, March 20 (217), which, if the year is 1890 (one possibility), would make him two years older than the real Vita. But then a person's age is not measurable by dates in this book anyway.
6 In *Also sprach Zarathustra*, "Von den Abtrünnigen 2" (KSA 4:230).
7 The sentence (Woolf 76), "The grandeur of their works was an argument ... habit facilitates success," is from William Hazlitt, "On Application to Study," Essay VI of *The Plain Speaker*, in *The Selected Writings of William Hazlitt*, 9 vols., ed. Duncan Wu (London: Pickering & Chatto, 1998), 8:55.
8 Nancy Armstrong, *How Novels Think: The Limits of British Individualism from 1719–1900* (New York: Columbia UP, 2005), 29. I have discussed Armstrong's argument in detail, with a different emphasis, in my *Aesthetics as Secular Millennialism*, 183–6.
9 Wittig 9, quoting from Colette Guillaumin, "Race et Nature: Système des marques, idée de groupe naturel et rapports sociaux," in *Pluriel* 11 (1977) (Wittig 102).
10 Wittig is referring to her own citation (36–7) of the famous exchange between Glaucon and Socrates at the end of *Republic* 9 (592 A-B).
11 The first list of names is introduced by the qualification: "CE QUI LES DÉSIGNE COMME L'ŒIL DES CYCLOPES, LEUR UNIQUE PRÉNOM," in Wittig, *Les Guérillères* (Paris: Les Éditions de Minuit, 1969), 15. Note the hovering between

singular and plural: the single eye of the (plural) Cyclopes corresponding to the unique given name of the (plural) women. Which disrupts the normal relation between the singular individual and its plural designations, not to mention the relation between the visible characteristic and the organ that perceives it.

12 For the instance of Goethe, and perhaps Heinrich von Kleist, see my *Goethe as Woman*.
13 Ingeborg Bachmann, *Malina* (Frankfurt/Main: Suhrkamp, 1997 [orig. 1971]), 119–21. Or Bachmann, *Malina*, trans. Philip Boehm (n.p.: Holmes & Meier, 1990), 73–5. References in the text are to both editions in the form, for the present instance, 119–21/73–5.
14 The translation reads "Are you ready?" which in German would be "Bist du bereit?" The original has "Bist du fertig?" suggesting that Malina knows the narrator has been up to something.
15 She quotes Kant on the impossibility of being indifferent to the issues he raises, from the "Vorrede" to the 1st edition of the *Critique of Pure Reason*, Kant, 4:8.

Conclusion

1 Interestingly enough, there is at least one long passage in Kafka's story that reads very much like a description, or even an advocacy, of what I have called the diaspora of the wise. I mean the long paragraph beginning "Muß ich das, wenn es für eine so abseitige …." See Franz Kafka, *Sämtliche Werke* (Frankfurt/Main: Suhrkamp, 2008), 1182–4.
2 An early (and eloquent) instance of the suspicion of New Criticism is Roy Harvey Pearce, "Historicism Once More," in his *Historicism Once More: Problems & Occasions for the American Scholar* (Princeton, NJ: Princeton UP, 1969), 3–45, esp. 8–25.
3 See *Aesthetics as Secular Millennialism*, esp. Ch. 9.
4 See *Aesthetics as Secular Millennialism*, esp. 38–51, 123–26, 204–5.
5 This is the whole basic argument of *Aesthetics as Secular Millennialism*.

BIBLIOGRAPHY

Anderson, Benedict. *Imagined Communities: Reflections on the Origin and Spread of Nationalism*. Revised Edition. London: Verso, 2006.
Anderson, Philip W. "More Is Different: Broken Symmetry and the Nature of the Hierarchical Structure of Science." *Science* 177, no. 4047 (August 1972): 393–6.
Angress, R. K. "Lessing's Criticism of Cronegk: *Nathan in Ovo?*" *Lessing Yearbook* 4 (1972): 27–36.
Aristotle. *The Nicomachean Ethics*. Loeb Classical Library. Cambridge, MA: Harvard UP, 1934.
Armstrong, Nancy. *How Novels Think: The Limits of British Individualism from 1719–1900*. New York: Columbia UP, 2005.
Attridge, Derek. "Ethical Modernism: Servants as Others in J.M. Coetzee's Early Fiction." *Poetics Today* 25, no. 4 (2004): 653–71.
Attridge, Derek. "Miller's Tale." In *The J. Hillis Miller Reader*, ed. Julian Wolfreys. Stanford, CA: Stanford UP, 2005, 78–82.
Bachmann, Ingeborg. *Malina*. Frankfurt/Main: Suhrkamp, 1997; orig. 1971.
Bachmann, Ingeborg. *Malina*, trans. Philip Boehm. N.p.: Holmes & Meier, 1990.
Baron, Hans. *In Search of Florentine Civic Humanism: Essays on the Transition from Medieval to Modern Thought*. 2 vols. Princeton, NJ: Princeton UP, 1988.
Baumgarten, Alexander Gottlieb. *Meditationes philosophicae de nonnullis ad poema pertinentibus: Philosophische Betrachtungen über einige Bedingungen des Gedichtes*, ed. and trans. Heinz Paetzold. Hamburg: Felix Meiner, 1983; orig. 1735.
Baumgarten, Alexander Gottlieb. *Reflections on Poetry*, trans. Karl Aschenbrenner and William B. Holther. Berkeley: U. of California Press, 1954.
Beauvoir, Simone de. *The Second Sex*, trans. Constance Borde and Sheila Malovany-Chevallier. New York: Vintage, 2011; orig. French, 1949.
Benjamin, Walter. *Illuminations*, trans. Harry Zohn. New York: Schocken, 1985.
Bennett, Benjamin. *Aesthetics as Secular Millennialism: Its Trail from Baumgarten and Kant to Walt Disney and Hitler*. Lewisburg, PA: Bucknell UP, 2013.
Bennett, Benjamin. *All Theater Is Revolutionary Theater*. Ithaca, NY: Cornell UP, 2005.
Bennett, Benjamin. *Beyond Theory: Eighteenth-Century German Literature and the Poetics of Irony*. Ithaca, NY: Cornell UP, 1993.
Bennett, Benjamin. *The Dark Side of Literacy: Literature and Learning Not to Read*. New York: Fordham UP, 2008.
Bennett, Benjamin. "Freud and the Denationalization of Literature." *artUS* (2010/11): 50–7.
Bennett, Benjamin. "The Future of the Infinitive." *The Serif* 8, no. 3 (September 1971): 14–19.
Bennett, Benjamin. *Goethe as Woman: The Undoing of Literature*. Detroit, MI: Wayne State UP, 2001.

Bennett, Benjamin. "It's a Word! It's a Claim! …: Modernism and Related Instances of an Inherently Discredited Conceptual Type." *artUS*, Special Issue 5/6 (January, February, 2005): 10–15.

Bennett, Benjamin. "Nietzsche's Idea of Myth: The Birth of Tragedy from the Spirit of Eighteenth-Century Aesthetics." *PMLA* 94 (1979): 420–33.

Bennett, Benjamin. "Reason, Error and the Shape of History: Lessing's Nathan and Lessing's God." *Lessing Yearbook* 9 (1977): 60–80.

Blake, William. *The Complete Poetry and Prose of William Blake*, ed. David V. Erdman. Newly Revised Edition. New York: Anchor Books, 1988.

Blumenthal-Barby, Martin. *Inconceivable Effects: Ethics through Twentieth-Century German Literature, Thought, and Film*. Ithaca, NY: Cornell UP, 2013.

Brooks, Cleanth. *The Well Wrought Urn: Studies in the Structure of Poetry*. New York: Harcourt, Brace, 1947.

Cassirer, Ernst. "Lessings Denkstil" (1917). In *Gotthold Ephraim Lessing*, eds. Gerhard Bauer and Sibylle Bauer. Wege der Forschung, vol. 211. Darmstadt: Wissenschaftliche Buchgesellschaft, 1968, 54–73.

Cohn, Dorrit. *Transparent Minds: Narrative Modes for Presenting Consciousness in Fiction*. Princeton, NJ: Princeton UP, 1978.

Corngold, Stanley. "The Curtain Half Drawn: Prereading in Flaubert and Kafka." In *The Comparative Perspective on Literature: Approaches to Theory and Practice*, eds. Clayton Koelb and Susan Noakes. Ithaca, NY: Cornell UP, 1988, 263–83.

Culler, Jonathan. "The Closeness of Close Reading." *ADE Bulletin* 149 (2010): 20–5.

Curthoys, Ned. "A Diasporic Reading of Nathan the Wise." *Comparative Literature Studies* 47 (2010): 70–95.

Diderot, Denis. *Œuvres*, ed. Laurent Versini. 5 vols. Paris: Robert Laffont, 1994ff.

Fick, Monika. *Lessing-Handbuch: Leben—Werk—Wirkung*. Stuttgart: Metzler, 2000.

Fore, Devin. *Realism after Modernism: The Rehumanization of Art and Literature*. Cambridge, MA: MIT Press, 2012.

Freud, Sigmund. *Gesammelte Werke: Chronologisch geordnet*, plus *Nachtragsband*. 18 vols. Frankfurt/Main: Fischer, 1999. Abbreviated "GW."

Freud, Sigmund. *The Standard Edition of the Complete Psychological Works of Sigmund Freud*, eds. and trans. James Strachey et al. 24 vols. London: Hogarth Press, 1953–74. Abbreviated "SE."

Freud, Sigmund. *Moses and Monotheism*, trans. Katherine Jones. New York: Vintage, 1955.

Freud, Sigmund. *Sigmund Freud. Karl Abraham. Briefe 1907–1926*, eds. Hilda C. Abraham and Ernst L. Freud. 2nd ed. Frankfurt/Main: Fischer, 1980.

Freud, Sigmund. Ralph Manheim and R. F. C. Hull, trans. *The Freud/Jung Letters: The Correspondence between Sigmund Freud and C. G. Jung*. Princeton, NJ: Princeton UP, 1974.

Freud, Sigmund. *Letters of Sigmund Freud*, ed. Ernst L. Freud. New York: Basic Books, 1975.

Freudiana: From the Collections of the Jewish National and University Library, ed. Reuben Klingsberg. Jerusalem, 1973.

Frye, Northrop. *Anatomy of Criticism: Four Essays* (1957). New York: Atheneum, 1966.

Gallop, Jane. "Close Reading in 2009." *ADE Bulletin* 149 (2010): 15–19.

Goethe, Johann Wolfgang von. *Goethes Werke*, "Weimarer Ausgabe." 143 vols. Weimar: Böhlau, 1887–1918. Abbreviated "WA."

Gresser, Moshe. *Dual Allegiance: Freud as a Modern Jew*. Albany: SUNY, 1994.

Guicciardini, Francesco. *Opere*, ed. Emanuella Lugnani Scarano. 3 vols. Turin: UTET, 1970.
Guillory, John. "Close Reading: Prologue and Epilogue." *ADE Bulletin* 149 (2010): 8–14.
Habermas, Jürgen. *Erläuterungen zur Diskursethik*. Frankfurt/Main: Suhrkamp, 1991.
Habermas, Jürgen. *Moralbewußtsein und kommunikatives Handeln*. Frankfurt/Main: Suhrkamp, 1983.
Habermas, Jürgen. *Theorie des kommunikativen Handelns*. 2 vols. Frankfurt/Main: Suhrkamp, 1981.
Habermas, Jürgen. *Justification and Application: Remarks on Discourse Ethics*, trans. Ciaran Cronin. Cambridge, MA: MIT Press, 1993.
Habermas, Jürgen. *Moral Consciousness and Communicative Action*, trans. Christian Lenhardt and Shierry Weber Nicholsen. Cambridge, MA: MIT Press, 1990.
Habermas, Jürgen. *The Structural Transformation of the Public Sphere: An Inquiry into a Category of Bourgeois Society*. Cambridge, MA: MIT Press, 1991.
Habermas, Jürgen. *The Theory of Communicative Action*, trans. Thomas McCarthy. 2 vols. Boston, MA: Beacon Press, 1984.
Hazlitt, William. *The Selected Writings of William Hazlitt*, ed. Duncan Wu. 9 vols. London: Pickering & Chatto, 1998.
Heller, Peter. *Dialectics and Nihilism*. N.p.: U. Mass., 1966.
Hess, Jonathan. *Reconstituting the Body Politic: Enlightenment, Public Culture and the Invention of Aesthetic Autonomy*. Detroit: Wayne State, 1999.
Hobson, Marian. *The Object of Art: The Theory of Illusion in Eighteenth-Century France*. Cambridge: Cambridge UP, 1982.
Jacobi, Friedrich Heinrich. *Werke*. 6 vols. Leipzig, 1812 ff.
Jolley, Nicholas. *Leibniz*. London: Routledge, 2005.
Kafka, Franz. *Sämtliche Werke*. Frankfurt/Main: Suhrkamp, 2008.
Kant, Immanuel. *Kants Werke*. Akademie-Textausgabe. 9 vols. Berlin: de Gruyter, 1968; rpt. of 1902ff.
Kant, Immanuel. *Kant's Foundations of Ethics*, trans. Leo Rauch. Millis, MA: Agora, 1995. Abbreviated "F."
Kant, Immanuel. *Religion within the Boundaries of Mere Reason and Other Writings*, trans. and eds. Allen Wood and George Di Giovanni. Cambridge: Cambridge UP, 1998. Abbreviated "R."
Keen, Steve. *Can We Avoid Another Financial Crisis?* Cambridge, MA: Polity, 2017.
Klein, Dennis B. *Jewish Origins of the Psychoanalytic Movement*. Chicago: U. of Chicago, 1985.
Kristeva, Julia. Σημειωτική: *Recherches pour une sémanalyse*. Paris: Seuil, 1969.
Lacan, Jacques. *The Four Fundamental Concepts of Psycho-Analysis*, trans. Alan Sheridan. New York: Norton, 1978; orig. French 1973.
Landon, William J. *Politics, Patriotism and Language: Niccolò Machiavelli's "Secular Patria" and the Creation of an Italian National Identity*. New York: Peter Lang, 2005.
Laqueur, Thomas. *Making SEX: Body and Gender from the Greeks to Freud*. Cambridge, MA: Harvard UP, 1990.
Leibniz, Gottfried Wilhelm. *Die philosophischen Schriften*, ed. C. J. Gerhardt. 7 vols. Berlin: Weidmannsche Buchhandlung, 1875ff.
Leibniz, Gottfried Wilhelm. *Theodicy*. Teddington, Middlesex: The Echo Library, 2008.
Lessing, Gotthold Ephraim. *Gotthold Ephraim Lessing: Sämtliche Werke*, eds. Karl Lachmann and Franz Muncker. 17 vols. Berlin: de Gruyter, 1979. Abbreviated "LM."

Lessing, Gotthold Ephraim. *Gotthold Ephraim Lessings sämtliche Schriften*, eds. Karl Lachmann and Franz Muncker. 23 vols. 3rd ed. Stuttgart, 1886–1924. Abbreviated "LM."

Leventhal, Robert S. *The Disciplines of Interpretation: Lessing, Herder, Schlegel and Hermeneutics in Germany 1750–1800*. Berlin: de Gruyter, 1994.

Lévi-Strauss, Claude. *The Elementary Structures of Kinship*, trans. James Harle Bell et al. Boston, MA: Beacon Press., 1969.

Machiavelli, Niccolò. *Opere politiche*, ed. Mario Puppo. Florence: Le Monnier, 1967.

Machiavelli, Niccolò. *Opere*. 8 vols. Milan: Feltrinelli, 1960.

Machiavelli, Niccolò. *Discorso intorno alla nostra lingua*, ed. Paolo Trovato. Padua: Antenore, 1982.

MacIntyre, Alasdair. *Whose Justice? Which Rationality?* Notre Dame: U. of Notre Dame Press. 1988.

Maimonides (Rabbi Moses ben Maimon). *The Guide for the Perplexed*, trans. M. Friedländer. 2nd ed. New York: Dover, 1956; orig. 1904.

Mendelssohn, Moses. *Gesammelte Schriften: Jubiläumsausgabe*. 24 vols. Berlin: F. Frommann, 1971 ff.; rpt. of 1929.

Miller, J. Hillis. *The Ethics of Reading: Kant, de Man, Eliot, Trollope, James, and Benjamin*. New York: Columbia UP, 1987.

Miller, J. Hillis. "The Ethics of Reading: Vast Gaps and Parting Hours." In *American Criticism in the Poststructuralist Age*, ed. Ira Konigsberg. Ann Arbor: Michigan UP, 1981: 19–41.

Moretti, Franco. *Distant Reading*. London: Verso, 2013.

Mufti, Aamir R. *Enlightenment in the Colony: The Jewish Question and the Crisis of Postcolonial Culture*. Princeton, NJ: Princeton UP, 2007.

Müller, Heiner. *Werke*, ed. Frank Hörnigk. 12 vols. Frankfurt/Main: Suhrkamp, 1998–2008.

Müller, Heiner. *"Jenseits der Nation": Heiner Müller im Interview mit Frank M. Raddatz*. Berlin: Rotbuch, 1991.

Nietzsche, Friedrich. *Sämtliche Werke: Kritische Studienausgabe in 15 Bänden*, eds. Giorgio Colli and Mazzino Montinari. 15 vols. Munich and Berlin: dtv, 1980. Abbreviated "KSA."

Nietzsche, Friedrich. *Thus Spoke Zarathustra*, trans. R. J. Hollingdale. London: Penguin, 2003.

Nietzsche, Friedrich. *On the Genealogy of Morals, Ecce Homo*, trans. Walter Kaufmann and R. J. Hollingdale. New York: Vintage, 1989. Abbreviated "GoM."

Nietzsche, Friedrich. *The Birth of Tragedy and The Genealogy of Morals*, trans. Francis Golffing. New York: Doubleday Anchor, 1956. Abbreviated "BoT."

Niewöhner, Friedrich. *Veritas sive Varietas: Lessings Toleranzparabel und das Buch Von den drei Betrügern*. Heidelberg: Lambert Schneider, 1988.

Niewöhner, Friedrich. "Das muslimische Familientreffen. Gotthold Ephraim Lessing und die Ringparabel, oder: Der Islam als natürliche Religion." *Frankfurter Allgemeine Zeitung*. 6 June 1996. No. 129, p. N6.

Nisbet, H. B. "The Hybrid Discourse of Lessing's *Erziehung des Menschengeschlechts*." *PEGS* 80 (2011): 69–77.

Pearce, Roy Harvey. *Historicism Once More: Problems & Occasions for the American Scholar*. Princeton, NJ: Princeton UP, 1969.

Politzer, Heinz. *Das Schweigen der Sirenen*. Stuttgart: Metzler, 1968.

Rorty, Richard. *Contingency, Irony, and Solidarity*. Cambridge: Cambridge UP, 1989.

Schulte-Sasse, Jochen, ed. *Lessing/Mendelssohn/Nicolai: Briefwechsel über das Trauerspiel.* München: Winkler, 1972.
Shohat, Ella. *Taboo Memories, Diasporic Voices.* Durham, NC: Duke UP, 2006.
Siebers, Tobin. *The Ethics of Criticism.* Ithaca, NY: Cornell UP, 1988.
Smith, John H. *Dialogues between Faith and Reason: The Death and Return of God in Modern German Thought.* Ithaca, NY: Cornell UP, 2011.
Stevens, Wallace. *The Collected Poems of Wallace Stevens* (1954). New York: Knopf, 2000.
Strawson, P. F. *Freedom and Resentment and Other Essays.* London: Routledge, 2008.
Taylor, Charles. *Sources of the Self: The Making of the Modern Identity.* Cambridge, MA: Harvard UP, 1989.
Wellmon, Chad. *Organizing Enlightenment: Information Overload and the Invention of the Modern Research University.* Baltimore, MD: Johns Hopkins UP, 2015.
Wernsing, Armin Volkmar. "Nathan der Spieler." *Wirkendes Wort* 20 (1970): 52–9.
Wilcox, John T. "What Aphorism Does Nietzsche Explicate in *Genealogy of Morals*, Essay III?" *Journal of the History of Philosophy* 35 (1997): 593–610.
Williams, Bernard. *Ethics and the Limits of Philosophy.* Cambridge, MA: Harvard UP, 1985.
Wimsatt, W. K., and Monroe Beardsley. "The Intentional Fallacy" (1946). In Wimsatt. *The Verbal Icon: Studies in the Meaning of Poetry.* Lexington: U. of Kentucky Press, 1967: 2–18.
Winckelmann, Johann Joachim. *Kleine Schriften. Vorreden. Entwürfe*, ed. Walther Rehm. Berlin: de Gruyter, 1968.
Wittgenstein, Ludwig. "Wittgenstein's Lecture on Ethics." *The Philosophical Review* 74, no. 1 (Jan. 1965): 3–12.
Wittig, Monique. *The Straight Mind and Other Essays.* Boston, MA: Beacon Press, 1992.
Wittig, Monique. *Les Guérillères.* Paris: Les Éditions de Minuit, 1969.
Woolf, Virginia. *Orlando: A Biography.* Notes by Maria DiBattista. New York: Harvest Books, 2006.
Woolf, Virginia. *A Room of One's Own.* New York: Harvest Books, 1989.
Woolf, Virginia. *The Diary of Virginia Woolf*, ed. Anne Olivier Bell. 5 vols. London: Hogarth, 1977–84.
Yerushalmi, Yosef Hayim. *Freud's Moses: Judaism Terminable and Interminable.* New Haven, CT: Yale UP, 1991.

PERSON INDEX

Abraham, Karl 93
Adler, Alfred 92
Adorno, Theodor 56
Althusser, Louis 155
Anderson, Benedict 187 n.3
Anderson, Philip W. 7
Angress, Ruth K. 182 n.4
Apel, Karl-Otto 120
Arendt, Hannah 17, 177
Aristophanes 102
Aristotle 55–6, 59, 67, 157, 162
Armstrong, Nancy 155–7
Attridge, Derek 14, 17
Augustine 59, 183 n.5
Austen, Jane 149–52, 159

Bachmann, Ingeborg 9, 14, 166–71, 178
Baron, Hans 129
Baumgarten, Alexander Gottlieb 19
Bayle, Pierre 59, 60
Beardsley, Monroe 175
Beauvoir, Simone de 27, 141–2, 146, 154, 160–1
Beckett, Samuel 22
Beethoven, Ludwig van 34
Behn, Aphra 152, 160
Benjamin, Walter 18, 185 n.6
Blake, William 148
Blumenthal-Barby, Martin 11, 14, 17–18, 21–4, 26
Booth, Wayne 14
Borgia, Cesare 137
Brecht, Bertolt 22
Brontë, Charlotte 150, 159
Brontë, Emily 150, 152
Brooks, Cleanth 179 n.2
Buber, Martin 12, 117
Buddha (Siddhārtha Gautama) 39, 41–2

Cassirer, Ernst 71
Catherine the Great 56

Charles II of England 151
Cohn, Dorrit 187 n.3
Coleridge, Samuel Taylor 159
Corngold, Stanley 15
Curthoys, Ned 182 n.4, 184 n.13

Dante Alighieri 135–6, 181 n.11, 186–7 n.9
Davidson, Donald 120
Defoe, Daniel 155–7
De Man, Paul 180 n.2
Descartes, René 56, 59, 60, 152
Diderot, Denis 56
Dilthey, Wilhelm 175
Dubos, Jean-Baptiste 71

Euripides 30

Fichte, Johann Gottlieb 155
Fick, Monika 183 n.7
Fish, Stanley 16
Fore, Devin 22–3
Freud, Martha (née Bernays) 112
Freud, Sigmund 9, 13, 32, 66, 90, 91–115
  Beyond the Pleasure Principle 101–2, 105, 112
  Civilization and Its Discontents 102–4, 109–11, 126–8
  The Ego and the Id 103–8, 111
  Moses and Monotheism 95–7, 107, 109, 113–15
  Totem and Taboo 95, 100–2, 106, 108, 118, 122, 126–8, 158–9, 178
Frye, Northrop 20

Gadamer, Hans-Georg 16
Gewirth, Alan 121
Goethe, Johann Wolfgang von 34, 98–9, 137
Goeze, Johann Melchior 65–6
Greene, Graham 166

Gresser, Moshe 185 n.4
Guicciardini, Francesco 138–9
Guillaumin, Colette 187 n.9

Habermas, Jürgen 5–6, 8, 13, 16, 18, 24–6, 57, 109, 118–28, 135–6, 178
Hare, R. M. 121
Hazlitt, William 151, 157, 159
Hegel, Georg Wilhelm Friedrich 46, 123, 125, 127, 155
Heller, Peter 183 n.11
Hess, Jonathan 186 n.3
Hirsch, E. D., Jr. 16
Hobson, Marian 19
Hoffmann, E. T. A. 167
Horkheimer, Max 56
Hume, David 3
Hutcheson, Francis 3, 171

Iser, Wolfgang 16

Jacobi, Friedrich Heinrich 182 n.3
Jameson, Fredric 187 n.1
Jesus of Nazareth 40–2, 44, 51–3
John of Ruysbroeck 60
Jolley, Nicholas 59
Jung, Carl Gustav 92–3, 95, 104, 106–8
Jünger, Ernst 23

Kafka, Franz 173–4, 176–7
Kant, Immanuel 3, 7–8, 12–13, 17, 22, 25–8, 31, 38, 42–3, 55–9, 61–4, 65, 87–8, 109, 117–18, 123–4, 127, 129, 135–7, 140, 149, 152–5, 171, 176–8
Keen, Steve 7
King, William 182 n.8
Klein, Dennis B. 185 n.4
Kleist, Heinrich von 188 n.12
Koffler, Chaim 91
Kristeva, Julia 16

Lacan, Jacques 97–8, 100, 104–5, 108, 163, 165
Lamarck (Jean-Baptiste Pierre Antoine de Monet) 101
Landon, William J. 186 nn.7, 8, 187 n.12
Laqueur, Thomas 153

Leibniz, Gottfried Wilhelm 9, 13, 28, 57–8, 60–4, 65–6, 71, 87–8, 129, 131–2, 134, 136–7, 140, 153, 178
Theodicy 57–62, 136
Lessing, Gotthold Ephraim 9, 13, 65–8, 70–4, 76, 80–2, 84–90, 92, 94, 97, 111–14, 118, 122, 128, 137, 159
Education of the Human Race 65–73, 75–89, 92
Nathan the Wise 65–71, 73–9, 81–2, 84–8, 90, 92, 97, 111–12, 122, 159
Leventhal, Robert S. 183 n.9
Levinas, Emmanuel 12, 14, 17, 117
Lévi-Strauss, Claude 162
Lipps, Theodor 99
Luther, Martin 59–60

Machiavelli, Niccolò 9, 13, 28, 128–40, 153, 178
MacIntyre, Alasdair 14, 121
Maimonides (Moses ben Maimon) 89–90, 111
Malebranche, Nicolas 59
Mallarmé, Stéphane 37
McCarthy, Thomas 120–1
Mead, G. H. 119
Medici, Giovanni de' (Pope Leo X) 137–8
Medici, Lorenzo de' (Duke of Urbino) 137–9
Mendelssohn, Moses 70–1, 94
Miller, J. Hillis 14–17, 24
Mirabeau, Honoré Gabriel Riqueti, Comte de 4, 34
Montaigne, Michel de 7
Moore, G. E. 1, 121
Moretti, Franco 174–5
Moses 93, 95–7, 113–14, 159
Mufti, Aamir R. 183 n.4
Müller, Heiner 21–2

Napoleon Bonaparte 34–5
Nietzsche, Friedrich 4, 6–9, 12–13, 27, 29, 31, 35–40, 42, 44, 46, 48–53, 80–2, 87, 108, 110–14, 141, 148–50, 158, 171, 177–8
Antichrist 30, 38–46, 49–53, 114
Birth of Tragedy 29–31, 34–5, 39, 51
Genealogy of Morals 31–8, 42–4, 49–51

Thus Spoke Zarathustra 35, 36, 49, 56–7, 61–4, 80–2, 117–18, 122–3, 136
Niewöhner, Friedrich 182–3 n.4, 184 n.15
Nisbet, H. B. 183 n.7
Nussbaum, Martha 14

Ortega y Gasset, José 22

Paul the Apostle 52–3
Pearce, Roy Harvey 188 n.2
Plato 46, 59, 75, 102, 162–3
Politzer, Heinz 183 n.10

Rawls, John 119
Reimarus, Elise 76
Reimarus, Hermann Samuel 65, 67, 73
Rorty, Richard 13–14, 16, 27, 31, 46–53, 56–7, 60–4, 81–2, 87, 99, 110, 118, 122, 127–8, 132, 135–6, 163, 178
Rousseau, Jean-Jacques 56, 155

Sackville-West, Vita 144, 146
Saussure, Ferdinand de 104–5
Schleiermacher, Friedrich 175, 177
Schopenhauer, Arthur 31
Shaftesbury, Anthony Ashley Cooper, third Earl of 3, 171
Shakespeare, William 149–51, 159
Shelley, Percy Bysshe 21
Shohat, Ella 184 n.13
Siebers, Tobin 14–15, 20–1, 24
Smith, Adam 3
Smith, John H. 136, 181 n.4
Socrates 29–31, 34, 39, 46, 51, 163
Spinoza, Baruch 60

Sterne, Laurence 145–6
Stevens, Wallace 21
Strawson, P. F. 3–7, 16, 24, 26, 121–2, 171, 178

Taylor, Charles 119–20
Tolstoy, Leo 150–1, 159
Toulmin, Stephen 121
Tugendhat, Ernst 119

Valla, Lorenzo 59, 60

Warburton, William 85, 88
Weizmann, Chaim 91
Wellmon, Chad 136–7
Wernsing, Armin Volkmar 183 n.8
White, Alan R. 121
Wilcox, John T. 181 n.9
Williams, Bernard 119
Wimsatt, W. K. 175
Winckelmann, Johann Joachim 31, 52
Wittgenstein, Ludwig 1–3, 5–8, 11, 13, 20–1, 26–7, 82, 88, 117–18, 122, 135, 171, 174
Wittig, Monique 9, 14, 27, 110, 141, 157, 160–6, 170–1, 178
Woolf, Leonard 144
Woolf, Virginia 9, 14, 144, 146–52, 154, 157, 159–61, 163–6, 170–1, 178
  Orlando 144–6, 148–9, 151, 154, 157–8, 160–1, 165–6
  A Room of One's Own 146–52, 159–60, 164

Yerushalmi, Yosef Hayim 185 nn.4, 5

SUBJECT INDEX

aphorism 35–7, 49, 181 n.9, 187 n.1
ascetic ideal 32–8, 40, 42–3, 51

bad conscience 32–3
becoming woman 154, 157–61
Buddhism 39–42, 43

categorical imperative 7–8, 13, 56, 123, 125, 155
Christianity 38, 70, 75, 79, 81, 89, 95, 114, 182 n.4
  anti-Christianity 38, 42, 45, 53, 70
  as dishonest 43, 49
  and doctrine 33, 39, 41
  and Jesus 40
  and Jews 32, 40, 41, 51, 75–7, 79, 85
  and literal-mindedness 77
  and selfishness 75
  and slave morality 32, 42
  use of Christianity 51
constructionist fallacy 7–8, 118
culture 29–31, 37, 47, 50, 51, 63, 69, 85, 86, 119, 141–2, 152, 175, 176
  cultural particularity and humanity 73, 82, 184 n.13
  of doctrines and of methods 39, 41–4

diaspora 85–7, 89, 91–2, 94, 112–14, 118, 158–9, 165, 184 n.13, 185 n.4, 188 n.1

enlightenment 13, 56, 65, 68, 70, 84, 125
eternal recurrence 77, 80–2
ethics 1–9, 11–14, 30, 31, 52, 55, 56–7, 63, 86, 109, 117–18, 119, 120, 131–2, 135, 149, 158, 173, 178
  and autonomy 3, 5, 22, 25, 44–5, 61–2, 113, 123–4, 155–8, 164
  of becoming 157–9
  and community 5–7, 12–13, 16–18, 20, 21, 27, 50, 51, 63, 81, 87, 88, 115, 117–18, 123–4, 153, 174

dilemma of 7, 34–5, 157
discourse 5, 13, 24–6, 120, 123, 125, 127
ethical gap 5, 121–8
ethical philosophy 12, 117, 119
existence of 1–3
feminist (*see* feminist ethics)
history of 8–9, 10–14, 152–3, 157, 173
honesty 43–4, 48–51, 53, 110, 111–12, 114, 118, 127, 129, 135, 150, 178
and irony (*see* Irony); of reading, 14–17, 174
and the lifeworld 5, 24–5, 26, 119, 122, 124–7
literary 17–20
as method (see *Method*)
micro/macro 8
objectivist and subjectivist 121
and politics 55–6, 127–9, 135, 166
possibility of 7–8, 10, 26, 35, 48, 49, 62, 63, 117, 154, 177
propositional 8, 12–13, 14, 25–7, 48–9, 53, 56, 63, 87, 109, 112, 117, 118, 121, 127, 152–4, 158, 159, 166, 173, 177, 178
rhetorical 13–14, 27, 50, 61–2, 64, 117, 135–7, 140, 153, 154, 158, 173, 178
and universality 4, 6–7, 12–13, 17–18, 20–2, 25, 56, 86, 88, 117
Europe 18–19, 38, 40, 42, 93, 113, 146, 154
elite intellectual class 21, 63, 134, 136, 153, 173, 176
and gendered language 141, 143–4
pre-Kantian 63, 136, 153, 173

feminism 7, 14, 21, 27, 110, 141, 143–4, 149, 154, 158, 160, 166, 170, 171, 173
feminist ethics 144, 149, 152, 158, 160, 164, 166

gender 21, 115
  the body 153, 154, 156, 163

both genders in an individual 147
changing gender 145, 146, 148, 151
gender difference as impossible to
    understand 143, 145, 153, 154, 158,
    161, 162
history of 149, 152–3, 157
and "the human" (see "the human")
male/female binary 115, 142, 152,
    160, 162
as natural 142, 161
and power relations 141, 142, 143, 152
and sex 141–4, 145
the world as feminine 146–9

hermeneutics 45, 139, 175, 177, 181 n.11,
    183 n.9
humanism 8, 13, 21–3, 117, 177, 184 n.13
the human
    as concept 21–23, 143, 153, 155
    as gendered 143

the individual 26, 27, 40, 48, 56, 67, 74, 76,
    78, 83–4, 89, 97, 104–7, 108, 110–11,
    126, 147, 152–7, 158, 163, 183 n.9,
    188 n.11
    as free 152–5, 157
    the problem of 67, 103–4,
        117–18, 155–7
irony 14, 26–8, 34, 46, 57, 60–1, 63–4, 76,
    86–7, 89, 101, 111, 137, 157, 160, 163,
    171, 176
    and community 7, 31, 46–7, 50, 51,
        52–3, 64, 81–6, 87, 88, 118, 123, 163
    ethics of irony 13, 31, 48–50, 51, 56, 62–
        63, 65, 81, 84, 87–90, 112, 114–15,
        117–18, 122–4, 127–9, 136–7, 149,
        152, 154, 158, 163, 173–4, 176–8
    irony of God 74–9, 81, 183 n.9
    and the public 47–8, 50, 51, 52
    radical 27, 48, 81, 83, 84, 86, 87, 88, 113
    and the Socratic 29–31
    and understanding/lying 27, 43–6, 48,
        50, 149

Jewish ethics 13, 66, 87–90, 112, 114, 152,
    158, 173
Jewish people 40, 42, 51, 74, 79, 82–4, 87,
    89, 91–4, 113–15, 118, 157–9, 184
    n.13, 185 n.4

as community of ironists (see irony: and
    community)
the diaspora (see diaspora)
as educators of humanity 84–6
and heroic obedience 75, 83, 85
and slave morality 32
Job, Book of 57, 78, 88–90, 92, 111–13,
    114, 184 n.16

language 16, 24, 50, 98, 104–7, 126,
    134–7, 163
cryptic language 87, 96–7, 98, 113, 114,
    118, 128, 132, 136, 146, 170
different and disjointed idioms/
    languages 62, 129–34, 137, 141, 144,
    173, 177
existence of 2–3
and gender 141, 143
limits of (collision; boundary) 2–3, 6–7,
    27, 82, 117
words as remembered objects 104–5
literature 11, 17–20, 26, 50, 179 n.7
    and aesthetic criteria 18–19
    comparative 19
    concept of 11, 18–20
    as ethical phenomenon 23
    and the human 21–3
    instability of 20
    national literature 19

master discourse 64, 135, 173, 176–7,
    186 n.9
method 7–9, 12–13, 30, 38–40, 41, 42, 44,
    46, 48, 49–50, 52, 53, 63, 64, 81, 83,
    86, 110–12, 117, 118–21, 131, 133,
    135, 136, 149, 150, 174, 176, 177–8,
    184 n.13
morality (see Ethics and morality)
Moses 83, 93, 95–7, 107, 109, 113–14, 159,
    185 n.4

New Criticism 174, 188 n.2
nihilism 29–30, 35, 37, 38, 39, 82
novel 19, 23, 37, 144, 145, 146, 148, 150–1,
    154, 155, 157, 169, 180 n.10, 187 n.3

psychoanalysis 13, 66, 91–5, 111–12,
    113–14, 185 n.10
    and civilization 94, 103–4, 109, 111, 126

and the critique of theorizing 107–10
and diaspora (*see* diaspora)
ego and id 103–8, 110–11
the ethical imperative of 109
as metapsychology 99
multiplicity of viewpoints 100, 110–11
and theory 98–102
the unconscious 94, 97–101, 104, 105–8, 109, 111
as wisdom 95–8

reading 15–16
and the absence of truth claims 37, 170
active reading as generating meaning 97
as an art 44
close/deep reading 8–9, 27, 42, 66, 174–6
distant reading 174–6
ethics of (*see* ethics: of reading)
as event 14–15, 18
impenetrable barrier between the real world and fictional text 169–70
and reaching beyond meaning 170–1
and systems of conventions 175–6
reason 8, 12, 29, 55, 57–8, 61, 82, 85, 93, 114, 122, 123, 125, 152, 153, 155, 186 n.3
determinate reason 60
distant reading 174–6
reason activated by error and revelation 70–4, 76–80
and tradition 66–7, 69–70
religion 2, 6, 12, 13, 30, 33, 39–41, 65, 66–7, 69, 81, 82, 84, 86, 94, 96, 97, 100, 112, 114, 136, 176, 183 n.7, 183 n.10
and the development of reason 72, 75–7, 79, 182 n.4
as ethical 56–8
as grounded in error 74
resentment 4, 6–7, 42

sexuality 156
heterosexuality 161–2
lesbian 161–3, 165
reproduction 142, 161–2
subjectivity 145, 153, 155, 163–5, 178, 187 n.3

theory 3–4, 7–8, 13, 17, 20, 23, 24, 19, 39, 49, 53, 56, 81, 92, 93–5, 98, 104–9, 119, 120, 122–7, 129, 132–3, 141, 148, 158, 185 n.11, 187 n.1
and the arbitrary 104–5, 109, 134
as a dishonest activity 107–8, 110–14, 118
and the fantastic; as quasi-visual 108
the necessity of 98, 108
theoretical closure 98–102, 103, 107–9, 122, 158

The "We" 38–40
and becoming 157–9
as gendered 158
of irony (*see* irony: and community)
membership of 5–7, 16, 18, 64, 117–18, 121, 123
and the structure of moral sentiments; as universal 6, 12–13, 56, 88, 157, 163
as untheorizable 87, 118, 158, 115
wisdom 21, 34, 58, 86–7, 90, 93, 97–8, 112–14, 118, 148, 183 n.4
woman 141–2, 145, 146–7, 149, 151, 153–4, 157–61, 163, 169, 180 n.13
writing 15, 16, 18, 19, 42, 47, 50, 129, 130, 135, 137, 144, 156–7, 160, 164, 175
ethical writing 13, 15, 35–8
history of 149–52, 154, 157, 160
ways of writing 11, 37, 148
with integrity 150–1, 154, 159

Zionism 91, 184 nn.1, 13

www.ingramcontent.com/pod-product-compliance
Lightning Source LLC
Chambersburg PA
CBHW052043300426
44117CB00012B/1951